Nature's Work of Art

Nature's Work of Art

The Human Body as Image of the World

LEONARD BARKAN

New Haven and London, Yale University Press

For my mother,
Frances Barkan,
and in memory of my father,
Benjamin Barkan

Contents

Acknowledgments

This study and its author are greatly indebted to a number of teachers, friends, and institutions. These debts are a joy to incur, an impossibility to repay, and a pleasure to acknowledge here. Thomas Greene, who directed this work in its long years as a dissertation, exhibited with stunning versatility such virtues as patience, wisdom, faith, high standards, respect, wit, tolerance, and friendship. Others who may be invited to share the blame include the extraordinary array of teachers I've had the pleasure to study with: David Cowden, who helped introduce me to the creative reading of literature; Susan Snyder, who reincarnates the glory of the Renaissance even as she forces undergraduates to read every word of *The Faerie Queene* (in three weeks!); Robert Brentano, who himself sets a standard for the life and work of a scholar which others can only dream about approaching; Marie Borroff, who possesses to a dazzling degree the skills of poetry, scholarship, criticism, teaching, and grace; E. Talbot Donaldson, whose mind and spirit have often recalled to me that the greatest glory of a humanist is to be human.

One great debt to a teacher I cannot acknowledge in person: to the late Rosalie L. Colie I owe more than even she could have guessed—from the practical matters of critical approach to the ineffable realms of spirit, guidance, and love. There are too many other mentors at Yale to mention all, but let me acknowledge A. Bartlett Giamatti, Alvin Kernan, and Traugott Lawler, who read the manuscript and offered extremely helpful suggestions, and A. Dwight Culler, who had the respect for me and the nerve to prevent me from changing the subject of my dissertation when I yearned for the primrose path of an easier topic.

I have been as fortunate in my friends as in my teachers. This book is, at least in part, the direct or indirect product of many long and long-remembered conversations with Albert R. Braunmuller, Lee Bliss Braunmuller, Elizabeth Coffin, E. Donald Elliott, Jr., Marjorie B. Garber, Thomas Laqueur, and Peter Schwenger; and I am, at least in part, the product of their respect and affection. Students like Ronald Martinez, Louis Montrose, and Frank Whigham have taught me more about the Renaissance than I have taught them.

Finally there are those whose practical assistance has been indispensable. The Yale University Press has faced difficulties with efficiency and grace: I particularly thank Whitney Blake, its editor-in-chief, and James Heaney, my manuscript editor. My gratitude also to Lucinda Rubio, Kathleen DeLand, and Sherryll Mleynek for their very important work with the manuscript. Research grants from the academic senate of the University of California, San Diego, and one of the National Endowment for the Humanities Summer Stipends for Younger Humanists were instrumental to my research and well-being. Similarly welcome aid, financial and spiritual, came from Yale's Prize Committee, who awarded this study a Theron Rockwell Field Dissertation Prize for 1972. Last, and perhaps greatest, I want to acknowledge the aid of the Sterling and Beinecke Libraries at Yale, the University Research Library at U.C.L.A., and the Bodleian Library at Oxford; and I want to thank their patient and helpful staff members.

La Jolla
11 February 1974

Introduction

When the simplest of all English Renaissance poets uses the simplest of all titles, the reader may anticipate the expression of some very basic truth. What, then, is George Herbert's picture of "Man"?[1]

> For Man is ev'ry thing,
> And more: He is a tree, yet bears more fruit;
> A beast, yet is, or should be more:
> Reason and speech we onely bring.
> Parrats may thank us, if they are not mute,
> They go upon the score.
>
> [7–12]

Man contains everything in the cosmos. All of nature:

> Herbs gladly cure our flesh; because that they
> Finde their acquaintance there.
>
> [23–24]

All of geography:

> Each thing is full of dutie:
> Waters united are our navigation;
> Distinguished, our habitation;
> Below, our drink; above, our meat;
> Both are our cleanliness.
>
> [37–41]

Man is inscribed as the central term in the sphere of the heavens:

> The starres have us to bed;
> Night draws the curtain, which the sunne withdraws;

1. Citations are to *The Works of George Herbert,* ed. F. E. Hutchinson (Oxford: Clarendon Press, 1964).

1

Musick and light attend our head.
All things unto our flesh are kinde
In their descent and being: to our minde
In their ascent and cause.

[32–36]

Yet for all this, man is not infinite; rather, he is able to contain the whole cosmos because he is a miracle of symmetry and proportion:

Man is all symmetrie,
Full of proportions, one limbe to another,
And all to all the world besides:
Each part may call the furthest, brother:
For head with foot hath private amitie,
And both with moons and tides.

[13–18]

This combination of total inclusiveness and miniature proportion represents an essential and typical view of man in the Renaissance: man is a little world. But Herbert does not create this picture in purely abstract terms. When he refers to man as house, tree, beast, sphere, world, palace, he is speaking not of the human condition but of the human body. Only the human body can be the image of a microcosm which is at once objective, infinite, and proportional.

The subject of the human body is very nearly as vast as the subject of man. The purpose of this introduction is to explain how this essay limits that subject to a group of concerns narrow enough for useful study and broad enough to form something like a complete statement. All imaginative thought attempts to bridge the gap between man and what is outside him. One method of bridging this gap is to see these two points of reference as fundamentally similar. Out of the desire to simplify man's relation to the cosmos arises the idea that man is a microcosm, a miniature cosmos. Whether viewed in terms of the most primitive or the most sophisticated cosmologies, this notion has more than a little truth in it. Biologically, behaviorally, intellectually, spiritually, man does partake of, and thus epitomize, all the elements in the cosmos. To confront the literary background and use of this idea would be to write an encyclopedia of all knowledge.

When the idea of a microcosm shifts from man to his body alone, there is considerably less literal truth. Having excluded man's behavior, thought, feelings, and his place among the zoological phyla, we are left with a purely concrete body whose oneness with the cosmos (except in chemical terms) is largely imaginary. His flesh does not resemble purple dust, his eyes are nothing like the sun, and his shape bears no resemblance to any empirical mapping of the world or the universe. Yet in an urge to understand the cosmos and man's place in it men have for several thousand years tried to turn this falsehood into a truth by distorting either the human body or the cosmos or both. They were not all liars. Most of these men knew that they were distorting the truth and did it for didactic or poetic purposes. The individuals who concern us here were not primarily interested in the human body for its own sake; they were not pure scientists or graphic estheticians. They could distort the truth about the concrete features of man and cosmos because they were concerned instead with abstract truths which could be drawn from concrete falsehoods. The act of drawing figurative truth out of literal falsity is the making of a metaphor. This study is concerned with the history and varieties of one particular metaphor, its origins in imagined truth, and its poetic use as a vehicle for a wide range of ideas.

Further limitations of the subject develop from specific ways in which the metaphor was made. The most important attribute of the body as a metaphoric vehicle is that it is a complete and finite system, highly complex but at the same time familiar and immediate. Thus Phineas Fletcher, who writes almost exclusively in truisms, speaks of it in *The Purple Island* as[2]

> A place too seldome view'd, yet still in view;
> Neare as our selves, yet farthest from our care;
>   Which we by leaving finde, by seeking lost;
>   A forrain home, a strange, though native coast;
> Most obvious to all, yet most unknown to most.
>
>   [1.34]

The body is remote not only because we tend to forget it but also because it is "compos'd with curious art" (1.43), so that it needs to be explicated by a poet or a scientist or, in Fletcher's case, a very little bit of both. Yet unlike larger and more abstract systems, e.g., God, the cosmos, or the commonwealth, the human body is finite in size and therefore in complexity. The first step in unraveling this complexity is

2. Citations are to *The Poetical Works of Giles and Phineas Fletcher,* ed. F. S. Boas (Cambridge: Cambridge University Press, 1908).

to postulate that the system of man's body is both exhaustive and all-inclusive, that it has everything it needs and nothing superfluous.

This sense of coherence and completeness brings us to an important characteristic of the metaphors which most concern us in this essay, whether in literature or in the background history of ideas. The focus here will be upon the use of the human body in a complete and systematic way. Thus I will not be interested in eyes, hearts, hands, or any other parts of the body which have in themselves sustained great poetic life, but rather in the creation of a system out of a group of parts, a system which is brought into parallel with another system postulated outside of man. The line between random catalogues and true systems may not be easy to draw, in that what Ptolemy suggested in a catalogue may be turned by Paracelsus into a system, or may have been implicitly a system in the first place. There are, of course, degrees of systematization, a difference, for example, between "My heart then quak'd, then dazled were mine eyes, / One hand forgott to rule, th' other to fight,"[3] and Spenser's House of Alma. Yet both are closed systems, each complete in its own way.

A corollary of this completeness of system is that the metaphor is multiple. Once man is viewed in the concrete terms of his fleshly house, he is inevitably subdivided into a number of parts, for, though the system of his body is closed and finite, it is clearly composed of a large number of separate elements. This concrete multiplicity becomes the vehicle for either concrete or abstract multiplicity in the world around him. Thus the human body as a metaphoric vehicle has considerable range, whether in philosophy or literature, since it is capable of subdividing its referent into a great number of parts, while at the same time controlling the total range by means of the body's essential unity.

The most sophisticated works which make use of the human body metaphor in any extended way invariably use it allegorically, even though, like *Coriolanus* or *Astrophil and Stella*, the works may not be allegories. As Rosemund Tuve has pointed out, allegory is extended metaphor, and thus an extended and consistent use of the human body image in a work is allegorical because it produces a continuous line of

3. *Astrophil and Stella,* Sonnet 53, in *The Poems of Sir Philip Sidney,* ed. W. A. Ringler (Oxford: Clarendon Press, 1962).

action parallel to the narrative itself.[4] The action of human characters in the world may have an analogue in action within the body, similar to the more familiar analogues of action on the plane of abstract virtues, or amongst the gods, or in the heavenly bodies of the cosmos. Furthermore, allegory is inherently concerned with breaking up single abstractions into concrete multiples which can be realized poetically. The system of the human body, both unified and diverse, forms the perfect vehicle for allegory, as Angus Fletcher has pointed out in speaking of the allegorical poet:

> He takes a grand large-scale analogy and breaks it up into its elements, as for example Sin may be subdivided into at least seven aspects to which are applied specific iconographic labels. When each part of the human body is made to stand for a particular part of the body politic, the subdividing process shows the most obvious kind of unity in diversity; both bodies are being anatomized and the parts of both are found to correspond isomorphically to each other.[5]

As we shall see, the commonwealth is not the only body to which the human body can be analogous, nor is the use of the metaphor always so obvious.

But the human body is more than simply an alternative theater of action, subject to comparison with abstractions and cosmic events. After so firmly separating man's body from man at the beginning of this introduction, it is important to bring man back together at this point. The human body is simultaneously abstract and concrete, general and specific. Images of man's body not only form a parallel to the action of the protagonists but are also identical to it, insofar as the characters' bodies take an important place in the action. In *Sejanus*, for instance, the body is not only an analogue to the commonwealth but also a concrete and specific object which Sejanus and Tiberius have depraved; and in *Astrophil and Stella* the body is not only the figurative territory occupied by Venus and her minions but is also representationally the literal bodies of the two title characters, one hot with lust, the other beautifully desirable. The allegory of the human body is projected by the actions of the characters and then projects back into it.

4. *Elizabethan and Metaphysical Imagery* (Chicago: University of Chicago Press, 1965), pp. 105–06.
5. *Allegory: the Theory of a Symbolic Mode* (Ithaca: Cornell University Press, 1964), p. 71.

Most of what follows will be an attempt to bring together strands of thought which have not been systematically viewed before and then to use this material in order to gain some new insights into the presuppositions and the literary practices of certain Renaissance poets. At the same time, however, there is something like an overall thesis. It is a truism that in the Renaissance men turned from pure contemplation of God to contemplation of themselves. This we see in Leonardo, in Montaigne, in Shakespeare. This study fixes upon one aspect of that contemplation, the idea that men are multiple rather than single beings, and suggests that that aspect, at least, was of special interest to the Renaissance. In order to depict man as a creature of great complexity and multiplicity, poets fixed upon the image of his multiple body and used it to subdivide him. In the philosophical tradition, the thrust of argument is away from man: human complexity is assumed, and the body is used rather as a figure for the world's complexity, whether cosmic, political, or architectural. But in the poetic tradition the thrust returns to man, proving that the complexity of the human body and of the worlds analogous to it are figures for the multiple nature of man himself. Thus *The Faerie Queene* is a limitless landscape of the world, a vast number of men who are themselves multiple and subdivided, and finally a single, perhaps perfect, human being who contains in body and spirit all the virtues of the heroes and all the struggles necessary to gain and keep those virtues.

Finally, a note upon the form of this work. I have subdivided the idea of the human body as microcosm into three relatively distinct comparisons: the human body and the cosmos, which is the domain of natural philosophy and science; the human body and the commonwealth, based upon social and political philosophy; and the human body and man-made constructions, the domain of estheticians and architects. These categories are neither mutually exclusive nor collectively exhaustive, but they help to make a vast idea easier to approach. Each of these chapters tries to do several things at once: to depict the history of an idea, to suggest poetic techniques which the idea may have produced, and to read one or more imaginative works in such a way that the history sheds light upon the critical reading and the critical reading upon the history. Each of these chapters is neither exclusively historical nor exclusively critical but rather something midway between the two: an attempt to define a habit of thought. The cause of such a habit of thought is to be found in the history of ideas, and the effect in poetic imagery and metaphor. This study attempts, in terms of one idea, to travel that whole distance. Having made this journey, it then goes on to consider two great sixteenth-century poems in a more purely critical fashion. The readings of *Astrophil and Stella* and *The Faerie Queene* use the habits of thought associated here with the human body as microcosm to rethink the works from the points of view of imagery, structure, and meaning.

1

Natural Philosophy:

The Human Body and the Cosmos

Behind the sophisticated image of the human body as microcosm in Herbert's "Man is ev'ry thing, / And more," lies much in the history of thought and of the imagination. The cosmological view of the individual man, which characterized the study of natural philosophy at least until the Copernican Revolution and can be said to have returned with atomic theory, is the most general and all-embracing context in which to view the microcosmic idea. For Western civilization, to study man was to study the cosmos, and to know the cosmos was to know oneself. The present chapter attempts to summarize the interrelations of these studies of self and cosmos as they have animated natural philosophy.

In the life of the primitive man, the self, and hence the body, is the only wholeness which can be grasped. Anthropomorphism is, *faute de mieux*, this man's only cosmology; and through this simple immediacy he may have experienced an epiphanic and total union with the cosmos that can only be reattained by the richest poetic images of more sophisticated times.[1] In post-literate times, this union becomes less purely

1. The anthropocentric microcosm—a world conceived in terms of the human body—is a highly significant chapter in the history of primitive thought, and despite its relevance to the subject at hand, it can only be alluded to here. For primitive examples, see Mircea Eliade, *Images and Symbols*, trans. Philip Mairet (New York: Sheed and Ward, 1961); and Gilbert Durand, *Les Structures Anthropologiques de l'Imaginaire* (Paris: Presses Universitaires de France, 1960), pp. 33–43. In post-primitive times, the idea of an anthropomorphic cosmos tends to blend with that of a cosmo-morphic man. C. A. Lobeck, in

anthropomorphic, less literal, and more logical. From Plato's time well into the Renaissance, the arts and sciences are recurrently concerned with defining, limiting, and interpreting this union of man and the cosmos. What is for Plato a logical cosmology will become an unquestioned presupposition for later studies of chemistry, astronomy, mathematics, and the natural world. As we proceed through this survey, it will become clear that these studies, parallel but separate in classical and early medieval times, ultimately unite in an anthropomorphic cosmology which finds, in the Renaissance, a great analogical world view imaged forth in a human body invested with allegorical significance.

1

The primitive belief in a literally anthropomorphic cosmos is partly recapitulated in the literary image of the human body as microcosm, but between these two imaginative conceptions lies a great deal of logic and scientific thought. Plato's *Timaeus* is probably the fullest and earliest logical exposition of a microcosmic world view, and his argument, particularly in respect to the human body, can stand as a conceptual framework for all that follows.

The groundwork of Plato's argument is laid by two presuppositions: first, the cosmos is a living creature, and second, it is a copy in the transitory world of "becoming" of a divine original which exists in the world of "being." The cosmos must be a living creature because, as the work of the supremely good creator, it must be endowed with the supreme virtue, i.e., intelligence implanted in a soul. And anything

---

Aglaophamus (Darmstadt: Wissenschaftliche Buchgesellschaft, 1961), cites some primitive Orphic verses in which the physical features of the world like sky, sun, stars, and waters all compose the body of Zeus, who is at once ruler of the world and the world itself. Plutarch, in *Of the Face Appearing in the Orb of the Moon* (in *Morals*, trans. William W. Goodwin [Boston, 1870], 5: 252–53), refers to a more complete correspondence by which the stars are the world's eyes, the moon its liver, the sun its heart, etc.; and Chalcidius's influential commentary on Plato's *Timaeus* extends animism in the same direction. Elsewhere the notion of a man-shaped cosmos is treated more figuratively. Socrates, in *Philebus* 28–30, proves that the universe has a soul by finding, one by one, each element of man's body in the universe and postulating that if it is an anthropomorphic body, it must have a soul. A more clearcut case is Carolus Bovillus (*Liber de Sensu* [Paris, 1570], p. 17), who endows the cosmos with anthropomorphic organs and with human behavioral patterns and sensations.

possessing intelligence must be a living creature. The second presuppo-
sition, suggesting a doctrine of likenesses, leads inevitably to the micro-
cosmic metaphor. "Our world must necessarily be a likeness of
something," says Timaeus at the outset (29b).[2] The search for that
something gives rise to the notion of an infinite regress of likenesses
beginning with man and proceeding all the way to the eternal prin-
ciple. The idea of the animate cosmos cuts both ways: if endowing the
cosmos with life brings it that much closer to an eternal principle, it
also brings it closer to every being that is endowed with life. This
animism is an important step in Plato's logical harmonization of the
cosmos, and by endowing both the world and man with life, he paves
the way toward other more physical similarities between them. The
notion of an infinite regress of likenesses will later become extremely
significant in sophisticated poetic uses of the microcosmic metaphor.
If man's body is a likeness of the cosmos, then it may also contain
miniatures of itself within it, each of which may contain still further
miniatures.[3]

  Plato stops far short of such a poetic figure as this, but he makes it
very clear that the cosmos is as much a copy of all the organisms it
contains as it is of the principle which gave it birth. The cosmos is seen
as a unit containing all other units:

> What was the living creature in whose likeness he framed the world? We must not
> suppose that it was any creature that ranks only as a species; for no copy of that
> which is incomplete can ever be good. Let us rather say that the world is like, above
> all things, to that Living Creature of which all other living creatures, severally and
> in their families, are parts. For that embraces and contains within itself all the intel-
> ligible living creatures, just as this world contains ourselves and all other creatures
> that have been formed as things visible. For the god, wishing to make this world
> most nearly like that intelligible thing which is best and in every way complete,

2. Citations are to Francis Macdonald Cornford, *Plato's Cosmology: the Timaeus of
Plato Translated with a Running Commentary* (New York: Harcourt Brace, 1937; rpt.,
1952).

3. This infinite regress is crucial to the whole microcosmic vision of the body. Individ-
ual parts of the body become human characters with bodies. Shakespeare makes the
belly smile in *Coriolanus*, and each part of Phineas Fletcher's purple island is itself an
island. Ernst Robert Curtius, in *European Literature and the Latin Middle Ages*, trans.
Willard Trask (New York: Pantheon, 1953; rpt., 1963), pp. 136–38, reports that patristic
literature reverted constantly to syntheses among the senses within the body, e.g., "the
hand of the heart," "the head of the soul," "the belly of the heart," "the neck of the
mind," "the groins of the bowels." Augustine and Donne both speak of prayer as a
bending of the knees of the heart.

fashioned it as a single visible living creature, containing within itself all living
things whose nature is of the same order.

[30c,d]

As at many other points, Plato here stops short of saying that the
"other living creatures" are actually identical to the cosmos, but he does
suggest that the nature of the cosmos as organism is determined by the
nature of the organisms which collectively inhabit it.

As Plato's description of the cosmos becomes more concrete, the
actual relations among the likenesses become clearer. He sees the
universe as a composite which is specifically physical:

> And for shape he gave it that which is fitting and akin to its nature. For the living
> creature that was to embrace all living creatures, the fitting shape would be the
> figure that comprehends in itself all the figures there are; accordingly, he turned its
> shape rounded and spherical, equidistant every way from centre to extremity—a
> figure the most perfect and uniform of all; for he judged uniformity to be im-
> measurably better than its opposite.

[33b]

This is the logical, as well as historical, beginning of the corporeal
metaphor arising out of microcosmic principles. The cosmos contains
all smaller organisms and therefore its shape must be that geometric
form which contains all smaller—or less perfect—forms. This line of
argument will be highly significant in creating the analogy between
man's body on the one hand and the cosmos or cosmic elements within
the body on the other. The body may not reproduce the appearance of
its constituent cosmic elements, but its form may be determined by
their collective form.

As Plato approaches an actual description of the world's body, he
makes one more implicit presupposition that suggests the notion of a
physically anthropomorphic cosmos, even though his explicit intent is
to deny this anthropomorphism:

> It had no need of eyes, for nothing visible was left outside; nor of hearing, for there
> was nothing outside to be heard. There was no surrounding air to require breathing,
> nor yet was it in need of any organ to receive food into itself. . . . It had no need of
> hands to grasp with or to defend itself, nor yet of feet or anything that would serve
> to stand upon.

[33c,d]

The presupposition of a human anatomy in the cosmos may well be as
significant for us as is its denial. Plato draws upon this primitive

anthropomorphism in order to demonstrate the weakness of the human condition: our senses, which we take to be our strengths, are seen as weaknesses when we realize how unnecessary they are to the gods' diviner being, the cosmos.[4]

Plato's description of man and his body—in parallel to his description of the cosmos—further helps to lay the foundation for microcosmic metaphor. He has already established that the cosmos is a supremely multiple thing whose physical unity is determined by the bodily nature of its multiple constituents. The next logical step in his argument, as well as in the derivation of a microcosmic human body, involves an understanding that man—particularly in his physical aspect—is also a composite of many elements, whose physical form is determined by these elements:

> Having received the immortal principle of a mortal creature, imitating their own maker [the creator's sons] borrowed from the world portions of fire and earth, water and air, on condition that these loans should be repaid, and cemented together what they took, not with the indissoluble bonds whereby they were themselves held together, but welding them with a multitude of rivets too small to be seen and so making each body a unity of all the portions.
>
> [42d,43a]

This description summarizes the picture of physical man that all microcosmic allegorists will later elaborate. Man is a composite being; the materials which fasten his constituent elements together are too small to be seen, but the fusion is not so perfect that we cannot detect what these separate constituents are. The cosmos is also composite and made of the same constituents as man; but in this case the unification is so perfect that exact definition of these constituents is very difficult. Consequently, research into the constituent elements of man's body is a kind of first step toward understanding the more veiled mysteries of creator and cosmos.

Plato's own research consists of an attempt to explain the structure of the body. He views the body as containing different levels of a corporealized soul, and by reason of this emphasis upon hierarchy, he describes the body in terms of a covert architectural or social metaphor.

---

4. This citation was of central importance to Neoplatonic philosophy. Proclus understood it to suggest that all the profoundest mysteries were not only inaccessible to the senses but also specifically graspable only after anesthesia of some sort. See *In Platonis Timaeum Commentaria*, 39E, ed. Ernst Diehl (Amsterdam: Hakkert, 1965), pp. 95–105.

The divine part of the corporeal soul is separated from the mortal by means of an isthmus, the neck, so that the two are kept apart but do not remain incommunicado. The noblest part of the mortal soul, "which is of a manly spirit and ambitious of victory," is fittingly placed in the highest part of the torso, the breast, "that it might be in hearing of the discourse of reason and join with it in restraining by force the desires, whenever these should not willingly consent to obey the word of command from the citadel" (70a). The heart is the center, or "guard-room," so that if there is a problem, "then every sentient part of the body should quickly, through all the narrow channels, be made aware of the commands and threats and hearken with entire obedience, and so suffer the noblest part to be the leader among them all" (70b). The lower parts of the body serve lower purposes. The stomach is stationed low in the torso, "as it were a manger for the body's nourishment." Appetite, tethered there "like a beast untamed," is placed far from the top so that "it might cause the least possible tumult and clamour and allow the highest part to take thought in peace for the common profit of each and all." Without actually using the metaphor, then, Plato represents the body as a little world of incarnate conflicting powers.

Yet Plato does not offer a heavily moralized reading of the body's structure. The one feature which he rigorously moralizes is the structure of torso and limbs. Plato is somewhat embarrassed by the attachment of such unanalogous features as torso and limbs to the perfect symbolic sphere of the head: "Accordingly, that the head might not roll upon the ground with its heights and hollows of all sorts, and have no means to surmount the one or to climb out of the other, they gave it the body as a vehicle for ease of travel" (44d,e). The spherical shape of the cosmos is the perfect shape because a sphere can move totally without any change of place, "round and revolving in a circle, solitary but able by reason of its excellence to bear itself company, needing no other acquaintance or friend but sufficient to itself" (34b). But man's body, which is not totally effective in confining the immortal soul,

> suffered violent motions; so that the whole creature moved, but advanced at hazard without order or method having all the six motions; for they went forward and backward, and again to right and left, and up and down, straying every way in all the six directions.
>
> [43a,b]

The limbs, for which physical parallels in the cosmos seemed too far-fetched to Plato, are treated as relevant to man's moral condition but not to the moral perfection of the cosmos. If the human body is part of a poetic metaphor in the *Timaeus*, then, it deliberately stands as a partial analogue to that perfection represented by the cosmos, demonstrating to man how high he can rise and how low he can sink.

Thus the scientific process of the dialogue moralizes man's condition implicitly by juxtaposing his body with the world's. As Cornford expresses it,

> The kernel of Plato's ethics is the doctrine that man's reason is divine and that his business is to become like the divine by reproducing in his own nature the beauty and harmony revealed in the cosmos, which is itself a god, a living creature with soul in body and reason in soul.[5]

For man, then, who is also a living creature with soul in body and reason in soul, the analogies between body and world are guideposts, much like the "signatures" which later natural philosophers will find in all of God's minute creations. Sorting out and ordering chaos by means of analogies is the necessary work of man in the cosmos—not unlike the original work of the creator—and the microcosmic metaphor of the body comes to stand for the proper perception of one's place in the cosmos. The search for the proper place, in cosmological terms, is the study of the ways in which the multiplicities of the world's body can be united with the multiplicities of man's.

2

Four approaches to cosmology arise from such speculation as Plato's and become the systems by which the bodies of greater and lesser worlds are united: the chemical geocosm, envisaging a world composed of the four elements; the astral geocosm, presupposing a heavenly cosmos that is both physical and spiritual; a numerical geocosm made up of abstract mathematical relations; and a natural geocosm comprised of the objects of this world as immediately beheld by the senses.

The system of the four elements—earth, air, fire, and water—is perhaps the most ancient of the cosmogonies which have persisted through Western thought. It represents what we might call a chemical

5. Cornford, *Plato's Cosmology*, p. 34.

geocosm, accounting for the origin and nature of the universe in terms of the constituent parts of matter. While the constituents are conceived of as pure essences beyond the experience of mortal man, they nonetheless resemble four perfectly common substances whose properties, at least in the diluted form we can observe, are familiar and can be studied in order to grasp the nature of their interaction within the cosmic sphere. The elements make up the world and the human body alike. The familiar and observable play among the elements in the world is itself a miniature version of the chemical principles underlying the creation, and as a miniature, the system of elements is parallel to the creator's own miniature, the human body. In order to understand the whole of creation, which is presumed beyond empirical grasp, the natural philosopher juxtaposes two kinds of entities which are familiar and graspable: the four elements and the human body. The four elements, diluted in the form we know them, are to their pure and essential form as the human body is to the macrocosm.

The actual content of the theory of the four elements in antiquity is not, however, so conscious of its presuppositions as the above explanation might suggest. The origin of the system can be credited to the Asiatic thinkers who influenced the pre-Socratic philosophers, but its most complete expression is to be found in the fragments of Empedocles (ca. 500–430 B.C.), where a cosmic system is built out of the four elements, whose relations are governed by attraction and repulsion, or love and hate. For Empedocles, the elements are the essential mediation between the One as principle of creation and the Many as objects or evidences of creation, just as they mediate between abstract essences and things.[6]

The four elements constitute a cosmos which is inevitably in flux, in which man's ultimate good consists in his centrifugal efforts against the forever centripetal spirit of negation. The Empedoclean fragments suggest a rather specific program of centripetal and centrifugal movements. The four elements are ruled alternately by love and strife. Love unites them into a single sphere, while strife fragments them into

6. So too his philosophy mediates chronologically. See Jean Bollack, *Empédocle* (Paris: Les Editions de Minuit, 1965) 1:19, "Empédocle se situe à la crête de deux versants. Derrière lui les Ioniens . . . qui réduisent toutes choses à l'Un et, devant lui, les modernes, Anaxagore et les Abdéritains, qui multiplient à l'infini les principes, *homéomeries, semences,* atomes, et les dérobent au regard."

separate concentric spheres. The process occurs in a continuous cycle. During the period of love, the cosmos is one single harmonious sphere with strife surrounding its outer surface. Strife initiates its reign by breaking through that outer surface, forcing love toward the center and separating the elements into four individual concentric spheres. The period of strife is at its height when love is isolated at the center, but immediately thereafter it starts to move outward, uniting the elements as it goes. These unions and combinations of elements eventually create a perfect sphere forcing strife again to the outer shell.[7] This process illustrates two of the crucial habits of thought associated with the microcosmic metaphor of the body: it asserts that the human condition is essentially changeable and multiple, and it expresses that condition in terms of a concrete construction subject to the laws of physics and geometry. The human body is parallel to this macrocosm of love and strife: first because it too contains the four elements and the two forces, and second because it too is a concrete construction subject to the laws of geometry and physics.

In the Empedoclean macrocosm the body is a quintessential image of *discordia concors*: it contains the fragmented multiplicity of the elements, but it unites them harmoniously. The sexual act is to the microcosm as the power of love to the macrocosm. In the history of the cosmos the original creation of the human body took place at the time of the perfect sphere. Out of what might have been a chaos of limbs and members, there came the beautiful and symmetrical form we know. The individual human reproductive act is parallel to the whole movement of the cosmos. Two bodies unite, members seeking out like members, in a symmetry that produces a seed containing the same symmetry in miniature, just as the body itself contains the symmetry of the macrocosm.

Empedocles, for all his purported invention of the four elements, does little to make them concrete, individual, or differentiated. The body is an image of the wholeness possible among them. It is appropriate, then, that his picture of the universe in a complete state of strife is concerned almost entirely with monstrous bodies: disconnected limbs and animals' heads attached to human torsos.[8] The human body as we have it is a perfection of harmony, a reminder of the power of

7. See D. O'Brien, *Empedocles' Cosmic Cycle* (Cambridge: Cambridge University Press, 1969), pp. 1–2.

8. See especially Fragment 495, in Bollack, *Empédocle* 2:177.

love during these times in which strife is gaining on us. Its chemistry of elements, which joins it to the cosmos, is not so much a union in content between man and the world as a description of the human condition.

For Empedocles, the equality and integrity of the elements are such that even in the perfect sphere they never really mix but remain discrete, even when minute. When Plato takes over the system in the *Timaeus*, the elements develop considerably more fluidity and dynamism. We can compare, for instance, two descriptions of the origin of bone. In Empedocles' system, bone contains four parts of fire, two of earth, one of air, and one of water. Plato is less interested in providing a cookbook than in exploring the dynamics of the creator and the hydraulics of the creation itself. Thus, his account of the origin of bone:

> Having sifted out earth that was pure and smooth, he kneaded it and soaked it with marrow; then he plunged the stuff into fire, next dipped it in water, and again in fire and once more in water; by thus shifting it several times from one to the other he made it insoluble by either.
>
> [73e]

These two accounts of the origin of bone stand in the same relation as the two parts of any culinary recipe, the list of ingredients and the instructions; and the difference between them is telling for later allegorizations of composite man. For Empedocles, as for his predecessor Anaxagoras, each kind of matter was made up of a vast number of homogeneous particles. The four elements are not parts of our actual experience in the world but rather pure types of matter. His composite man is the result of a divine recipe which scarcely takes into account the ways in which the four elements, as primary parts of our familiar universe, would act upon each other.

Plato, on the other hand, describes a process which anyone might attempt if he only had the purest forms of the four elements. Thus not only is man made of earth, air, fire, and water, but these elements have individual identities and a familiar relationship among themselves. The elements within us, though refined and mixed so that their primary and familiar form is barely perceptible, are cousins to matter which we can directly perceive in the world around us, whether that external matter be primary or itself composite. Conclusions we might draw empirically about relations among the primary elements in nature become valid when translated into the terms of the human body.

Once the constituent elements of man's body are truly identified

with those of the cosmos, human experience can be seen as a series of
confrontations among like and unlike elements in micro- and macro-
cosm. The most interesting example of this confrontation also repre-
sents one of the few instances where Plato asserts that anatomical and
cosmic events are identical. He has been discussing the formation of
the blood, made from the particles we take in, then digested by means
of fire and hence stained red:

> This we call blood, on which the flesh and the whole body feed, so that every mem-
> ber draws water therefrom to replenish the base of the depleted part. The manner of
> this replenishment and wasting is like that movement of all things in the universe
> which carries each thing towards its own kind. For the elements besetting us out-
> side are always dissolving and distributing our substance, sending each kind of body
> on its way to join its fellows; while on the other hand the substances in the blood,
> when they are broken up small within us and find themselves comprehended by the
> individual living creature, framed like a heaven to include them, are constrained to
> reproduce the movement of the universe.
>
> [80e,81a,b]

This description epitomizes one traditional scientific ground for the
microcosmic metaphor. Blood is itself a microcosm, a purée of the
universe. Man's experience in the cosmos demonstrates that all parti-
cles are seeking their fellows; so, too, the puréed particles in our blood.
Our body is a cosmos, "framed like a heaven to include them," and the
search of like for like, which is a kind of vital force, animates the world
within. The particles of the universe which we have consumed are
"constrained" to reproduce the cosmos by this vital force. In this
tradition, then, the body imitates the cosmos by its wholeness; they do
not resemble one another physically, but each of them is a complete
world. The microcosm repeats the dynamic motions of the macrocosm,
whether in abstraction and essence, as in Empedocles' cycles of *philia*
and *neikos*, or in Plato's biochemistry conceived in the image of world
geography.[9]

9. Other examples of the confrontation between internal and external elements in-
clude Plato's explanations of eyesight and his discussion of the relation between the flesh
and weather conditions. Sight he takes to be the noblest of the senses, resulting from a
particular alliance between the elements of fire within and without the human body:
"Such fire as has the property, not of burning, but of yielding a gentle light, they con-
trived should become the proper body of each day. For the pure fire within us is akin to
this and they caused it to flow through the eyes. . . . Accordingly, whenever there is
daylight round us, the visual current issues forth, like to like and coalesces with it and is
formed into a single homogeneous body in a direct line with the eyes, in whatever quar-

The geographical microcosm that arises out of the chemical is both extended and limited by the applications of the theory of the elements to medicine. From the earliest times, the four elements within the body were felt to be distinctive in form and to be individually associated with bodily substances. In Empedocles the four elements created the body by a series of quasi-geographical processes, but their pure form then departed from the microcosm, leaving traces only in the blood, which contains them all and which circulates in imitation of macrocosmic motions.[10] This rather monistic conception is in keeping with Empedocles' vision of the body as essentially unified. Contemporaries of his, however, envisaged the anatomy as containing a multitude of forces. In the Hippocratic tradition these were limited to four, viz., the hot, the cold, the moist, and the dry, which ally themselves quite neatly with the four elements.[11] Up to this point the biochemistry remains microcosmic: the body contains familiar constituent parts, and health or disease can be predicted by an observation of these elements or forces as they operate among themselves in the microcosm.

The next step, taken in a treatise called *The Nature of Man*, which Aristotle attributed to Polybus, is the conception of the four humours, blood, phlegm, yellow bile, and black bile.[12] Though these were originally associated with the four elements in the macrocosm, they eventually lost their cosmic relevance and developed exclusively corporeal

---

ter the stream issuing from within strikes upon any object it encounters outside" (45b,c). As far as the flesh is concerned, Plato offers a relatively empirical explanation of confrontation among the elements: "[the flesh] contained in itself a warm moisture, which in summer it might sweat forth and so spread a native coolness all over the body by moistening it outside, while in winter, on the other hand, we should have this fire as a fair protection against the assaults of the beleaguering frost outside" (74c). Earth, air, fire, and water have their corresponding properties: dryness, coldness, heat, and moisture; and both the human body and the climate are composed of these properties. Flesh is predominantly fire and water, "warm moisture," while summer is fire and earth and winter is air and water. By some unexplained process, like elements are neutralized in the confrontation of flesh with the two seasons. In the winter, body temperature warms us and in the summer, perspiration cools us. The anatomical properties are metaphorically identical to natural properties in the cosmos both in terms of their constituent elements and in terms of the actual heat (like hot weather) we feel inside us and the perspiration (like rain) we feel on our skin.

10. See Bollack, *Empédocle*, 1:242–43; also Fragment 551 in idem, 2:204–07.

11. The Hippocratic treatise *De Victu*, for instance, suggests that dropsy is an excess of water and can be remedied as one might deal with inundation on land. See Walter Pagel, *Paracelsus* (Basel: S. Karger, 1958), p. 214 n.

12. See Rudolf Allers, "Microcosmus," *Traditio* 2 (1944): 347.

significations. The link is not completely forgotten. As late as 1120, Henricus Francigena asserts: "Mundus iste ex quatuor constat. . . . Continet enim hominem qui microcosmus dicitur . . . qui ex quatuor elementis constat, . . . sed etiam ex quatuor humoribus qui similes propterea sortiti sunt."[13] Nonetheless, in the classical and medieval periods, the concrete metaphor of the corporeal microcosm which underlies the origins of the humour theory remains submerged. Only when the rather abstruse designations for the humours are abandoned in favor of anatomical substances more familiar and more closely linked to the chemical geocosm is the image of *homo microcosmus* re-awakened. In the twelfth-century *Quod Homo sit Minor Mundus* of Robert Grosseteste, for example, the elements are internalized more simply: earth as flesh, water as blood, air as breath, and fire as vital heat.[14] Such associations make microcosmic analogies possible: Grosseteste, for instance, suggests that the head makes use of the four internal elements just as the heavens use the four external ones. Yet the general evolution of the idea from elements to humours, complexions, and lastly, personality types, tends to submerge and destroy the connections between the multiples of the world's body and those of man's. Nevertheless, such a submerged idea is the most fertile ground for metaphor in the mind of a poet who can create a sympathetic confrontation between, say, a melancholy disposition and the earth, out of which— back in the days of Empedocles—that disposition sprung.

The number of the elements, which was itself invested with significance by the Greeks and others, leads us to another vision of the universe, which we may call the numerical or proportional geocosm. The theory of the four elements, as has been suggested, attempts to define the matter of the cosmos, but, apart from certain suggestions about its dynamic motions, does little to explain its form. A microcosmic analogy based upon the elements can suggest merely that man's body resembles the cosmos in constituent parts, and for metaphoric purposes such an equation is very limited.

The numerical geocosm represents just the opposite vision. Its originator, Pythagoras, struggling with the Ionic belief that there was a single, primary matter and unable to reconcile this with the fact of

13. Ibid., pp. 345–46 n.
14. In *Die Philosophischen Werke*, ed. Ludwig Baur (Münster: Aschendorff, 1912), pp. 77–78.

there being different objects in the world, rejected matter in favor of structure as determining the "nature" of a thing.[15] This structure he saw in geometric and proportional terms, borrowing especially from his discovery that the nature of musical tones was spatial and geometric. Plato, in fact, uses the proportional system in the *Timaeus* to derive the four elements. First he explains the nature of geometric proportion. Then, assuming the two most opposed elements, fire and earth, he demonstrates how a solid entity like the cosmos would require two geometric means instead of one:

> Accordingly the god set water and air between fire and earth, and made them, so far as was possible, proportional to one another, so that as fire is to air, so is air to water, and as air is to water, so is water to earth, and thus he bound together the frame of a world visible and tangible.
>
> [32b]

Neither Plato nor Pythagoras specifically connects the numerical geocosm with the microcosm; yet the nature of their mathematical speculations is extremely influential for the microcosmic tradition. In the Pythagorean system, the whole cosmos is a series of entities standing in geometric proportion to one another. This proportion, or *analogia*, specifies a microcosmic relation among all the constituents of the cosmos. The human body as microcosm is the quintessential *analogia*: as the creator is to man's body, so is man's body to the world. They do not have to be identical, but the body must be a proportional reduction. Like the mathematician, the natural philosopher can supply missing terms once the nature of the ratio is specified and two of the terms are given. The world and man's body can specify the deity, or the deity and man's body can specify the world.[16]

Chemistry provides the matter and geometry the form of the cosmos; the astral microcosm incorporates both systems in its own vision of wholeness. Astrology, from its very origins in Chaldean observation of the heavens, offered the Greeks a synthetic vision, at once mystical and natural, at once chemical and arithmetical. The geography of the

15. For Pythagoras, see Allers, "Microcosmos," pp. 341–43 and R. G. Collingwood, *The Idea of Nature* (Oxford: Oxford University Press, 1965), pp. 49–55.

16. On the body itself, we are told by Aristotle and Macrobius that Pythagoras saw the soul as the harmony of the body; thus it too is a proportional reduction or microcosm.

heavens is a physical version of the abstract world order, while astral influences and relations among the bodies are a spiritual version of the cosmos. These are the two components of the astral geocosm, and the science of astrology consists in the exact definition of the heavens through empirical means for the purpose of grasping the links which underlie the physical system. The astrological vision, then, includes the naturalistic and chemical studies we associated with the four elements, for planets and signs of the zodiac are entities whose physical essence must be grasped;[17] it also includes the study of geometry and proportion, since astral influence can only be determined through an exact knowledge of the mathematical relations among the heavenly bodies.

Astrology is microcosmic from its inception: man is the crucial and central term in the astral cosmos, and since all the bodies in the cosmos influence all the others, man must contain within him the distillation of the whole astral system. But what is the nature of this essence which the astral cosmos and the microcosm share? In the most ancient Eastern astrology, which influenced the Greeks of the Golden Age, this essence is in part simple and in part mystical. On the one hand the planets and zodiacal signs are connected with heroes and divinities possessing specific personalities and destinies that could stand as constituent parts of each individual; on the other hand, the connection between the astral body with its significations and the individual is vague and spiritual. Only with the Stoics, who brought astrology into the mainstream of Western thought, do these mystical connections come to be scrutinized:

> L'influence des astres sur la terre devint pour eux un cas particulier de la "sympathie" ou solidarité de toutes les parties de l'univers: solidarité non pas idéale, morale, mais matérielle comme la substance de l'être, et réalisée à tout moment par un échange de molécules ou de mouvements propagés.[18]

The earth was felt to nourish the heavens; and this nourishment returned in subtler and more obscure forms, as both physical and spiritual influences on human life. The indisputable physical influences of the heavens on the tides and the weather, for example, became proofs of spiritual influences.

17. See the chart harmonizing zodiacal signs, seasons, ages, elements, winds, qualities, conditions, humours, temperaments, and colors in Jean Seznec, *The Survival of the Pagan Gods*, trans. B. F. Sessions (New York: Pantheon, 1953; rpt., 1961), p. 47.
18. A. Bouché-Leclerq, *L'Astrologie Grecque* (Paris, 1899), p. 75. .

The tension between the physical aspect of the astrological system, which is logical, and the spiritual, which is mystic, can be resolved when the emphasis is shifted from man to man's body, and in this sense the system is important to our study. Only within the human body, seen here as a system governed by the elements, humours, and complexions, are the physical and spiritual truly united. The organs of the body can be parallel to the various heavenly bodies, and the relations among the organs, which can be read both medically and in terms of personality and destiny, can be seen as indicative of the astral influences within the microcosm and between the microcosm and the macrocosm. Thus as early as 400 B.C., the world of astral influences is closely connected with microcosmic theory and gives rise not only to astral biology but also to astral geography and botany.[19] Throughout this early time and well into the Hellenistic period when astrology flowered, the superimposing of the human body upon the cosmos was a means of uniting the multiplicity of substances in the world and defining the nature of the spirit.

The union of astrology with the body arises, then, out of the search for parallel wholeness; and ancient astrology had two cosmic systems in which the body could be inscribed: the zodiacal, emphasized by the great Egyptian astrologers of the first centuries of the Christian Era like Ptolemy and Manilius, and the planetary, emphasized by the much earlier Chaldeans. Each system has its own kind of power over the individual and its own links to parts of man's body. The zodiacal signs are present at birth and govern the permanent and abiding nature of anatomical features, while the planets, as their configuration changes in the cosmos, determine the day-to-day alterations within our bodies.

The features of anatomy and cosmography which are paired are not so important as are the principles by which the pair was brought together. The planetary and zodiacal systems differ in this respect. The planets are literally astral bodies whose concrete features are irrelevant to human anatomy. They are present in the human body because astrology endowed them with human spiritual values, which were then seated—either logically or imaginatively—in specific parts of the anatomy. Consequently, phlegm is of Saturn, famed for melancholy disposition; male reproductive organs of Mars, associated with heat

19. Wilhelm and Hans Georg Gundel, *Astrologumena* (Wiesbaden: Steiner, 1966), p. 80 n.

and passion; olfactory sense of Venus, goddess of love and therefore of
perfumes. Other associations are made with more spiritual values of
the planet–gods: Mercury is associated with reason and is therefore
present in the tongue; while still others are more empirical, such as the
sun being present in the eyes.

The planetary system is joined with the human body not astronom-
ically, but by the metamorphosis of the planets into gods who have
human form and personality. If we carry this system beyond its orig-
inally narrow imaginative limits, the cosmos can form an external
stage on which dramas can be acted out and then mirrored in the work-
ing of our anatomy. If we restrict ourselves purely to the plane of
anatomy, these dramas are as predictable as all planetary motion; but
with the attribution of anthropomorphic significance to the planets
via the lives of the gods, the dramas within one human anatomy or
among various people have a greater potential field of variety.

The zodiacal system offered a more physical, and more anthropo-
centric, junction of man's body and the world's. Since the signs of the
zodiac had little concrete astronomical form, they could take the shape
of man's body and their permanent positions in a circle around our
anatomy, equivalent to their positions in the circle of the heavens. A
seventeenth-century translation of Manilius will serve to summarize
the zodiacal system of correspondences:

> For as in Man, the work of Hands Divine,
> Each Member lies allotted to a Sign;
> And as the Body is the common care
> Of all the Signs, each Limb enjoys a share:
> (The Rame defends the Head, the Neck the Bull,
> The Arms bright Twins are subject to your Rule;
> I' th' Shoulders Leo, and the Crab's obey'd
> I' th' Breast, and in the Guts the modest Maid;
> I' th' Buttocks Libra, Scorpio warms desires
> I' th' secret parts, and spreads unruly fires:
> The thighs, the Centaur, and the Goat commands
> The Knees, and binds them up with double bands.
> The parted Legs in cold Aquarius meet,
> And Pisces gives protection to the Feet.)[20]

The correspondences themselves, unlike those of the planets, are far-

---

20. Marcus Manilius, *The Five Books of M. Manilius*, trans. Thomas Creech (London,
1697), pp. 32–33.

fetched and often based on trivial physical resemblances: Aries, seen exclusively as a head, therefore located there; Pisces at the feet simply because there are two of them, though, as Bouché-Leclerq dryly points out, fish have no feet; Taurus, an animal with a strong neck, at the neck; Gemini, again because of doubleness, at the arms and shoulders; Cancer, because of its strong shell, at the chest; Libra, at the breasts or the buttocks, which balance the body, etc. The correspondences are unimportant, but the physical system by which a sphere of different forces was placed around the human body was very influential. Since our nonspherical bodies could not be made identical with a spherical cosmos, the zodiac was itself transformed into a kind of oval casing for the body, called the Melothesia, or zodiacal man. This represents a primitive version of our metaphor. Man's body is viewed as a whole rather than in a list of anatomical parts, and is isomorphic with the heavens. The astrologers inscribe the individual in a man-shaped cosmic circle so that the multiplicity of the universe is contained and logically structured within him. The planetary system brought tiny bits of the gods into our bodies; but the zodiacal system makes of our bodies a spherical cosmos and perfect replica of the external one.

The picture of the natural geocosm which arises in the Middle Ages out of interpretations of Genesis 1:26 ("Let us make man in our image"), is holistic, like astrology, but it derives from a rather different combination of the chemical and mathematical visions. Genesis 1:26 clearly meant to locate man physically and spiritually in relation to God; but the problem for cabalistic exegetes was that God transcended physical form. Thus the medieval Jewish philosophers make use of the method of *analogia*: God's body and man's are joined together in the world's body.

The leap from God's body to the world's was performed by a curious rationalization. When God said, "Let *us* make man, . . . ," He was not speaking with royal plurality but rather, according to *Bereshit Rabba* (sixth century), He was assembled in congress with the works of heaven and earth, which He had after all made on an earlier day.[21] This is no isolated bit of choplogic: it is maintained by most interpreters, including such diverse natural philosophers as Philo Judaeus and the seventeenth-century Helkanah Crooke, who dramatizes this council of

21. Cited in George Perrigo Conger, *Theories of Macrocosms and Microcosms in the History of Philosophy* (New York: Columbia University Press, 1922), p. 38.

heaven and earth and uses it to exalt man above all other creations. These biblical interpreters believe in an extremely straightforward physical microcosm. The parallels they conceive of between anatomy and cosmography are very concrete ones which demonstrate simply that man is made of the same materials as his world.

Having used the structural method of the proportional geocosm, this approach to the cosmos goes on to be more concerned with matter than with form. If God is in the world and the world is in man, then both man's body and the world's must be exhaustively read and analyzed if man is to grasp God. For these interpreters, the body may be a mere container of all the world's constituent parts. The basic purpose was to praise God for the limitless variety of the cosmos and for His remarkable achievement in abstracting every single cosmic element into man. At the simplest level of cabalistic interpretation, these parallels do not form a coherent system, and the union between man and God's image is largely forgotten in the face of scientific analogies between man and the earth. Thus in the *Pirke* of Rabbi Eliezer (eighth century) man is made of four colors of dust, red for the blood, black for the intestines, white for the bones, and yellow for the nerves. This represents neither a call to worship nor a vision of God's image in man. Other commentators on Genesis turned man into a more complete world in himself and thus more nearly a replica of God. Shabethai Donolo extended the notion of God creating man in His image to the natural limit, where man is himself a creator.[22] Man was made of the four humours, air his blood, water his phlegm, fire his black bile, and earth his yellow bile. God created the four elements and out of them made man. Man in turn is capable of producing these elements. He produces air when he breathes; he produces water by breathing against a hard object which then becomes damp; he can produce fire by means of a glass; and he can produce a solid mass by boiling a kettle of water for a long time. This exegesis views man in the light of a coherent and complete system, the four elements. It investigates the elements in empirical or scientific terms, and it concludes by demonstrating man's similarity to God not in terms of physical image, but in reference to the concrete substances both man and God can create.

This is primarily a natural vision of the microcosm. In order to see the place of his body and spirit in the cosmos, the religious man does not have to be a savant: a chemist isolating the pure elements, a

22. Conger, *Theories*, pp. 38–40.

mathematician assigning numbers and proportions to the parts of creation, or an astrologer reading the heavens. He merely has to observe the world around him with a properly allegorizing frame of mind. The cabalistic tradition is more important for the later method of the metaphor than even the system of *analogia*, for it is not chemistry, mathematics, or astronomy, but rather metaphysics, the leap from the commonest features of the world to spiritual and corporeal equivalents. When Rabbi Nathan, in his *Abot* (eighth or ninth century), suggests that man, being of one substance with the universe, has within him all its powers and capacities to deal with its difficulties, he is turning Genesis back upon itself, seeing man created in God's image as a god-like world.[23] As we proceed through the later syncretistic development of the metaphor, it will become clear that the elements, the proportions, and the heavens are joined with a metaphysical or allegorizing turn of mind in order to see man through his body as both multiple and unified, like the world.

3

These ancient and relatively simple visions of the universe all presuppose an actual equivalence of body and cosmos. In each case the equivalence is couched in rather mystical terms: the essences of the chemical geocosm, the numbers of the proportional geocosm, the *sympatheia* between heavenly and human bodies in the astral geocosm, and the image of God in the world of the monotheistic geocosm. Yet despite the implicit mystical leaps, these natural philosophies consider the microcosmic idea a direct, even scientific clue to the nature of things. But Platonic and Pauline Christianity, which viewed the body

23. The *Abot* of Rabbi Nathan includes perhaps the longest of all lists of parallels between the cosmos and man's body. An exhaustive human and cosmic system is built not by means of a short, complete series like the four elements, but rather by sheer length and inclusiveness. For this commentator and the rabbinical sources he is relaying, the identity itself is an act of devotion. It must be total and it need not be logical. Thus apart from a couple of normal analogies (forests and hair, king and head) most are highly idiosyncratic, e. g., wild beasts and worms, fresh water and saliva, smelly waters and mucus. But Rabbi Nathan finds a kind of ethical system in the midst of his act of devotion. Here the microcosmic human body makes man a replica of God not by scientific casuistry but by the suggestion that God has implanted in man all the powers he needs to live almost as a god. Such parallels as horses with shoulders, warriors with arms, advisors with kidneys, and heaven with the tongue, make man truly a little world. See Kaim Pollak, ed. *Rabbi Nathans System der Ethik und Moral* (Budapest, 1905).

as a mere shell, coupled with a certain degree of anatomical empiricism in the Middle Ages and the Renaissance, tended to diversify the microcosmic idea into two strands: the figurative microcosm, which views man—rather than his body—as a précis of all creation and seeks in that perception a spiritual or intellectual truth, and the literal microcosm, which assumes an equivalence of man's body and the cosmos and uses this equivalence as some sort of scientific key to the nature of the world and man. Since this is a study of the human body, and since the notion of man in general as microcosm is a vast and separate chapter in the history of philosophy, we shall concentrate upon the literal microcosm. Yet the figurative microcosm cannot be excluded from a study that attempts to fill in the background to Renaissance poetry. The great images of the body as microcosm are often combinations of the figurative and literal visions; the concrete details of man's body and the world's are the vehicles of the metaphor, and the spiritual union of man and the cosmos is the tenor.

In the literary image of the body as microcosm, the literal and figurative visions are joined; but in the history of natural philosophy through the Middle Ages and the Renaissance, the figurative tradition remained independent from the literal and very much more in the mainstream of thought. The figurative view of man as microcosm arises out of a great variety of philosophical traditions and periods, but it is always composed of two parts: a method, the metaphoric imagination that transforms a non-human phenomenon into an equivalent within human experience, and a content, the idea that man contains everything which he can perceive in the world around him. These are the presuppositions of humanism, whether classical, medieval, or Renaissance. The method praises man's mind, and the content praises his condition.

Homo omnis creatura is the keystone of medieval humanism. In such an early expression as the works of Philo Judaeus, for example, we find elements that characterize it throughout its history. No one could more perfectly epitomize the influence of the four geocosms than Philo: a Platonist versed in the *Timaeus* and the lore of the four elements, he was also a numerological philosopher,[24] an Alexandrian of the first century

24. See his treatment of the number seven in "On the Creation," in *Works*, trans. F. H.

living at the center of astronomy and astrology, and finally a learned Jew engaged in interpreting the Old Testament, including such verses as "let us make man in our image." The force of all these traditions in Philo's thought led him to be perhaps the inventor of symbolic scriptural interpretation, even though his influence upon Christian authors was not so great as that of his countryman, Clement of Alexandria. Philo approaches Mosaic Scripture as a text which is neither direct in its moral meanings, nor so oblique as to be imaginary or mythical. For Philo, the interpreter of Mosaic Scripture must accept it as literal, but also be prepared to expound it figuratively or allegorically in order to decipher the moral or spiritual meaning which Moses "refrained . . . from stating abruptly."[25]

Philo reads the cosmos literally and allegorically much as he reads Scripture. When expounding upon the creation of Eve, for instance, he combines these views in seeing man as having

> the power of holding together, of growing, of conscious life, of thought, and countless other powers, varying both in species and genus. Lifeless things, like stones and blocks of wood, share with all others the power of holding together, of which the bones in us, which are not unlike stones, partake. "Growth" extends to plants, and there are parts in us, such as our nails and hair, resembling plants; "growth" is coherence capable of moving itself. Conscious life is the power to grow, with the additional power of receiving impressions and being the subject of impulses. This is shared also by creatures without reason. Indeed our mind contains a part that is analogous to the conscious life of a creature without reason.[26]

Philo reads man, his body, and the cosmos allegorically in order to prove that man contains all the orders of creation within him.

But the extent of man's inclusiveness is less interesting than the regularity and order of the picture. To superimpose man upon the cosmos is to structure both entities. Man is ordered by means of his various powers and capacities; and the cosmos is ordered by a sequence of levels of creation. The human body may offer the most concrete kind of structure, but when the microcosmic idea is only figurative, man and the cosmos are structured intellectually. Philo emphasizes

---

Colson and G. H. Whitaker (London: Heinemann, 1929), 1:89–127.

25. "On the Creation," *Works*, 1:6.
26. "Allegorical Interpretation of Genesis," in Philo, *Works*, 1:238–40.

abstract hierarchy—here stones, plants, and beasts—since hierarchy is a basic intellectual structure with quasi-visual significances and with close connections to the Ptolemaic world picture.[27] Man's hierarchy of powers becomes, in the figurative tradition, the spiritual equivalent of the hierarchy of corporeal beings among the various orders of creation. The connection between the plant life in the cosmos and the abstract power of growth within man is the raw material of metaphor.

The celebration of man throughout the Middle Ages closely follows Philo's formulation. Gregory the Great's version of *homo omnis creatura* is probably the most influential: "Omnis enim creaturae habet homo. Homini namque esse cum lapidis, vivere cum arboribus, sentire cum animalibus, intelligere cum angelis."[28] The microcosmic picture of man's condition remains essentially orderly and hierarchical. It is not necessarily assumed that either man or the cosmos is in and of itself well ordered—indeed, much medieval thought is opposed to that idea—but both take on a system and hierarchy when juxtaposed because they can indeed only be related by means of abstract conceptual order. This order may be the four elements, Aristotle's three souls, the four orders of being, or even the planetary system. The celebration of man always resides in the fact that he is at once in the middle of the hierarchy and yet also outside it, being able to contain all of it within him. Man is seen as having a symmetrical external relation to the creation but a multiplicity of creation within him. Though he is intrinsically lower than the order of angels, yet he is greater in being more multiple.

Homo omnis creatura was such a commonplace of medieval humanism that it must have seemed old-fashioned and scholastic to the men of the early Renaissance. The absolute equivalence of man's powers with those of the other orders begins to be questioned even in the thirteenth and fourteenth centuries. Even Aquinas introduces a "quodammodo" to the familiar formula: "homo dicitur minor mundus quia omnes creaturae mundi quodammodo inveniuntur in eo."[29] The figurative idea of man as microcosm does not by any means lose its appeal to Renaissance philosophers, but it becomes yet more abstract and

27. See also "On the Creation," *Works* 1: 50, where he produces a hierarchy moving from fish to land animals to birds to man.

28. Cited in Allers, "Microcosmus," p. 345.

29. *Summa Theologica*, 1, q. 91. a. 1c., Blackfriars Edition (New York: McGraw Hill, 1963), 13:18.

intellectual. While the image is still intended to order and harmonize multiplicity, the order is much less likely to be strictly hierarchical and concrete or visual in any way.

Nicholas Cusanus, whom Ernst Cassirer sees as the philosophical springboard of the Renaissance, rejects the Aristotelian and scholastic notion of a hierarchy or continuum which moves step by step from the inanimate to the angelic.[30] The Divine is so infinitely separated from all other orders that the comparative distance between man and beast, for example, is negligible. The created universe, the contemplation of which is essential to the microcosmic metaphor, is no longer an image of perfect wholeness or order. Given the infinite separation of the Divine, all within the created world is a great deal more random and relative than the scholastics had believed:

> The earth is not a comparative part of the world, nor is it an aliquot part of the world; for the world has neither a maximum nor a minimum and, in consequence, has neither a middle nor aliquot parts. With man or animal we have the same thing, for, though the hand of man seems to bear a relation to his body through its weight it is not an aliquot part of man; and the same assertion has to be made of magnitude and figure.[31]

These proportional relationships break down because everything within the creation depends upon point of view, i.e., these familiar proportions represent only our limited point of view.

Cusanus does not reject the idea of man as microcosm. He calls the ancient idea "reasonable," but since the union of man and cosmos cannot be based upon proportional relationship, it is achieved only through the humanity of Christ. Man does contain all the orders of being, and these produce in man "the perfection of all things." This perfection alone explains how Christ could have become a man. In this way Cusanus resolves the paradox between man as the middle of creation and man superior to all the orders by his inclusiveness. The former is man's humanity and the later his relation to Christ as man. This abstract version of the microcosm, often found in Renaissance philosophy, tends to remove the impression of man's multiplicity. The multiplicity is so perfectly ordered in the inclusiveness of Christ—or some

30. See Ernst Cassirer, *The Individual and the Cosmos in Renaissance Philosophy* (Oxford: Clarendon Press, 1963), pp. 7–73.
31. Nicholas Cusanus, *Of Learned Ignorance*, trans. Germain Heron (London: Routledge and Kegan Paul, 1954), 2:12; p. 113.

other more abstract principle—that the vision of man is neither diverse enough nor ordered enough to create a powerful tension between harmony and fragmentation.

But Cusanus represents only one side of the Renaissance picture. The same endless, irreconcilable worlds which Cusanus harmonizes so easily in the person of Christ can be for others a vast and frightening cosmos in which man must find his place. This is particularly true for Pico della Mirandola. For the Renaissance Neoplatonists, man is a chameleon in a cosmos of bewildering multiplicity. The One behind the Many is to be as diligently sought as Cusanus seeks Christ, but the Many of the cosmos thwarts man in his search. Pico describes man's condition in the familiar medieval terms of the microcosm. This union of man with the multiple cosmos serves to make man the ultimate chameleon, admirable in his multiplicity and yet really seeking the One in the Many.[32]

The speech of God to Adam in *De Hominis Dignitate* summarizes *homo omnis creatura* as Pico sees him:

> O Adam, I have given you neither a determined place, nor a single physiognomy, nor any specific gift, since the place, the physiognomy, and gifts which you wish for you shall have, according to your wish and will. As for the others, their defined nature is ruled by laws which I have prescribed; while you are not limited by any barrier but your own will, in which power I have placed you so that you determine your own nature. I have installed you in the middle of the world in order that you examine there most comfortably around you all that exists in the world. I have made you neither heavenly or earthly, neither mortal nor immortal, so that, master of yourself and having as it were the honor and duty of fashioning and modeling your own being, you will compose it in the form which you prefer. You can degenerate into lower forms, which are animal, or you can, by a decision of your spirit, be regenerated in higher forms which are divine.[33]

This represents perhaps the fullest microcosmic assertion of man's general condition in the Renaissance. It is at once a celebration of man's multiplicity ("Who would not admire this chameleon," Pico says later in *De Hominis Dignitate*) and a frightening view of man's need to unify his own multiplicity, for it is clear from God's speech to Adam that if man does not choose or does not act he is nothing. Having no innate qualities, but rather being an amalgam of those qualities which

32. See introduction to *Heptaplus* in *De Hominis Dignitate, Heptaplus, De Ente et Uno e Scritti Vari*, ed. Eugenio Garin (Florence: Vallecchi, 1942).
33. Pico, *De Hominis*, ed. Garin, pp. 104–06.

are assigned to the other orders, man alone is multiple, and thus he alone can hope to find the One through the Many.[34] Pico views the body as only one element in man's chameleon-like condition, but as we approach the more literal tradition, we can begin to see that the same mixture of celebration and fear can be contained within the microcosm of the body alone.

The intersection of the ideas of man as microcosm and his body as microcosm is what we might call the epistemological microcosm. According to this persistent train of thought, man contains all things because he has the capacity to know all things. The origin of the epistemological microcosm may be the Aristotelian idea that the human soul is a kind of microcosm.[35] This vision differs from those preceding in depending upon man's active participation. The individual attains a microcosmic state by knowing the macrocosm so well that it becomes a part of him. Combined with the vision of man as an innate microcosm, this idea has a particularly dramatic force: man is made of the same elements as the cosmos, and hence by knowing the cosmos he knows himself, makes of his brain the true microcosm. The human mind as microcosm returns to that same combination of unity and multiplicity which is the substance of all microcosmic visions. The mind attempts to contain all things but also to categorize them, as is apparent from Cassirer's description of Cusanus's epistemology:

> The mind attains genuine insight not when it reproduces external existence, but only when it 'explicates' itself and its own nature. . . . In fact everything logical—the ten predicates, the five universals, etc.—is included in this basic power of the mind. It is the necessary prerequisite to all 'discretion', i.e., all categorization of multiplicity according to species and classes; and it is the necessary prerequisite to the possibility of tracing the empirical–mutable back to strictly defined laws.[36]

Yet though Cusanus distinguishes between the mind reproducing the cosmos and the mind rederiving it within itself, the poetic life of the idea is more concerned with an equivalence between subject and object, between the mind and what it knows. Thus while the Aristotelians may view the soul as attaining a microcosmic state through knowledge and transformation, the Platonists are more likely to envision the

34. See Cassirer, *Individual*, p. 85.
35. See Aristotle, *De Anima*, 431b, 21, trans. R. D. Hicks (Amsterdam: Hakkert, 1965), p. 542.
36. Cassirer, *Individual*, p. 41.

brain itself as a physical wholeness which may contain shadows of all
the ultimate realities. Andrew Marvell's words on the subject are
probably the most famous:

> The Mind, that Ocean where each kind
> Does straight its own resemblance find;
> Yet it creates, transcending these
> Far other Worlds, and other Seas.[37]

In the English Renaissance, particularly in popular literature of a
quasi-scientific type, the idea of the brain as a little world becomes the
ideal means of not having to distinguish between spiritual and corpo-
real microcosms or between the literal and figurative union of man's
body with the cosmos. The mind can become a character combing the
physical world for all it contains and attempting to master that world.
Such is the premise in Nathaniel Wanley's description, written in 1678:

> The brain is so vigorous and active it insinuates itself into all places and times;
> reaches the heights, searches the depths, peers into all those recluded cabinets of
> nature wherein she hath stored up the choicer and abstrussest pieces of all her
> workmanship, and these it contemplates and admires.[38]

What is perhaps most significant about Wanley's description is that the
method he ascribes to the brain epitomizes the whole microcosmic
tradition from Plato onward: the union of man and the cosmos obliges
man to know the cosmos and through it himself. By turning the brain
into a person, Wanley begins to literalize the microcosm; but only an
emphasis, whether mystical or empirical, on man's body as microcosm
can give the idea a concrete structure.

4

To see man's spirit, or soul, or his whole condition as all-inclusive is
to make a humanistic assertion of man's infinity. But in a poetic image,
sheer infinity is neither realizable nor powerful. Man's body, on the

37. "The Garden," in Andrew Marvell, *The Poems and Letters*, ed. H. M. Margoliouth
(Oxford: Clarendon Press, 1952), ll. 43–46.
38. Nathaniel Wanley, *The Wonders of the Little World* (London, 1788), p. 6. Also
compare Sir John Davies, *Nosce Teipsum* in *Silver Poets of the Sixteenth Century*, ed.
Gerald Bullett (London: Dent, 1947), p. 361: "Then what vast body must we make the
mind, / Wherein are men, beasts, trees, towns, seas, and lands, / And yet each thing a
proper place doth find, / And each thing in the true proportion stands?"

other hand, is the very image of his finiteness, his limitations, his mortality. When this body becomes a miniature of the cosmos—as in all the ancient geocosms described earlier—and when the body as microcosm becomes invested with all the implications of infinitude associated with *homo omnis creatura*, then the body expresses at once man's vastness and his limitations. Consider, for example, Menaphon's description of Tamburlaine's body:[39]

> Of stature tall and straightly fashioned,
> Like his desire, lift upwards and divine,
> So large of limbs, his joints so strongly knit,
> Such breadth of shoulders as might mainly bear
> Old Atlas' burden. 'Twixt his manly pitch,
> A pearl more worth than all the world is placed,
> Wherein by curious sovereignty of art
> Are fixed his piercing instruments of sight,
> Whose fiery circles near encompassed
> A heaven of heavenly bodies in their spheres,
> That guides his steps and actions to the throne
> Where honor sits invested royally.
> Pale of complexion, wrought in him with passion,
> Thirsting with sovereignty, with love of arms,
> His lofty brows in folds do figure death,
> And in their smoothness amity and life.
> About them hangs a knot of amber hair,
> Wrapped in curls, as fierce Achilles' was,
> On which the breath of heaven delights to play,
> Making it dance with wanton majesty.
> His arms and fingers, long and sinewy,
> Betokening valor and excess of strength—
> In every part proportioned like the man
> Should make the world subdued to Tamburlaine.
>
> [Pt. 1.2.1.7–30]

Every aspect of the hero's body subdues the world to him because in each feature Menaphon reads some infinite aspect of the cosmos. Tamburlaine's head is the whole globe, which he, like Atlas, can carry upon his shoulders; but at the same time the head is equated with the whole astral macrocosm containing the astrological reading of the hero's own fate and that of the whole world. Tamburlaine's Promethean grandeur can be imaged forth in his body.

39. Citations are to *The Complete Plays of Christopher Marlowe*, ed. Irving Ribner (New York: Odyssey, 1963).

At the same time, the body bespeaks the hopelessness of Tam-
burlaine's overreaching, of which Zenocrate's dying words are a clear
omen:

> I fare, my lord, as other empresses,
> That, when this frail and transitory flesh
> Hath sucked the measure of that vital air
> That feeds the body with his dated health,
> Wane with enforced and necessary change.
>
> [Pt. 2.2.4.42–46]

Given this tension between infinity and mortality, the body is indeed a
place of "elements / Warring within our breasts for regiment." The
war is not only between the greatness and paltriness of man but also
among the tensions implied in all his cosmic multiplicity. This is
crucial to the Renaissance vision of man's body as microcosm: natural
philosophers search the world for vast multiplicities which can be
contained in the actual fabric of man's body. This search is usually an
act of humanism and celebration: but implied within it, and elaborated
by authors like Marlowe, Donne, or Browne, is a potentially destruc-
tive tension and fragmentation within this infinite containment of man.
Tamburlaine is destroyed not only by the death which can so easily
ravage his frail body but also by the war among the greatnesses within
that body.

The factual data that feed into this poetic vision of the body are
derived largely from mystical and anti-empirical strands of natural
philosophy developing out of those geocosms mentioned earlier in this
chapter. Throughout the Middle Ages and well into the Renaissance of
the fifteenth and sixteenth centuries, the astral, numerical, chemical,
and natural systems became increasingly syncretized and unified around
the figure of man so that together they represented a microcosmic
vision of man containing a vast but orderly quantity of the cosmos.[40]

More important, perhaps, than the syncretism among the various
systems is the fact that each union of man's body with the cosmos was a
search for man's infinity and for his capacity to order that infinity.

---

40. See Seznec, *Survival*, pp. 63–68. Compare also the tradition of including astrologi-
cal signs and emblems in sixteenth-century portraits. Otto Benesch, in *The Art of the
Renaissance in Northern Europe* (London: Phaidon, 1965), p. 64, says of Lucas Cranach's
portrait of Johannes Cuspinian: "A star and the professor's astrological bird fill the sky.
Sidereal and elementary forces entangle man in their magic play."

Astrology, for instance, was popular well into the Renaissance, despite the censure of the church; and the melothesia—man's body inscribed in the circle of the heavens—is one of the most popular images of Renaissance astrology. For most of this period the melothesia, and the astral relationships that it implies, represent multiplicity ordered in complete harmony. This is the impression one carries away from Chaucer's reference in *A Treatise on the Astrolabe*: "And everich of these 12 signes hath respect to a certeyn parcel of the body of a man, and hath it in governaunce."[41] The same harmony underlies the great Renaissance vogue of astrological medicine. From the early Middle Ages, it had been felt that surgeons must operate on a given part of the body only at a time when the moon was in the sign governing that organ. By the sixteenth century, there is an enormous body of works on medical astrology.[42] They are nearly all syncretistic views of cosmology, anatomy, human destiny, and what we would call biochemistry.

Marsilio Ficino, the great fifteenth-century philosopher, epitomizes this harmonizing view of astrology. Cassirer's description makes the microcosmic premise clear:

> The astrological vision of the world had always been bound to the idea of the microcosm. Indeed astrology seemed to be nothing other than the simple consequence and carrying out of that idea. Ficino's presentation . . . begins with the thought that inasmuch as the world is not an aggregate of dead elements but rather an animate being, there can be in it no more "parts" that possess an independent existence next to and outside the whole. What appears externally to be a part of the universe is, when more deeply grasped, to be understood as an *organ* possessing its definite place and necessary function in the whole complex of life of the cosmos. The unity of this universal complex of activities must necessarily be articulated through a multiplicity of organs. But this differentiation does not signify an isolation of the part from the whole; rather it signifies an ever new expression of the whole, a particular aspect of its self-presentation.[43]

Ficino turns the melothesia around so as to conceive of the universe anthropomorphically rather than the reverse. Man and his body become yet more orderly and hierarchical when their form is imposed upon the cosmos.

41. *The Works of Geoffrey Chaucer*, ed. F. N. Robinson (Boston: Houghton Mifflin, 1961), p. 549.

42. See D. C. Allen, *The Star-Crossed Renaissance* (Durham: Duke University Press, 1966), pp. 247–55.

43. Cassirer, *Individual*, p. 110.

This conservative and harmonistic view of the astral cosmos persists even into the seventeenth-century work of Robert Fludd.[44] A century earlier, however, it undergoes a revolution in the writings of Paracelsus. The great German astrologer, physician, and alchemist saw much the same fragmentation of the idea of astral harmony and hierarchy as Cusanus had, a hundred years before, in his treatment of man as microcosm. The absolute *donnée* of Paracelsus's system is the complete correspondence, part by part, of macrocosm and microcosm. Yet though this correspondence lends a harmony to the world picture, Paracelsus so vastly multiplies the number of bodies and correspondences that in this very harmony there lies multiplicity. In his astrological medicine, for instance, each disease has its own cosmic body which touches each individual who is afflicted. The cosmos of the disease confronts the cosmos of the individual, in which each anatomical element has a planetary cycle. These cycles, whose physical counterparts are circular motions which Paracelsus discerned within the anatomy, must keep the body in health just as the sun by its cycle keeps the earth in health. At the same time, the disease itself has a body analogous to the cosmos and the microcosm. Man is inscribed in a hyperorganized cosmos; but the very extent of analogous cosmic bodies stresses the multiplicity and fragmentation of man's body and condition over its unity. The result in the Paracelsian system is not unlike that of Pico's speech of God to Adam: man's body is so vast a world, analogous to so many others, that his condition necessitates enormous moral insight and personal fortitude to control and harmonize such great worlds.[45]

In the literary life of the astral microcosm, this multiplicity is continually set over against the underlying harmony of a system in which man and cosmos are perfectly parallel. Tamburlaine seems excessively favored by the astral destinies within him, and then is suddenly abandoned by them on one of the dangerous "critical days" of his final

44. See J. B. Craven, *Doctor Robert Fludd* (Kirkwall: Occult Research Press, 1962), pp. 93–99.

45. The extremity of this microcosmism was one of the subjects of the censure of Paracelsus by Erastus (1523–1583). According to Pagel, *Paracelsus*, pp. 323–24, Erastus asserted that the microcosmic idea "may pass as a pleasant allegory; but it is simply foolish to assume that the human body contains the virtues and materials of all parts of the outside world. . . . How many of the innumerable microcosms that must exist does man contain? Or, why can he not fly, lay eggs, live in the sea, grow fruit or remedial arcana, if he really contains all other objects of nature?"

illness.[46] The system of planetary alliances increases the tension and strife between Palamon and Arcite in *The Knight's Tale*. Poets of Chaucer's time and later can use the great system of astral correspondences to depict a harmonized and hierarchical cosmos while the same complex of forces within man's body can suggest too vast an infinity for the individual man to control. The most significant correspondence within the system is between cosmology and self-knowledge;[47] and while Tamburlaine's cosmology is accurate, his self-knowledge, drawn upon that cosmology, is destined for a tragic fall.[48]

The numerical and chemical visions of the cosmos undergo much the same development as the astrological, a growing tension between the harmonious hierarchy and great inclusiveness which leads toward multiplicity and fragmentation. As early as Philo's *On the Creation*, there is an extremely lengthy treatment of the number seven, arising from the number of days of creation, but serving in dozens of ways to unite aspects of that creation, including man's body and the cosmos. By the fourteenth century, geometric and numerical systems could be used with great erudition to structure the universe graphically, juxtaposing seasons, months, minerals, ages of man, zodiacal signs, continents, and of course parts of the body.[49] Again the hierarchies and systems which correspond to man's body proliferate so greatly in the Renaissance that the values of proportion and *analogia* that were so comforting to the Middle Ages could now place excessive multiplicity in man's condition.[50] Perhaps the best literary example is Spenser's *Cantos of Mutability*, where Dame Mutability produces an orderly procession of all the units which measure time, less as an image of order and hierarchy than of man's helplessness in the face of anarchy and change.[51]

46. See Johnstone Parr, *Tamburlaine's Malady* (University, Ala.: University of Alabama Press, 1953), pp. 3–24.

47. See Cassirer, *Individual*, pp. 112–19.

48. Compare the astrological *discordia concors* in the medal of Federigo da Montefeltro by Clemente da Urbino. See Edgar Wind, *Pagan Mysteries in the Renaissance* (New Haven: Yale University Press, 1958; rpt., 1967), pp. 95–96.

49. Seznec, *Survival*, pp. 124–25.

50. The work of Opicinus de Canistris is an especially good example. See Richard Georg Salomon, *Opicinus de Canistris* (London: Warburg Institute, 1936).

51. This argument is strengthened by, though not dependent upon, Alastair Fowler's connection of the number seven, the book of the poem in which the fragment is putatively placed, with a massive series of mutable factors in the cosmos. See *Spenser and the Numbers of Time* (London: Routledge and Kegan Paul, 1964), p. 58.

The system of the elements proliferates in much the same way. Once it is joined with the humours and complexions, the system becomes more corporeal, but loses some of its cosmic origins. Nevertheless, it is also joined to larger cosmic systems, planetary and numerological. Here too we see man overwhelmed by the sheer number of analogous hierarchies. While Empedocles had viewed the force of strife as by its very nature external to the elements themselves, since they were an image of wholeness and concord, the poets of the Renaissance are more likely to see the chemical microcosm in Tamburlaine's terms "of four elements / Warring within our breasts for regiment." William Hammond writes that

> The elements, that do man's house compose
> Are all his chiefest foes;
> Fire, Air, earth, water all are at debate,
> Which shall predominate.[52]

In a more dynamic vein and reminiscent of Menaphon's picture of Tamburlaine, there is the Gentlemen's description of King Lear, which builds a cosmos and then internalizes it:[53]

> Contending with the fretful elements;
> Bids the wind blow the earth into the sea,
> Or swell the curled waters 'bove the main,
> That things might change or cease; tears his white hair,
> Which the impetuous blasts, with eyeless rage,
> Catch in their fury, and make nothing of;
> Strives in his little world of man to out-storm
> The to-and-fro conflicting wind and rain.

[3.1.4–11]

Lear's fall is much more clearly destined than is Tamburlaine's, since in the confrontation of the world and Lear's body it is the cosmos which can "make nothing of" him, rather than the reverse.

The vision of the natural geocosm that best demonstrates the proliferation and multiplicity of correspondences is the doctrine of signatures. The intent behind this doctrine is ultimately devotional, and the logic is similar to Plato's presentation of a multiple god and multiple microcosm made in god's image. Jacob Boehme (1575–1624) says

52. "On the Death of My Dear Brother," cited in Marjorie Nicolson, *The Breaking of the Circle* (New York: Columbia University Press, 1960; rpt., 1965), p. 14.
53. Citation is to *King Lear*, ed. Kenneth Muir (Cambridge: Harvard University Press, 1959).

in the second chapter of *Aurora* that God transcends the body of the universe but is still present in it, "for when we say ALL, or from eternity to eternity, or ALL in ALL, then we understand the entire GOD";[54] and in *Signatura Rerum*, "Man has all the forms of all the three worlds lying in him; for he is a complete image of God; or the Being of all beings."[55] These steps of logic have been seen on earlier occasions, but here these totalities are made to suggest that the natural world contains creations that are sympathetic to particular features of our internal anatomy, and further, that these natural creations are somehow signed so that they bear a veiled similarity to the part of our anatomy which they can be made to treat. Thus according to Henry More, "Walnuts bear the whole signature of the head. The outward green cortex answers to the Pericranium, and a salt made of it is singularly good for wounds in that part, as the kernel is good for the brains, which it resembles."[56]

Whether walnuts and the head (or orchids and the pubis, eyebright and the eyes, etc.) are in any sense identical is hidden behind the mystical system that gives rise to the doctrine. Those who believed in signatures generally ignored the logical relation between the thing in the natural world and in our anatomy. They used visual parallels, physical structure, and medical data to create a relation which is essentially metaphorical and "metaphysical," in the sense of the seventeenth-century poets. We are obliged to search the world with a metaphysical allegorizing eye in order to perceive these signatures. The physical health which we can attain by searching out these signatures will bring spiritual health as it brings understanding.

In the works of Jacob Boehme, the doctrine of signatures gave rise to a whole new set of literal and figurative microcosmic parallels. Just as he found signed objects didactically as well as materially joined with parts of the microcosm, he saw a double parallel between the world's body and man's: flesh signifies earth and comes from the earth, blood signifies water and comes from water, etc. A part of the anatomy "signifies" its analogous part of the cosmos by bearing all the moral meaning which could be assigned to that part of the cosmos. The flesh signifies the earth "congealed and without motion; so the flesh hath no reason but is moved only by the power of the stars, which reign in the

54. *The Aurora*, trans. John Sparrow (London: Watkins, 1914; rpt., 1960), p. 56.
55. *The Signature of All Things*, ed. Clifford Bax (London: Dent, 1912), p. 108.
56. *An Antidote Against Atheism* (London, 1653), p. 100.

flesh and veins."[57] The moralizing here is reciprocal in that it depends partly on allegorizing the cosmos and partly on allegorizing the body.

This complete mutuality produces a kind of internal cosmos by commingling internal and external terms. The overall image is a kind of planetary one, but he rarely strays so far from anatomical fact that we are forced to doubt his astrology. Perhaps the best example is his description of the veins as signifying the powerful flowings out from the stars, "and [they] *are* also the powerful outgoings of the stars, for the stars with their powers reign in the veins and drive forth the form, shape and condition in man."[58]

The nearer the hierarchies of natural correspondences come to empirical science, the more vivid and multiple is the world which man contains within him. Thomas Browne is led from the doctrine of signatures to muse upon physiognomy, and here he defines the multiplicity and at the same time the danger of man's condition:

> Now there are besides these Characters in our faces, certaine mysticall figures in our hands, which I dare not call meere dashes, strokes, *a la volee*, or at randome, because delineated by a pencill, that never workes in vaine; and hereof I take more particular notice, because I carry that in mine owne hand, which I could never read of, nor discover in another.[59]

"I carry that in mine owne hand, which I could never read of" is an epitome of the microcosmic reading of the body as that presented itself to creative minds of the Renaissance. All these systems arising out of medieval science had been intended to place man yet more comfortably in cosmic hierarchies. But in the sixteenth and seventeenth centuries the comfortable equation between cosmological knowledge and self-knowledge is to disappear before the philosophical implications of multiplicity inherent in man as envisioned by these systems and before the beginnings of modern empirical science, which was to impugn the whole hierarchical idea.

5

Empirical science was not always capable of liberating itself from the

57. *The Aurora*, p. 59.
58. Ibid., p. 56.
59. Thomas Browne, *Religio Medici and Other Works*, ed. L. C. Martin (Oxford: Clarendon Press, 1964), p. 57.

primitivism of the microcosmic ideal. As Lynn Thorndike has pointed out, the line between experimental science and mysticism or magic in medieval and Renaissance times is very fine.[60] One might almost say that the experiments which succeeded we now call science and those which failed we call magic. The same drive which Paracelsus felt to contemplate the creation and understand the connections among its elements had led Leonardo da Vinci to the task of painstakingly sketching the human anatomy. Paracelsus's method was inductive and Da Vinci's deductive, but both were attempting to read the book of nature, in which the human body is a major chapter.[61]

The microcosmic idea persists in Leonardo's notebooks as a rich and meaningful figure of speech often used to clarify anatomy by reference to simple cosmology or geography. For Leonardo, the union of man and the world is a basic moral supposition:

> Now you see that the hope and the desire of returning to the first state of chaos, is like the moth to the light. . . . But this desire is the very quintessence, the spirit of the elements, which finding itself imprisoned with the soul is ever longing to return from the human body to its giver. And you must know that this same longing is that quintessence, inseparable from nature, and that man is the image of the world.[62]

The essence of man's union with the world lies in mortality and change, in the movements, both in time and place, of all the features of mortal creation.

The human body is an image of this union because of its mortality, and because of the ceaseless change within it, a subject which remained of paramount interest to Leonardo as anatomist. Hence he is most likely to draw explanatory parallels to the cosmos when he is speaking of the body's motions:

> The waters return with constant motion from the lowest depths of the sea to the utmost height of the mountains, not obeying the nature of heavier bodies [i.e., the law of gravity]; and in this they resemble the blood of animated beings which always moves from the sea of the heart and flows towards the top of the head; and here it may burst a vein, as the blood rises from below to the level of the burst vein.

60. See Thorndike, *A History of Magic and Experimental Science* (New York: Macmillan, 1923–1941).

61. See Cassirer, *Individual*, pp. 53–55, on the connection between the natural philosophy of Campanella, Paracelsus, etc., and the science of Leonardo, Galileo, and Kepler.

62. *The Literary Works of Leonardo Da Vinci*, ed. Jean Paul Richter (London: Oxford University Press, 1939), 2:242.

When the water rushes out from the burst vein in the earth, it obeys the law of other bodies that are heavier than the air, since it always seeks low places.

This picture of cosmic and microcosmic motion has a double force: as an image both of harmonious regularity and of ceaseless change. It may be connected with the movement of time, as elsewhere in Leonardo's notebooks: "the man who with constant longing awaits with joy each new springtime . . . does not perceive that he is longing for his own destruction."[63] Or the orderliness of the body's circulation may emphasize how well unified is the little world of man, as in William Harvey's dedication to King Charles of *De Motu Cordis*:

> The heart of animals is the foundation of their life, the sovereign of everything within them, the sun of their microcosm, that upon which all growth depends, from which all power proceeds. The King, in like manner, is the foundation of his kingdom, the sun of the world around him, the heart of the republic, the fountain whence all power, all grace doth flow. . . . Almost all things human are done after human examples, and many things in a king are after the pattern of the heart. The knowledge of his heart, therefore, will not be useless to a Prince, as embracing a kind of Divine example of his functions,—and it has still been usual with men to compare small things with great. Here . . . you may at once contemplate the prime mover in the body of man, and the emblem of your own sovereign power.[64]

When these men impose the form of the body upon the world, they create an organic system which is at once ordered and fragmented.[65] Unlike the natural philosophers discussed earlier, they do not take the parallel at all literally—an anthropocentric microcosm is even harder to believe empirically than a cosmocentric—but the same lesson, of diversity contained within unity, is drawn whether the body is imposed upon the world or the world upon the body. Milton, also in close touch with the empirical science of his time, images forth the cosmos as a vast anthropomorphic digestive system:[66]

63. Ibid., 2:105, 242.

64. *The Works of William Harvey, M. D.,* trans. Robert Willis (London, 1847), pp. 3–4.

65. Leonardo also uses the image of the body to describe the ordering of his own work on anatomy: "Thus, in fifteen entire figures, you will have set before you the microcosm on the same plan as, before me, was adopted by Ptolemy in his cosmography; and so I will afterwards divide them into limbs as he divided the whole world into provinces" (*Works* 2 : 88).

66. Citation is to *The Poems of John Milton*, ed. John Carey and Alastair Fowler (London: Longmans, 1968).

> For know, whatever was created, needs
> To be sustained and fed; of elements
> The grosser feeds the purer, earth the sea,
> Earth and the sea feed air, the air those fires
> Ethereal, and as lowest first the moon;
> Whence in her visage round those spots unpurged
> Vapours not yet into her substance turned.
> Nor doth the moon no nourishment exhale
> From her moist continent to higher orbs.
> The sun that light imparts to all, receives
> From all his alimental recompense
> In humid exhalations, and at even
> Sups with the ocean.
>
> [5.414–26]

The syncretistic combination of science and lyricism—the final image in the above lines being purely visual and with no background in cosmology—merely serves to demonstrate how many traditions could feed into the image of a microcosmic human body.

The poetry of the English Renaissance was written by men who generally combined the arcane imagination of a Paracelsus with the scientific awareness, if not the deductive method, of a Leonardo. Many of the more empirical minds of the fifteenth and sixteenth centuries struggle with the question of whether the body is a literal or a figurative microcosm. Thomas Browne, a man of both science and literature, speaks of his quandry in *Religio Medici*:

> to call ourselves a Microcosm, or little world, I thought it onely a pleasant trope of Rhetorick, till my neare judgement and second thoughts told me there was a reall truth therein.[67]

He resolved his doubts with a humanistic version of the old idea that man includes all the orders of being. His contemporary, barber-surgeon Helkanah Crooke, struggles with the same analogy:

> The body also, as far as it was possible, carieth the image of God, not in figure as Audius and his followers the anthropomorphites have sottishly dream't, he being an infinite ocean of essence, transcendent, and above all comprehension of nature or time . . . but because the admirable structure, and accomplished perfection of the body, carieth in it a representation of all the most glorious and perfect workes of God, as being an Epitome or Compend of the whole creation, by which he is rather signified than expressed. And hence it is that man is called a Microcosme or little

67. *Religio Medici*, p. 33.

worlde. . . . The divines call him *omnem creaturam*, every creature, because he is in power (in a manner) All things; not for matter and substance, as Empedocles would have it, but analogically by participation or reception of the severall species or kinds of things.

Here the analogy is obscured behind a shower of similes; the quandary can only be resolved by what passes in *Microcosmographia* for flights of poetry:

The head, the Castle and tower of the soule, the seat of reason, the mansion house of wisdom, the treasury of memory, judgment, and discourse, wherein mankinde is most like to the angels or intelligencies, obtaining the loftiest and most eminent place in the body; doth it not elegantly resemble that supreame and angelicall part of the whole?[68]

6

This, then, is the tradition which presented itself to the Renaissance creative mind. An overall equation between concrete realities, comprehending a vast number of smaller concrete equations, could also express the spiritual relation between men and the world, between subject and object. The poet could draw upon primitive conceptions, upon ancient science, upon contemporary cosmological traditions, upon the prevailing natural philosophy, upon the heuristic devices of a thousand thinkers, even upon the writings of those empirical scientists who purposed to disprove the whole tradition.

For the creative artist, as for the natural philosopher or mystic, the idea that the human body is a microcosm represents a potential key to man's place in the world. When an equation between man and the world is assumed, then the subject–object problem becomes identical with the problem of self-knowledge. In studying cosmology, man comes to know himself; and in identifying the parallels of microcosm and macrocosm and understanding the relations of like to like in the two worlds, man grasps self and world at once. The existence of the parallels is a means for understanding each world in relation to the other, and at the same time an ever present proof that a harmonistic place of man in the cosmos can be found if only the parallels are successfully delineated.

The bodies of man and the world are of the greatest importance in

68. Helkanah Crooke, *Microcosmographia* (London, 1615), pp. 2–3, 6.

this search because they can be objectively contemplated. Through their multiplicity and diversity of relations, the unifying principle of harmony may show itself. Surely this is the nature of Sir John Davies' contemplation in *Nosce Teipsum*:

> THE lights of heaven, which are the World's fair eyes,
> Look down into the World, the World to see;
> And as they turn, or wander in the skies,
> Survey all things that on this centre be.
> And yet the lights which in my tower do shine,
> Mine eyes which view all objects, nigh and far,
> Look not into this little world of mine.
> Nor see my face wherein they fixed are.[69]

The physical parallels between the two worlds bear the promise of harmony, but when the poet actually contemplates and compares them, he discovers that man, unlike the cosmos, cannot harmonize subject and object, cannot be at once both the eyes and the object viewed. Davies' assertion is decidedly paradoxical, though no more so than Plato's moralization of microcosmic parallels in the *Timaeus*: the assumption of unity and harmony between the two worlds is most valid in that it reveals the tension and multiplicity within man which separates him from the greater world of which he is a type.

We have seen how the harmonistic cosmology of the ancient and medieval epochs, which produced the microcosmic idea, gave way in the early Renaissance to an elaboration and proliferation of parallel schemes so numerous that multiplicity and diversity began to contend with the harmony inherent in a system of parallel worlds. The cosmological poetry of the Renaissance is in many respects a product of these two forces, the belief in harmonious, analogous *cosmoi* and in the existence of an *embarras de richesses* of complexities in the world and in man. Since both forces have their roots in medieval orthodoxy, I feel the cosmological art they produced is a great deal more conservative than critics like Marjorie Nicolson have believed. The imaginative works which have come to be associated with the "new science" are saturated with the analogy of macrocosm and microcosm. That analogy is the pillar of the old science, whether in the harmonistic form of St. Gregory's *homo omnis creatura* or the more bewildering diversity of Pico or Paracelsus. By 1600 the new science is altering the terms of the

69. In *Silver Poets*, ed. Bullett, p. 350.

universal analogy system beyond all recognition. But the poets of the time are reacting less to the advent of the new than to the last exaggerated gasps of the old.

It has become clear that through the Middle Ages and the Renaissance the literal analogy of man's body with the world's moved farther and farther out of the mainstream of philosophical and scientific thought, and toward myth and mysticism. The more out-of-date the idea becomes as science, the richer it is as a convention between poet and audience. Davies may lament that "all disorder and misrule is new," and Donne, in a more famous lament, may complain that the "new Philosophy calls all in doubt," but the matter and fabric of their poetry are so steeped in the old science that critical emphasis upon Copernicus and Galileo may radically distort the balance.

In both these cosmological works, the poetics remain remarkably unshaken by new visions of the universe. Davies' cosmic dance epitomizes the old analogical view of the cosmos. It anthropomorphizes the cosmos in order to express the familiar tension between hierarchy and seemingly random motion. Donne's "First Anniversary," which comes much closer to grasping the new science, still celebrates and elaborates the old in its poetics. Elizabeth Drury, who has been given so many differing abstract identifications, seems to me the personification of man as harmonious microcosm. The poem plays upon the idea that in the old order man was the microcosm of the world, but since the bodies of the world and of man have so decayed, the world ought to re-form itself as a microcosm of Elizabeth Drury, "She to whom this world must it selfe refer, / As Suburbs, or the Microcosme of her" (235–36).[70] The lament over the diseases of the world, which occupies most of the poem, is written in the image of the old microcosmic idea, not so much discredited as rendered beyond man's reach by recent events.

Even when Donne specifically mentions the new philosophy, clearly referring to the science that will discredit the system of universal analogies, his fears seem as much responses to that proliferation of the analogical system which we saw in Cusanus, Pico, and Paracelsus as they are to the more contemporary discrediting of the Ptolemaic cosmology. Donne asserts that

> The Sun is lost, and th' earth, and no mans wit
> Can well direct him where to looke for it.

70. Citations are to *The Poems of John Donne*, ed. Herbert J. C. Grierson (Oxford: Clarendon Press, 1966).

> And freely men confesse that this world's spent,
> When in the Planets, and the Firmament
> They seeke so many new; they see that this
> Is crumbled out againe to his Atomies.
> 'Tis all in peeces, all cohaerence gone;
> All just supply, and all Relation.
>
> [207–14]

It would be absurd to argue that Donne does not have the Copernican world view in mind here; yet it is important for our purposes to see that he is speaking within and borrowing upon a tradition that goes back to a century before Copernicus's birth, when the analogical system became so strong that man got lost in its complexities. That proliferation, too, could be described in terms of losing the sun and the earth, finding new planets, and discovering that the universe "is crumbled out againe to his Atomies."[71] Thus there are as many tensions between harmony and diversity within the old system as there are between the old system and the new.[72]

But if the poetics of Donne and the "metaphysical" school (as well as of their more traditional predecessors and contemporaries) cannot be simply explained as a reaction to the fear inspired by the new science, what is their source? Here, too, the answer lies as much in the medieval heritage as in the Copernican revolution. The reason for the flowering, in the sixteenth and seventeenth centuries, of a cosmological art based upon the soon to be outmoded system of universal analogies is, at

71. Compare Sermon No. 10, in John Donne's *Sermons on the Psalms and Gospels*, ed. Evelyn M. Simpson (Berkeley: University of California Press, 1963), p. 223: "I need not call in new Philosophy, that denies a settlednesse, an acquiescence in the very body of the Earth, but makes the Earth to move in that place, where we thought the Sunne had moved; I need not that helpe, that the Earth it selfe is in Motion, to prove this, That nothing upon Earth is permanent."

72. Otto Benesch, in *Art of the Renaissance* (see especially pp. 101–21), discusses analogous developments in the graphic arts. The early sixteenth-century microcosmic works of Lucas Cranach or Albrecht Altdorfer, where figure and ground mirror each other in both harmony and complexity, give way at the end of the century to the mannerist art of Bruegel, in which the intricacies of the analogy between man's body and the world's constitute a source of tension and fragmentation. Thus Bruegel's work, which may have the appearance of "modernism" and of the dehumanizing effects of the new science, is, in fact, a reversion to the systems of the medieval imagination expressed in a particularly multifarious way. These northern masters can be fruitfully compared with Giuseppe Arcimboldi (1527–1593), whose output consists almost entirely of bodies composed of the world's objects and cosmic landscapes composed of the human body. This is an elaborately manneristic and self-conscious version of the old literal equivalence between macrocosm and microcosm. See Benno Geiger, *I Dipinti Ghiribizzosi di Giuseppe Arcimboldi* (Florence: Vallecchi, 1954).

least in part, a renewed interest in the parallel between God as Creator and the poet as creator. Though this idea is at least as old as Augustine and Plotinus,[73] it combines with what we have called the Renaissance proliferation of the analogical system so as to uncover in the cosmos an endless series of analogous constructions at once multiple and harmonious. This, as we have seen, is a natural outgrowth of the medieval system. Joseph Mazzeo sees in this system of analogies a definition of the "metaphysical" poetic:

> The universe was created by a God who was a "witty creator," an *"arguto favel-latore,"* a witty writer or talker. The world was a poem made up of conceits, . . . a "metaphysical" poem and God a "metaphysical" poet.

This esthetic, according to Mazzeo, presupposes

> a world full of metaphors, analogies, and conceits, and so far from being mere ornamentation, they are the law by which creation was effected. God wrote the book of nature in metaphor, and so it should be read. . . . The universe is a vast net of correspondences which unites the whole multiplicity of being. The poet approaches and creates his reality by a series of more or less elaborate correspondences.[74]

These remarks apply to more than the metaphysical school. They summarize the presuppositions which underlie the contemplation of parallel macrocosm and microcosm throughout the Renaissance, and they can apply as much to Spenser and Shakespeare as to Donne.

The human body is the central component in a system of universal correspondences which was as alive metaphorically to Donne as it had been literally to Ptolemy or St. Gregory. By understanding the objective links between man's body and the world's, the poet seeks to place himself in the cosmos. The correspondences themselves are comforting, but within their sheer number and elaborateness there is a multiplicity which can produce the *Angst* characteristic of English Renaissance poetry. The human body epitomizes this tension, being the most immediate cosmos with links to the remotest worlds. It is at once a naturally unified, organic whole harmoniously inscribed in the circle of the heavens, and also a dizzying collection of elements, astral bodies, numbers, and natural forces which stand in multiple relations with those entities in the macrocosm. The body is God's

73. See Tuve, *Elizabethan and Metaphysical Imagery*, p. 151.
74. Joseph Mazzeo, "Metaphysical Poetry and the Poetry of Correspondence," *Journal of the History of Ideas* 14 (1953): 228; 229–30.

metaphor for the world, and the Renaissance poet has no choice but to read it as such and to understand and develop its metaphorical properties.

7

"Thou art a figurative, a metaphorical God," Donne asserts in his *Devotions upon Emergent Occasions* (p. 124),[75] and no work of the English Renaissance illustrates more fully the close connections between literary metaphor and the belief in a universal system of analogies. Written during a serious illness which Donne suffered in the latter part of 1623, the *Devotions* consist of twenty-three triads each made up of a freewheeling, intellectual meditation, an outspoken, even rebellious expostulation, and a humble but insistent prayer. The text for each triad is a distinct stage of the illness, upon which Donne meditates, expostulates, and reaches conclusions in prayer. The result of this insistent reference to the self and the illness is a vast intellectual superstructure built upon a metaphorical and literal contemplation of the poet's body.

Donne's imagination is so steeped in the old microcosmic traditions that even so late in his life as this, with so much of the new philosophy in his mind, he can derive all the great cosmic unities from the contemplation of his own body. He sees the universe as a great chain of analogies with man in the middle: "This is nature's nest of boxes: the heavens contain the earth; the earth, cities; cities, men. And all these are concentric." The concrete image of the body spreads over the cosmos: "the heavens have had their dropsy, they drowned the world; and they shall have their fever, and burn the world" (Meditation X, p. 63); over the hierarchy of society: "the heart in that body is the king, and the brain his council; and the whole magistracy, that ties all together, is the sinews which proceed from thence" (Meditation XII, p. 79); and over the microcosmic constructions of man: "into some rooms of his thy house, my body, temptations will come, infections will come; but be my heart thy bedchamber" (Prayer XI, p. 75).

The method of the whole work consists of drawing analogies between objective realities which are capable of capturing spiritual re-

75. Citations are to John Donne, *Devotions upon Emergent Occasions* (Ann Arbor: University of Michigan Press, 1965).

alities within themselves. Donne creates exhaustive hierarchies of concrete things which structure the objective cosmos in such a way as to make his farfetched "metaphysical" analogies seem more organic:

> From thy first book, the book of life, never shut to thee, but never thoroughly open to us; from thy second book, the book of nature, where though subobscurely and in shadows, thou hast expressed thine own image; from thy third book, the Scriptures, where thou hadst written all in the Old, and then lightedst us a candle to read it by, in the New Testament; to these thou hadst added the book of just and useful laws, established by them to whom thou hast committed thy people; to those, the manuals, the pocket, the bosom books of our own consciences; to those the particular books of all our particular sins; and to those, the books with seven seals.
>
> [Expostulation IX, pp. 60–1]

The verbal play on "book" turns the universe into another nest of concentric boxes, a single framework by which all the orders of God's creation can be understood in parallel series. In addition, by describing the hierarchy as one of "books," Donne can include by implication in the hierarchy the two most immediate, the work he is writing and his own body inspiring it, which he and the physicians are so assiduously reading.

This latter parallel suggests yet another nest of boxes, another framework of conceptual hierarchies: "I have cut up mine own anatomy, dissected myself, and they are gone to read upon me. . . . I offer not to counsel them who meet in consultation for my body now; but I open my infirmities, I anatomize my body to them" (Meditation IX, p. 56; Expostulation IX, p. 60). The human body lies at the center of this set of analogies: the physicians are studying it to identify the symptoms and cure the disease, and Donne is studying it to identify himself and purify his soul. This hierarchy of body and soul is essential to the work; and it illuminates the tradition of corporeal allegory. Donne believes in these hierarchical systems of which the human body is the nexus. Though he frequently disparages the body, he still sees it as central to God's universal plan and, more important, to man's interpretation of that plan, man's discovery of his own place in the universe and of his soul.

Donne's method, then, is inherently optimistic: he believes in a harmonious cosmology of concentric spheres and in the power of the mind to move through the hierarchy. This is a late Renaissance, self-conscious, and baroque version of the medieval world view. Yet it is also clear that the *Devotions* as a whole are far from an optimistic work. There is a tension about man's place in the cosmos and a terror of doubt that suggests all the fears inspired by the new philosophy, even at the same time that Donne's imagination returns so steadily to the microcosmic idea which is the backbone of the old philosophy. This combination—cosmological security united with personal insecurity—has been the cause of much critical comment upon the *Devotions,* as for example Joan Webber's:

> Taken as a whole, Donne's use of the microcosm–macrocosm analogies would probably have been seen, against the background of contemporary ideas, as a purposeful distortion of traditions, and a purposeful singling out for ironic symbol of aspects of tradition which could only be seen properly when viewed as parts of a whole great design.[76]

Mrs. Webber pinpoints a tension which is central to Donne's work, but I hope the present study demonstrates that he is not inventing or flouting tradition, but rather making a startling use of some very familiar tensions implicit in the old analogical world view.

If the *Devotions* are a gloomy meditation, then it is interesting that what Donne finds most depressing is just that cosmological identity which was a source of optimism and humanism in the early medieval scheme, while the traditional *contemptus mundi,* which despises the body as an obstacle to the soul, has very little place in this work. The spiritual anguish arises not from the paltriness of man or man's body but from their grandeur:

> It is too little to call man a little world; except God, man is a diminutive to nothing. Man consists of more pieces, more parts, than the world; than the world doth, nay, than the world is. And if those pieces were extended, and stretched out in man as they are in the world, man would be the giant, and the world the dwarf: the world but the map, and the man the world. If all the veins in our bodies were extended to rivers, and all the sinews to veins of mines, and all the muscles that lie upon one another, to hills, and all the bones to quarries of stones, and all the other pieces to the proportion of those which correspond to them in the world, the air would be too little for this orb of man to move in, the firmament would be but enough for this star; for, as the whole earth hath nothing, to which something in man doth not answer, so hath man many pieces of which the whole world hath no representation. Enlarge this meditation upon this great world, man, so far as to consider the

76. Joan Webber, *Contrary Music* (Madison: University of Wisconsin Press, 1963), p. 188.

immensity of the creatures this world produces; our creatures are our thoughts, creatures that are born giants; that reach from east to west, from earth to heaven; that do not only bestride all the sea and the land, but span the sun and firmament at once; my thoughts reach all, comprehend all.

[Meditation IV, p. 23]

I quote this at length because it is one of the great assertions of the microcosmic idea in Renaissance literature, and one of the most extreme. The parallels between man's body and the world's are so numerous, and the identities conceived so totally and literally, that the very zeal with which Donne makes the universal analogy causes the harmonic balance of smaller and greater worlds to be upset.

That "the world [is] but the map, and the man the world" is more than a *reductio ad absurdum* of an old-fashioned idea by means of new logic. Donne here expresses that same proliferation of the microcosmic idea which came with the early Renaissance. In the proper and harmonious relation of the great and little worlds, man fits physically and spiritually into systems that are much larger than he is and much more profoundly and mysteriously ordered, such as the cosmos or society. Hence, though all the worlds are ultimately controlled by God, man seems to be controlled in addition by all those other concentric worlds mediating between the spheres of God and man. Donne uses the logical analogy to internalize this whole conceptual universe of concentric forms in man's body, which is, in some respects, its pattern. Consequently, far from feeling the security of many intervening worlds between himself and God, man in this system constitutes all the worlds himself and is thus so great that he must face God alone.

The interchange of forms between man and the world in the *Devotions* has the effect of saddling each with the miseries of the other: the world's body becomes prey to the physical and spiritual ailments of man, and man's body becomes prey to the dizzying multiplicity and fragmentation of the world. We shall consider the ailments of the world's body first. All the imagery of an analogical cosmos is saturated with feelings of man's mortality, disease, and unhappiness. The center of "nature's nest of boxes" is "decay, ruin." All the physical systems which go to make up the world, such as land and sea or the four elements, are transformed into a negative view of the human condition. If man is a world, Donne meditates, himself will be the land, and misery the sea. . . . His misery, as the sea, swells above all the hills, and reaches to the remotest parts of this earth, man; who of himself is but dust, and coagulated and kneaded into earth by tears; his matter is earth, his form misery.

[Meditation VIII, p. 50]

In a similar way, the image of a diseased physical body spreads over the social hierarchy:

the heart alone is in the principality, and in the throne, as king, the rest as subjects. . . . And yet this is also another misery of this king of man, the heart, which is also applicable to the kings of this world, great men, that the venom and poison of every pestilential disease directs itself to the heart, affects that (pernicious affection), and the malignity of ill men is also directed upon the greatest and the best; and not only greatness but goodness loses the vigour of being an antidote or cordial against it.

[Meditation XI, pp. 70–71]

Here the body and the cosmos illuminate each other: society is as fragile as the individual man's body, and the body is as prone to internal discord as society.

Donne's interpretation of the world's presence within man's body is yet more revealing than his anthropomorphization of the world. He frequently expostulates that the grandeur and diversity which man gains by being a little world are nothing but a multiplicity of trials:

Is this the honour which man hath by being a little world, that he hath these earthquakes in himself, sudden shakings; these lightnings, sudden flashes; these thunders, sudden noises; these eclipses, sudden offuscations and darkening of his senses; these blazing stars, sudden fiery exhalations; these rivers of blood, sudden red waters?

[Meditation I, p. 8]

The Promethean overreaching which saw its birth in the medieval *homo omnis creatura* and its flowering in such a figure as Tamburlaine, who proudly carried all the elements and astral forces within him, is transformed here into a human condition of multiple strugglings and miseries. The grandeur of man's all inclusiveness is a grandeur of disease, and "the masters of that art can scarce number, not name all sicknesses" (Meditation IX, p. 57). Disease becomes the emblem of the human condition not because Donne is such a thoroughgoing pessimist, but because he envisions in the greatness of man's constituent parts the fearful possibility of disorder among them, and disease is "the disorder, the discord, the irregularity, the commotion and rebellion of the body" (Meditation XIX, p. 122). This is the disorder inherent in the microcosmic idea in the Renaissance, the chemical, astral, natural, social unrest of the parts which make up man's little world. Thus man in the *Devotions* is forever being built up so as to be torn down,[77] with the grandeur of his universality shrinking into helpless loneliness:

> what's become of man's great extent and proportion, when himself shrinks himself and consumes himself to a handful of dust. . . . His diseases are his own, but the physician is not; he hath them at home, but he must send for the physician.
>
> [Meditation IV, pp. 24–25]

Within this meditation, which begins "It is too little to call man a little world," Donne transforms man into a being so small that, far from containing the whole universe, he does not even have his own cure within him.

But the most significant negative version of the microcosm in the *Devotions* lies in Donne's recognition that when man includes the world within him, he includes a multiple capacity for discord and fragmentation. Throughout his disease, he realizes how the grandeur of man, expressed by the complexity of his body, heightens his inner conflict. At the very beginning Donne describes the disease in terms of corporeal fragmentation: "we are not sure we are ill; one hand asks the other by the pulse, and our eye asks our urine how we do. O multiplied misery!" (Meditation I, p. 8). Perfectly normal bodily functions become rhetorically absurd in this cosmic vision of the individual body as a little academy of confused persons.

As the disease steals upon him, he feels that his own cosmic identity shatters and fragments him: "Why dost thou melt me, scatter me" (Meditation II, p. 14), he asks God, and later quotes Ecclesiastes, "*Pray unto the Lord, and he will make thee whole*" (Meditation IV, p. 26). Though he is acutely conscious, in the midst of containing so much, that he does not include the natural power of physic (see Meditation IV), the emphasis remains upon the deadly strength of the great multiplicity within him:

> The pulse, the urine, the sweat, all have sworn to say nothing, to give no indication of any dangerous sickness. My forces are not enfeebled, I find no decay in my

---

77. The very structure of Meditation, Expostulation, and Prayer exemplifies this movement.

strength; my provisions are not cut off, I find no abhorring in mine appetite; my counsels are not corrupted nor infatuated, I find no false apprehensions to work upon mine understanding; and yet they see that invisibly, and I feel that insensibly, the disease prevails. The disease hath established a kingdom, an empire in me, and will have certain *arcana imperii*, secrets of state, by which it will proceed and not be bound to declare them.

[Meditation X, pp. 64–65]

In this picture, drawn from the political allegory of the body, the elements of man's multiplicity are independent but united in an evil enterprise. The very ability to contain the "kingdom" of this disease suggests that man the chameleon—to use Pico's term—has reached too far.

Donne's image is very much in the microcosmic tradition. Paracelsus viewed diseases as having cosmic bodies inhabiting the cosmic bodies of individuals, and the Petrarchan poets recurrently picture Cupid as invading the lover's body with his own kingdom. This is an essential image of human complexity in Renaissance literature, man containing a cosmic wholeness within himself which is at the same time a war with himself. Donne's disease, being largely without moral implication and unspecified, does not image forth a particular kind of internal complexity and dissension; but when Coriolanus assumes the body of the state within his own or Astrophil the kingdom of love within his own, specifics of the internal war become clearer.

For Donne here, the internal war is the basic nature of the human condition. He does not forsake his belief in wholenesses—in this case, the cosmic unity of the disease—or in the whole analogical system which enables his body to be a place in which to read the world. But the cosmic wholenesses which the body contains may be so vast that they are fragmented or at cross purposes with man himself. This tension of the microcosm is perhaps clearest when the disease is waning:

I am up, and I seem to stand, and I go round, and I am a new argument of the new Philosophy, that the earth moves round; why may I not believe that the whole earth moves, in a round motion, though that seems to me to stand, when as I seem to stand to my company, and yet am carried in a giddy and circular motion as I stand?

[Meditation XXI, pp. 139–40]

Donne's body here comes to contain the whole sphere of the heavens. Though the heavens are viewed in the Copernican system, the microcosmic idea is ancient and Ptolemaic. Donne grafts on the new philosophy because he wishes to emphasize the tension, randomness, and fragmentation which is possible within the microcosmic idea. The entire independence of subject and object is called into question in this passage. While man's body and the world's are inextricable from each other, Donne is completely separated from his visitors because the differences in their point of view cause them to see two completely different worlds. That insight represents the germ of the new philosophy, the idea that man's earthly point of view makes it impossible to see the movement of the earth. When Donne internalizes within his body such a fragmented cosmos as this, the last phase in the diversification is reached.

But the *Devotions* are not so purely negative as this historical approach to them may suggest. If the body and the cosmos are fragmented by their grandeur and multiplicity, they are also capable of uniting and being reunited. The multiple parts of man's body may seem at times completely separate and fragmented— "no part of my body, if it were cut off, would cure another part" (Meditation XXII, p. 147)—but at other times, the multiple components can perfect man in the service of God:

> As therefore thou hast imprinted in all thine elements of which our bodies consist two manifest qualities, so that as thy fire dries, so it heats too; and as thy water moists, so it cools too; so, O Lord, in these corrections which are the elements of our regeneration by which our souls are made thine, imprint thy two qualities, those two operations, that, as they scourge us, they may scourge us into the way to thee.
>
> [Prayer VII, p. 49]

In addition, the very greatness of man's body as a piece of workmanship and the extent of its analogous relations make it a fit habitation for God, since if it is a little world, it may well be one that God can live in. "Will God pretend to make a watch and leave out the spring?" Donne asks (Expostulation I, p. 10), and he comes to realize, in his more optimistic moments, that, as a great building, the body may be a fit temple for God. He prays, "Only be thou ever present to me, O my God, and this bedchamber and thy bedchamber shall be all one room, and the closing of these bodily eyes here, and the opening of the eyes of my soul there, all one act" (Prayer XIII, p. 88), thus uniting self with God, body, and soul, anatomy and architecture.

Finally, the same process which can transform one individual, via his body, into a vast and fragmented world can also unite many individuals into a larger, single, composite body. These are complementary processes which we shall observe not only in Donne but also in Shakespeare, Sidney, and Spenser. The famous passage from the *Devotions*, "No man is an island, entire of itself; every man is a piece of the continent, a part of the main" (Meditation XVII, p. 108), expresses this reunion via a larger body, at once anthropomorphic and geomorphic. This is the inherent paradox in that process of metamorphosis and fragmentation so dear to the Renaissance imagination: man can be torn apart by his own multiplicity, or exalted by it; man can be dismembered by his own multitude of component parts, or else reunited with the cosmos and God because they too are analogous bodies with component parts, and the single individual can find his place within those larger bodies.

That man can be exalted by the multiple cosmological significances of his body and his identity is nowhere clearer than in a poem Donne wrote during the same illness which produced the *Devotions*. The "Hymne to God my God, in my sicknesse" is a poem of transformation, in which Donne's body becomes the world. The more richly and fully he explores the implications of his micro-cosmology, the more unity and harmony and perfect sphericality to his little world. That his body is so protean proves his grandeur, but it is a grandeur in which the multiplicity of elements always gets back to the same identity, just as Paradise and Calvary are ultimately identical. The conceptual framework of the poem is as perfect and spherical as the cosmology. It is worth quoting in full, not to explicate further, but to epitomize the Renaissance traditions of corporeal transformation and *homo omnis creatura*:

> Since I am comming to that Holy roome,
> Where, with thy Quire of Saints for evermore,
> I shall be made thy Musique; As I come
> I tune the Instrument here at the dore,
> And what I must doe then, thinke now before.
>
> Whilst my Physitians by their love are growne
> Cosmographers, and I their Mapp, who lie
> Flat on this bed, that by them may be showne
> That this is my South-west discoverie
> *Per fretum febris*, by these streights to die,

I joy, that in these straits, I see my West;
    For, though theire currants yeeld returne to none,
What shall my West hurt me? As West and East
    In all flatt Maps (and I am one) are one,
    So death doth touch the Resurrection.

Is the Pacifique Sea my home? Or are
    The Easterne riches? Is *Jerusalem*?
Anyan, and *Magellan*, and *Gibraltare*,
    All streights, and none but streights, are wayes to them,
    Whether where *Japhet* dwelt, or *Cham*, or *Sem*.

We thinke that *Paradise* and *Calvarie*,
    Christs Crosse, and *Adams* tree, stood in one place;
Looke Lord, and finde both Adams met in me;
    As the first *Adams* sweat surrounds my face,
    May the last *Adams* blood my soule embrace.

So, in his purple wrapp'd receive mee Lord,
    By these his thornes give me his other Crowne;
And as to others soules I preach'd thy word,
    Be this my Text, my Sermon to mine owne,
    Therefore that he may raise the Lord throws down.[78]

To one inheritor of medieval and continental Renaissance traditions, then, a vision of man's perfect security in God's plan is inevitably joined with the image of *homo omnis creatura*. Cosmology, self-knowledge, and knowledge of God unite here in the poetic metamorphosis of the human body. The great distance which Donne travels from "no part of my body, if it were cut off, would cure another part" to "Looke Lord, and finde both Adams met in me" demonstrates the whole range of the metaphoric image of the body, from fragmentation to unity.

78. In *The Divine Poems of John Donne*, ed. Helen Gardner (Oxford: Clarendon Press, 1964). The assumption that the "Hymn to God, my God in my sicknesse" was written during the 1623 illness, rather than during Donne's terminal illness in 1630, has not gone unquestioned. Helen Gardner reviews the evidence and comes down on the side of 1623. I am inclined to agree. *Divine Poems*, pp. 132–35.

2

The Human Body and the Commonwealth

The image of the human body and its pervasiveness in thought and literature are reminders that not only the proper but in fact the only study of mankind is man. Great abstract entities like the cosmos or the commonwealth are interesting less in themselves than as constructions against which man can more readily measure man, and the use of the human body as an analogy for these constructs demonstrates the extent to which we reduce great abstract things to physical realities and individual human forms. This chapter will trace a path from the simplest and earliest anthropomorphic conceptions of the commonwealth all the way to the point where body politic, idealized body, and natural body are internalized in such figures as the heroes of *Sejanus* and *Coriolanus*. We shall begin with the classical, medieval, and Renaissance history of the anthropomorphic analogy for the commonwealth, proceed to a treatment of the poetic techniques which the analogy inspires, and conclude with a reading, in the terms of this analogy, of the two tragedies. A study of the history and technique of the analogy will, I think, demonstrate how the rhetorical, polemic, and scientific methods of the political theorists become the materials by which Jonson and Shakespeare construct metaphors, heroes, and worlds.

1

The anthropomorphic vision of the commonwealth is from the earliest times closely tied to an organic conception of the State. Just as Plato in the *Timaeus* was unable to grasp the principles of the cosmos

without resorting to the image of an animate being, so too he and those
who followed him assumed the State to be constructed like a living
organism. Ernest Barker's excellent summary of this organic theory of
the State will serve to suggest how natural the human body would
seem for its metaphoric expression:

> This is what we should call an "organic" conception of the State. . . . An organism
> is a unity, where each member is an instrument (or *organon*) in the general plan;
> where each member has its appointed purpose or function (*ergon*); where each
> member can only act, and be understood, and indeed exist, through the end and aim
> of the whole. But such is the unity of the State and such is the relation of the indi-
> vidual to the State: the State is an organism and its citizens are its members.[1]

As we saw in the *Timaeus*, it is at best risky to say that the anthropo-
morphic analogy arose out of the organic view of the state rather than
vice versa. It must always be remembered that the human body is both
phylogenetically and ontogenetically one of the first and most basic
entities the mind can grasp. In view of that fact, we can presuppose a
roughly three part development of the idea which links the anthropo-
morphic image with the organic view of the State. The first stage is
purely anthropomorphic: at a time when there is little empirical sense
of the cosmos as a whole, not much in the way of overarching com-
monwealth, and nothing like a man-made leviathan, the human body
is the only, as well as the most obvious, way of understanding a unity
of diversity. Consequently, abstract unities of diversity are seen in the
image of the body.[2] The second stage is the development and refine-
ment of an organic conception of the commonwealth out of the original
anthropomorphic conception. In this stage, once an organic theory has
been evolved, the original corporeal source has died imaginatively.
Thus in the above quotation from Professor Barker, we are not likely,
upon seeing the word *members*, to think immediately of arms and legs
even though the human body is the source for both the idea and the

1. Ernest Barker, *The Political Thought of Plato and Aristotle* (New York: Russell and
Russell, 1959), p. 127.
2. This stage is largely buried in preliterate history, but it may correspond with the
blatantly anthropomorphic vision of the godhead that Ruth Mohl discovered in the Rig-
Veda (*The Three Estates in Medieval and Renaissance Literature* [New York: Columbia
University Press, 1933], p. 263 n.) or with the vision of the pre-Socratic Metrodorus of
Lampsakos, who allegorized Olympus as a human organism, with Apollo as the bile,
Demeter as the liver, Dionysus as the spleen, and Zeus as the brain. See Wilhelm Nestle,
"Die Fabel des Menenius Agrippa," *Klio* 22 (1926–27): 354.

means of its expression. In the third stage the anthropomorphic vision is imaginatively reborn as a means either of expressing or of proving some version of the organic theory.

In classical literature from Plato to Seneca, the analogy between body and commonwealth is heuristic, idealized, and propagandistic rather than empirical, literal, or concrete. Thus the technique of comparing an abstract or distant thing with the human body may be similar to that in the *Timaeus*, but the underlying assumption differs. Plato believed the cosmos to be an actual animate being literally parallel in some respects to the human body. The State is not an animate body in the same sense. It is rather an artificial body, a necessary unity which society can evolve and whose terms can be clarified by an understanding of the natural unities of diversity to be found within the human body.

Since Plato's anthropomorphic analogy is largely heuristic, it rarely attempts to be exhaustively physical. He is more apt to compare the State with the individual man's life than with his body.[3] His more distinctly corporeal images treat disorder in the State as the sickness of a body, but this body is never elaborated or articulated. Socrates speaks of the city as "swollen and festering,"[4] and the Athenian in the *Laws* praises peace over mere armistice in terms of the corporeal analogy:

> And thus a victory of a city over itself turns out, it would seem, to be not so much a good as a necessary evil. It is as though one fancied that a diseased body which has been subjected to medical purgation were at its best in that condition, and ignored a body which has never stood in need of such treatment.[5]

Even in the *Republic*, which derives and defines the commonwealth along lines not too different from the derivation of the cosmos in the *Timaeus*, the analogy with the human body, though extremely pervasive, is imaginative rather than empirical and idealistic rather than corporeal. The difference in style and structure between the two great dialogues is an excellent indication of the different use of the analogy with the human body. The *Timaeus* is an almost uninterrupted monologue, a "scientific" proof issued by a single voice, while the *Republic* is constructed in the more argumentative form of questions and

---

3. *Laws* 829a. Citations are to Plato, *The Collected Dialogues*, ed. Edith Hamilton and Huntington Cairns (New York: Pantheon, 1966), p. 1395.

4. *Gorgias* 518e, p. 299.

5. *Laws* 628d, p. 1230.

answers. The analogy between the State and the body is the most trusty, and perhaps more frequently used, of Socrates' logical traps. By forcing his interlocutors to admit to an obvious anatomical premise, he induces them to accept the analogy in terms of the State. Socrates begins logically with the body, out of which he constructs a utopian State whose ultimate purpose is less public and political than personal and moral. In this way an image of the human body becomes an image of the self, but only once the body is transformed through some kind of analogy, in this case with the commonwealth.

To such a logical system as this, notions of complex physical correspondences or empirical identities of body and State would be superfluous and misleading. Plato concentrates on the generalized, idealized, and persuasive analogy between disease in the body and disorder in the State.[6] He creates this idealized image in order to argue against a more contractual view of the State. Thus it is enough that the analogy with the body be general and ideal so as to distinguish his State from one in which secession of members and dissolution of the contract are possible.

Aristotle rejected the Platonic notion of a supreme good as the ultimate reference point for analogous constructions like the body, the State, and the cosmos; at the same time, he did not go so far as the Stoics would in seeing the State as a contract ever reversible at the whim of any dissatisfied individual. He compromises by treating the State as an association, a perfectly functioning creation which is neither manmade, as the Stoics would have it, nor a particle in the ladder of ideal perfection, as Plato saw it. The principles which define this association, such as the combination of self-interest and the striving for good, are innately human but not reversible by individual men.

Since Aristotle's conception of the State is somewhat more mechanistic than Plato's, we would be right to expect that the later thinker uses the analogy with the body in a more specifically corporeal way, especially since the principal quality of Aristotle's association is the perfect working together of many parts, just as we are accustomed to find in images of the body. The analogy and its use are apparent at the very beginning of *The Politics*:

6. See especially *Republic* 372e, p. 619; 426a–c, pp. 667–68; 444c–d, p. 687, among others.

Furthermore the city or state has priority over the household and over any individual among us. For the whole must be prior to the parts. Separate hand or foot from the whole body and they will no longer be hand or foot. . . . It will have been ruined by such treatment, having no longer the power and the function which make it what it is.[7]

Aristotle does differentiate the parts more than Plato does. In fact in one of his works of natural science, *Of the Movement of Animals*, entirely concerned with corporeal diversity, he conversely draws the analogy of the commonwealth to explain animal organisms.[8] Nevertheless, Aristotle's analogy of the body with the State is still largely idealized and heuristic. As the above citation suggests, he is much more concerned with unity than diversity, he does not develop the different meanings, values, or purposes of the parts of the body, and he most certainly does not see the body as parallel to the State in any real or empirical way.

The anthropomorphic idea of the State and the analogy with the body appeared in numerous other guises in classical times. The analogy between State and body was already a commonplace in Plato's time not only among political philosophers using anatomical descriptions but also among physicians describing anatomy in social or political terms. A vision of the State as the perfect, and perhaps god-given, union of diverse elements was particularly attractive to the conservatives who watched the disintegrating polis of the later fifth century, torn between the extreme individualism of the sophists on the one hand and the split of the populace into factionalism on the other. This defense of the State as a commonweal, or *omonoia* becomes the prevailing note in the classical expressions of the anthropomorphic idea. In the Hellenistic period, the basic unit may be seen in broader terms than the polis, but throughout antiquity we find the familiar admonition to the individual to cooperate in the commonwealth as if he were a larger body. Cicero makes the same assertion in generalized terms in *De Officiis*:

Suppose, by way of comparison, that each one of our bodily members should conceive this idea and imagine that it could be strong and well if it should draw off to itself the health and strength of its neighbouring member, the whole body would

7. *The Politics* 1253a, 20, trans. T. A. Sinclair (Baltimore: Penguin, 1969), p. 29.
8. *De Motu Animalium*, trans. Farquharson in *The Works of Aristotle*, ed. J. A. Smith and W. D. Ross (Oxford: Clarendon Press, 1958), 703 a, 29–37.

necessarily be enfeebled and die; so, if each one of us should seize upon the property of his neighbours and take from each whatever he could appropriate to his own use, the bonds of human society must inevitably be annihilated.[9]

Seneca later makes exactly the opposite admonition by means of the analogy with the body:

> To injure one's country is a crime; consequently, also, to injure a fellow–citizen— for he is a part of the country, and if we reverence the whole, the parts are sacred —consequently to injure any man is a crime, for he is your fellow–citizen in the greater commonwealth. What if the hands should desire to harm the feet, or the eyes the hands? As all the members of the body are in harmony one with another because it is to the advantage of the whole that the individual members be un- harmed, so mankind should spare the individual man, because all are born for a life of fellowship, and society can be kept unharmed only by the mutual protection and love of its parts.[10]

The individual, then, is hallowed for the strength and significance of his role as a member of the larger body, and the reader is cautioned not so much against opposition to the State as against opposition to other individuals, who, like himself, are part of the State. Here the diversity implied in the analogy to the body begins to have as much imaginative life as the unity. Nevertheless, as in most classical expressions of the analogy, the image remains hypothetical, heuristic, and largely un- differentiated.

Surpassing Plato, Aristotle, and the Stoics in later influence and deriving from them were the Epistles of St. Paul. The doctrine of the *corpus mysticum* originates in Paul's Epistles, even though the phrase itself is of much later date.[11] Paul expands the analogy in several new directions: he understands its implications in new ways, and he uses it to promulgate sacramental, theological, and ecclesiastical doctrines which are, of course, completely alien to pre-Christian authors.

Paul's new understanding of the analogy is partially a result of Stoic influences carried somewhat further even than the passage from Seneca quoted above. We saw that Seneca's individualistic philosophy began to stress the diversity of the body image almost as much as its unity.

9. Cicero, *De Officiis* 3. 5. 22–23, trans. Walter Miller (London: Heinemann, 1913), p. 289.

10. Seneca, *De Ira* 2. 31.7, in *Moral Essays,* trans. John W. Basore (New York: Putnam, 1928), 1:237–39.

11. The term became current only in Carolingian times. See Henri de Lubac, "Corpus Mysticum," *Recherches de Science Réligieuse* 29 (1939): 429–80.

This sense of diversity can be immediately seen in the most famous and extended treatment of the human body analogy in the Epistles:

For to one is given by the Spirit the word of wisdom; to another the word of knowledge by the same Spirit; To another faith by the same Spirit; to another the gifts of healing by the same Spirit; To another the working of miracles; to another prophecy; to another discerning of spirits; to another divers kinds of tongues; to another the interpretation of tongues: But all these worketh that one and the selfsame Spirit, dividing to every man severally as he will. For as the body is one, and hath many members, and all the members of that one body, being many, are one body: so also is Christ. For by one Spirit we are all baptized into one body, whether we be Jews or Gentiles, whether we be bond or free; and have been all made to drink into one Spirit. For the body is not one member, but many. If the foot shall say, Because I am not the hand, I am not of the body; is it therefore not of the body? And if the ear shall say, Because I am not the eye, I am not of the body; is it therefore not of the body? If the whole body were an eye, where were the hearing? If the whole were hearing, where were the smelling? But now hath God set the members every one of them in the body, as it hath pleased him. And if they were all one member, where were the body? But now are they many members, yet but one body. And the eye cannot say unto the hand, I have no need of thee: nor again the head to the feet, I have no need of you. Nay, much more these members of the body, which seem to be more feeble, are necessary: And those members of the body, which we think to be less honorable, upon these we bestow more abundant honor; and our uncomely parts have more abundant comeliness. For our comely parts have no need: but God hath tempered the body together, having given more abundant honor to that part which lacked: That there should be no schism in the body: but that the members should have the same care one for another. And whether one member suffer, all the members suffer with it; or one member be honored, all the members rejoice with it. Now ye are the body of Christ, and members in particular. And God hath set some in the church, first apostles, secondarily prophets, thirdly teachers, after that miracles, then gifts of healings, helps, governments, diversities of tongues. Are all apostles? are all prophets? are all teachers? are all workers of miracles? Have all the gifts of healing? do all speak with tongues? do all interpret? But covet earnestly the best gifts: and yet show I unto you a more excellent way.

[1 Cor. 12:8–31]

This is by far the fullest treatment of the analogy between the human body and body politic up to its time, and despite its multiple reinterpretations by the medieval Church, the passage largely speaks for itself. Paul here enunciates some of the major specific strands of content which will animate and sustain the analogy well into Tudor times. He uses the analogy with the body to explain the diversity of the body politic (12,14), the specific differences among members (15,16), the need for a multiplicity of functions or organs (17,20), the importance of cooperation among these elements (21,25,26), and the essential significance of even the humblest members of the body (23,24).

It is not surprising that with classical and Hellenistic influences behind him, Paul could celebrate the diversity of both bodies politic and natural in this manner. The Apostle was faced with the problems of a Christian communion which was diversified in membership and spread over great distances. In addition, there was considerable partisanship within the Corinthian church itself, as its members were feeling certain democratic longings to which Paul was replying and which are specifically answered in verses eight to eleven. In Paul's later epistles written when there was less immediate danger of schism, the lesson of the human body analogy is less one of spiritual equality and cooperation among the members than of complete dependence of all the members upon the head, which is Christ. This notion is not so attractive as a selling point for the Church, but nonetheless closer to the heart of its mysteries. The later Pauline idea is also closely bound up with the meaning and unity of the mystical body, which is discussed below.

A corollary of the diversity which Paul saw in the image of the body is its actual physicality, another aspect which was largely missing from the earlier classical instances of the analogy. A more diversified image of the human body would likely be in more genuinely corporeal terms. The highpoint of this line of thought will come much later, when each organ of the body will be associated with a specific function within the body politic. Paul makes the analogy more corporeal, not so much by specific references to ear, eye, foot, etc., to which he does not give differentiated functions within the body politic, as by linking the idealized image of a human body with the real body that any one of the faithful carries around with him. This is particularly apparent earlier in First Corinthians:

> Meats for the belly, and the belly for meats: but God shall destroy both it and them. Now the body is not for fornication, but for the Lord; and the Lord for the body. And God hath both raised up the Lord, and will also raise up us by his own power. Know ye not that your bodies are the members of Christ? shall I then take the members of Christ, and make them the members of a harlot? God forbid. What! know ye not that he which is joined to a harlot is one body? for two, saith he, shall be one flesh.
>
> [1 Cor. 6:13–16]

The appetites and functions of the literal body are grafted onto the idealized, mystical body of Christ, and a union of bodies through a concupiscent sexual drive is violently contrasted with the union of bodies among the members of Christ's body.

The unity of the mystical body departs even more completely from the classical model than the diversity, for the unity is in the body of Christ. The most important departure from classical thought in Paul's use of the corporeal analogy is his belief in the absolute reality of the idealized body. The equivalence between body politic (or in this case, body of the faithful) and generalized human body, which was so purely heuristic a device for Socrates, is real and concrete for Paul, at the same time as it remains a useful heuristic device. The generalized human body can be "real" principally because it is specified and attached to Christ who, being human, had a human body. The body politic, which can be likened to the physical body of Christ (or any other human), is not merely similar, it *is* the body of Christ.

Two other equivalences complicate and elaborate the analogy. The Church is the body of Christ, and the Eucharist is the body of Christ. That the Church is the body of Christ is partly a mystery and partly a matter of political philosophy. The latter is clear from what has been said already : Paul means the Church when he speaks of the body politic, and the body politic is one with the body natural of Christ. The mystery is to be understood in terms of Christ's oneness with His Church; the Father, Paul tells us, "hath put all things under his feet, and gave him to be the head over all things to the church, Which is his body, the fullness of him that filleth all in all" (Ephesians 1:22-23). That the sacrament is the body of Christ lies, of course, in the mystery of the Eucharist. On the occasion of Christ's instituting the communion rite, He was sitting among the body of the faithful and was thus capable of transforming the Communion into His own body. We see here a very basic union of the body politic with the specified, though idealized, body natural of one individual. Thus the Pauline analogy of the human body with the commonwealth retains its classical rhetoric and idealization but adds diversity, some physicality, and identifies the ideal body as the body of Christ.

The notions of *res publica* and *corpus mysticum,* both evoked by anthropomorphic analogies, become in the Middle Ages vehicles for expression of that essentially medieval tension between the passionate vision of comprehensive cosmic unity and the overwhelming evidence of fragmentation and diversity within the world. This polarity has always been the substance of the microcosmic body image, and both the thought and the events of the Middle Ages give rise to a great flowering of this analogy. Two medieval developments in the anthropomorphic analogy stand out: the struggles for control of the overarching unity, particularly between the empire and the papacy, turn the analogy into a prime vehicle for propaganda, and the curiously physical imagination of the time, particularly in northern Europe, tends to transform a Platonic or Pauline idealized body into a real flesh and blood composite of many parts.

The ideal of unity is largely self-explanatory: it is usually a combination of some Platonic sequence of unities leading to a higher unity with an Aristotelean sense of association or mechanism governing the whole system. This is perhaps most succinctly expressed by Dante:

> Mankind in one sense is a whole (that is, in relation to its component parts), but in another sense it is itself a part. It is a whole in relation to particular kingdoms and peoples, as we have previously shown; but in relation to the wide universe it is, of course, a part. Therefore just as its component parts are brought to harmony in mankind, so mankind itself has to be brought into the harmony of its appropriate whole. The component parts of mankind are brought into harmony by a single principle (as may easily be gathered from the preceding argument); and mankind itself is similarly related to the whole universe, or to its principle (that is, God, the Monarch); this harmony is achieved by one principle only, the one Prince.[12]

But long before Dante, the unity was attacked and defeated by the actual complexity and fragmentation of the medieval world; and the medieval anthropomorphic analogy concentrates upon expressing versions of this diversity. In the first place, the implications of diversity within the *corpus mysticum* increased in importance as Church doctrine developed and as the Church assumed a larger role in governing. In Carolingian times *corpus mysticum* referred specifically and only to the consecrated Host. But by the twelfth century, its meaning moved in two other directions. First, in response to eleventh-century heresies proposing a purely mystical transubstantiation, the Church reaffirmed the actuality of the body and blood in the Eucharist, and second, because of the growing social importance of the Church, the *corpus*

12. *De Monarchia*, in *Monarchy and Three Political Letters*, trans. D. Nicholl (London: Weidenfeld and Nicolson, 1954), 1. 7, p. 12.

mysticum became more specifically identified with the body of the faithful.[13]

It is this sociological development which is of greatest importance to our metaphor. Writers in the early and high Middle Ages treating the complexities of the Church and later writers treating the complexities of the State specified and physicalized the anthropomorphic analogy with worlds of detail not dreamed of by Plato, Aristotle, or St. Paul. The transformation of the *corpus mysticum* from a sacramental to a social concept came just at the time when ideas of corporation were influencing medieval political thought. The jurists, who early felt the need to deal with this complex corporation, were the first to elaborate the different parts of the analogous body and to attach them to various orders within the society.

One twelfth-century codex glosses "princeps" and continues with further corporeal comparisons:

> Princeps: quasi primum caput. iudices enim capita sunt aliorum hominum, quia ab eis reguntur ut membra a suis capitibus; sed princeps est caput aliorum iudicum et ab eo reguntur. post principem sunt illustres, qui sunt quasi oculi imperatoris. post illustres sunt spectabiles, quasi manus. post spectabiles sunt clarissimi, quasi torax. post clarissimos sunt pedanei, quasi pedes imperatoris, et inferiores iudices similiter in ecclesia est quoddam caput primum iudicum: solus papa. post eum sunt patriarche; post patriarchas primates; post archiepiscopi; post hos episcopi.[14]

This pioneering venture in the elaborated anthropomorphic analogy is interesting in a number of ways. First, it multiplies the analogy beyond mere discussion of the head and members, for differentiation to that extent had existed ever since Platonic uses of the analogy. Second, the hierarchy within the commonwealth is not very specified (*illustres, spectabiles, clarissimi*), even though the parts of the body are clearly differentiated. Third, the pun on *pedanei* and *pedes* looks forward to the

13. See Ernst H. Kantorowicz, *The King's Two Bodies* (Princeton: Princeton University Press, 1957), pp. 194–206.

14. Cited in H. Fitting, *Juristische Schriften des Früheren Mittelalters* (Halle: Waisenhause, 1876), p. 148: "The sovereign, meaning the first head. For judges are the heads of other men, who are ruled by them just as limbs are ruled by their heads. But the sovereign is the head of judges, and they are ruled by him. After the sovereign there are the princes, who are like the eyes of the emperor. After the princes are the high lords who are like the hands. After the high lords are the nobles, like the chest. After the nobles are the petty judges, like the feet of the emperor, and also the lesser judges. Similarly in the church there is a certain first head of the judges: the pope alone. After him are the patriarchs, then the archbishops, then the bishops."

more corporeal and tortured analogies of the later Middle Ages and the Renaissance. Finally, it is significant that an ecclesiastical hierarchy follows the political, implying a similar alignment with parts of the body. The first and most basic challenge within the medieval mind to the doctrine of overarching unity was the obvious duality between Church and State.[15] This essential doubleness could cast considerable doubt on the idea that a single analogous body might contain both spiritual and temporal powers. Even this early in the medieval use of the analogy, two parallel bodies had to be invented.

John of Salisbury, in the twelfth century, is the first to attempt a lengthy and full-scale anatomy of the anthropomorphic state. *Policraticus* is a compendium of all the lore surrounding the organic theory of the State, to which he adds a good deal of metaphor and imagery which will be discussed in greater detail later. In addition to the familiar lessons of primacy and the need for cooperation among the members, John reproduces a work which he refers to as Plutarch's "The Instruction of Trajan," which may, in fact, be by John himself.[16] This work includes an elaborate anthropomorphic image of the State:

> The place of the head in the body of the commonwealth is filled by the prince, who is subject only to God and to those who exercise His office and represent Him on earth, even as in the human body the head is quickened and governed by the soul. The place of the heart is filled by the Senate, from which proceeds the initiation of good works and ill. The duties of eyes, ears, and tongue are claimed by the judges and the governors of provinces. Officials and soldiers correspond to the hands. Those who always attend upon the prince are likened to the sides. Financial officers and keepers . . . may be compared with the stomach and intestines, which, if they become congested through excessive avidity, and retain too tenaciously their accumulations, generate innumerable and incurable diseases, so that through their ailment the whole body is threatened with destruction. The husbandmen correspond to the feet, which always cleave to the soil, and need the more especially the care and foresight of the head, since while they walk upon the earth doing service with their bodies, they meet the more often with stones of stumbling, and therefore deserve aid and protection all the more justly since it is they who raise, sustain, and move forward the weight of the entire body.[17]

John brings to the analogy a kind of medieval realism. The functions

15. See Otto von Gierke, *Political Theories of the Middle Age*, trans. F. W. Maitland (Cambridge, Eng.: Cambridge University Press, 1900; rpt. 1958), pp. 10–11.
16. See Kantorowicz, *King's Two Bodies*, p. 199 n.
17. *Policraticus*, in *The Statesman's Book of John of Salisbury*, trans. J. Dickinson (New York: Knopf, 1927), 5.2, p. 65.

within the commonwealth are specified in detail, and, more important-
ly, the anatomical functions are understood in very concrete terms. Far
from the simple classical distinction between head and members, this
image explains each analogy either in terms of physical position of the
part of the body which the functionary might be most particularly
expected to use, or of some imaginative link between an anatomical
phenomenon and a political one. The Platonic idealized body and the
sacramental divine body are replaced by an extremely corporeal entity
which is at the same time only imaginatively and heuristically con-
nected with the body politic.[18]

The last word in medieval anthropomorphism is to be found in the
De Concordantia Catholica of Nicholas Cusanus, finished around 1433
and deriving ultimately from John of Salisbury. The work is quite long
and contains many forward looking notions about reform of the em-
pire; but at the very end it returns to a conservatively organic and
hierarchical vision of Church and State. This vision is expressed in an
elaborated anthropomorphic analogy, which drew upon the author's
considerable medical experience. Each part of the body contains both
body and soul, the former analogous to the imperial hierarchy and the
latter to the ecclesiastical. The most significantly "modern" quality in
Cusanus's analogy is his concern with physical and governmental
process, rather than static definition and equivalence. When he com-
pares the movement from God's will down to Church decrees, he is as
clever an anatomist as he is political theorist:

> As the smaller veins nourishing certain individual parts of the body can not bring
> life, strength and spirit, unless they flow from the common source so all provincial
> and local statutes must conform to the principles of canon laws.[19]

18. It is worth comparing John of Salisbury with Thomas Aquinas, who, writing about
a century later, is much less pictorially anthropomorphic. But Aquinas contributed
significantly to the physicalization of the analogy by redefining the body of Christ in the
sacrament as less a mystical, imaginary body than a real flesh-and-blood body. This
increasing tendency to speak of Christ's specific body and to understand that body as
physical goes hand in hand in the high Middle Ages with an increasing sense in the
Church of political involvement and complexity. Thus we see contemporary with
Aquinas the flourishing of the concept "body politic," which could be compared with
corporational *corpus mysticum* of the Church at the same time as others writing in the
tradition of John of Salisbury could remind their readers of the specific and anthropo-
morphic nature of that *corpus*.

19. Translated in Paul E. Sigmund, *Nicholas of Cusa and Medieval Political Thought*
(Cambridge, Mass.: Harvard University Press, 1963), p. 135.

Elsewhere in the work the analogy becomes a good deal more gro-
tesque in that grossly physical manner which one associates with the
later Middle Ages, particularly in Northern Europe.[20] Lawmaking, for
instance, is compared at some length with eating, including biting,
tasting, chewing, and digesting, though stopping short of the final
stages of the process beyond the stomach, which Cusanus compares
with the Great Council. Readers of Tudor literature and of Spenser
cannot fail to notice that in this late medieval period, in its exuberant
and graphic imagination, we have the source for so much of the
imaginative material of the subsequent time. The human body is a
prime matter for this imagination; and in the political works of the
Middle Ages it begins to bear not only the ideal and heuristic values we
saw in the classics but also some of the power of real anatomy and real
human life.

The rhetorical or propagandistic power which the analogy of the
human body developed in the Middle Ages should be clear from the
varieties of anthropomorphism discussed above. Nonetheless it is im-
portant to conclude with some mention of the political powder keg
which initiated the propaganda, the struggles between pope and
empire in the thirteenth and fourteenth centuries. As we saw above,
the split between spiritual and temporal power was one of the basic
challenges to the doctrine of unity long before the high Middle Ages;
and that doubleness within a Christian society which was still conceived
of as ultimately unified made the analogy of the body, with its combi-
nations of unity and diversity, particularly appropriate. Once the two
powers were actually diversified, the struggle often revolved around
the identity of the head and the form of the organic "body" of the
state. The papal side expressed the extreme doctrine of unity, holding
both swords in the Church, which, as Boniface VIII expressed in *Unam
Sanctam*, "represents one mystical body, the head of which is Christ,
and the head of Christ is God."[21] The standard form of the papal
argument in anthropomorphic terms was that Christian society was a
single mystical body which could not have two heads, one papal and
one imperial.

The imperial theory, though much less loudly heard in medieval

20. See J. Huizinga, *The Waning of the Middle Ages* (London: Arnold, 1924; rpt.
1954), passim, especially pp. 214–20.

21. Don Louis Tosti, *History of Pope Boniface VIII*, trans. E. J. Donnelly (New York:
Christian Press, 1911), p. 537.

times, may have proved more significant in the future. The emperors and the legists proposed a theory of coordinate power. This gives rise to the coordination between elements of soul and body, or imperial and ecclesiastical functionaries, which was apparent in the anthropomorphic conceits of the twelfth-century codex and of Nicholas Cusanus. It further gives rise to a system of graduated bodies, a kind of infinite regress which will be of prime importance in later imaginative treatments of the image. In either case, the image of the human body remains central to the propagandistic power of political theories, even at the same time as the body is physicalized or personified in actual or ideal terms.

Renaissance England represents in a way the heyday of the anthropomorphic image of the commonwealth; but rather than contributing new meanings and forms to the analogy, the English writers consolidated the classical and medieval visions with new imaginative force and with new applications to the political world around them. In order to understand the centrality of the organic political theory and its anthropomorphic expression, it will be necessary to suggest some idea of the nature and form of political thought in late medieval and Tudor England.

In the late Middle Ages, the characteristically English approach to the organic theory of the State stressed the importance of the whole realm to the government of the commonwealth at least as much as that of the king. The anthropomorphic image supports this contention by suggesting that the body politic can no more exist without its torso than without its head. This attitude emphasizes the organic and dynamic functions within the State and within the body. By going beyond the simple idea that the king is the head and all the other members are below, these theorists used the anthropomorphic analogy to suggest that the lifeblood of the commonwealth included the royal power, but not to the exclusion of all other bases of power. Thus Sir John Fortescue speaks of the law as central to the *corpus mysticum* of the commonwealth, "for just as the body is held together by the nerves, so is the *corpus mysticum* joined together and united into one by the Law."[22] In general, then, medieval English philosophy emphasized a common cooperation: the head is primary but not absolute.

22. *De Laudibus Legum Angliae,* ed. S. B. Chrimes (Cambridge, Eng.: Cambridge University Press, 1942), p. 28.

Given this traditional medieval viewpoint, we cannot help but see Henry VIII's assumption of absolute power, particularly over the Church, as an aggressively "modern" and antimedieval act. As late as 1542, Henry could still use the traditional anthropomorphic image of common cooperation, speaking of Parliament, "wherin we as head and you as members are conjoined and knit together in one body politic."[23] But Henry's takeover of the English church was an act which subsumed all those spiritual and ecclesiastical aspects of the *corpus mysticum*—those which men like Cusanus had labored to keep separate—into the narrower sphere of the body politic, of which he was without question the head. In this way the traditionally fluid relationship in England between head and members, to continue the anthropomorphic image that was often used for and against Henry, made it possible for all the limbs to be completely subsumed in the head. The confusion of bodies politic and mystical caused the integrity of the anthropomorphic image to break down completely.

But the expression of the organic theory and of the anthropomorphic analogy which is most significant in English thought is neither that of the late medieval period nor that of Henry VIII's reformation. Rather, when we think of the organic political theory in England, we think of the so-called Elizabethan world picture. This well known chapter in the history of ideas, with its sweeping cosmic parallels extending from the heavens all the way to the human body and on down to animals, plants, and stones, had strong political overtones, and the history sketched briefly above is intended to place the political ideas in their proper context. The "great chain of being" and the anthropomorphic image of the State that went with it in Renaissance England represent a definitely conservative political philosophy. This has frequently been pointed out. The Elizabethan world picture has been seen as an outdated world view about to be destroyed by the science of Copernicus, the politics of Machiavelli, and the morality of Montaigne.

What has not so frequently been pointed out is that the Elizabethan world picture, at least in England, is a contradiction as much of what preceded it as it is of what followed it. Raymond Southall has argued this point of view convincingly in *The Courtly Maker*. The Reformation, both of the continental dogmatic variety and of the English

---

23. *Letters and Papers Concerning the Reign of Henry VIII* (London: Longmans, 1899), 12:4 n. 3.

despotic variety, denies the medieval world picture in numerous ways. Those who oppose Henry in the early part of the sixteenth century are conservatives, and their cause is ultimately triumphant when Elizabeth, for the purposes of her own political order, promulgates the theory of cosmic correspondences. As Southall sees it,

> The doctrine of World Order was inconsistent both with the spirit of the old courtly tradition and with the new spirit of the Reformation; its promulgation as state doctrine by Elizabeth is simply a sign that the Reformation had been officially called to a halt.[24]

The English Renaissance picture of world order was above all a defense of the hierarchical *status quo*, and the human body was a useful analogy because, like society, it was clearly a strange and arbitrary combination of functions which all seemed to work perfectly together. Perhaps the prime lesson of the anthropomorphic analogy is the idea of cooperation: each member is only a part of the whole body, and therefore less than the whole, but the whole can only exist as the totality of its members. Otto von Gierke refers to this as the notion of membership, and he traces it back to late medieval thought. He quotes the fourteenth-century legist Baldus de Ubaldis: "imperium est in similitudine corporis humani, a quo, si abscinderetur auricula, non esset corpus perfectum sed monstruosum."[25] For an understanding of these concepts in Renaissance England, a more interesting source is

---

24. *The Courtly Maker* (Oxford: Clarendon Press, 1964), p. 55. The source of Southall's belief that the great chain of being was official rather than merely popular doctrine is the *Book of Homilies*. It is worth quoting in full: "Almighty God hath created and appointed all things, in heaven, earth, and waters, in a most excellent and perfect order. In heaven he hath appointed distinct (or several) orders, and states of archangels and angels. In earth, he hath assigned and appointed kings and princes, with other governors under them, all in good and necessary order. The water above is kept, and raineth down in due time and season. The sun, moon, stars, rainbow, thunder, lightning, clouds, and all birds of the air, do keep their order. The earth, trees, seeds, plants, herbs, corn, grass, and all manner of beasts, keep themselves in their order. All kinds of fishes in the sea, rivers and waters, with all fountains and springs, yea, the seas themselves, keep their comely course and order. And man himself also hath all his parts both within and without, as soul, heart, mind, memory, understanding, reason, speech, with all the singular corporal members of his body, in a profitable, necessary, and pleasant order. Every degree of people in their vocation, calling, and office, hath appointed to them their duty and order. Some are in high degree, some in low; some kings, and princes, some inferiors and servants; priests and laymen, masters and servants, fathers, husbands, and wives, rich and poor; and every one have need of other."

25. von Gierke, *Political Theories*, p. 134.

Thomas Starkey's *Dialogue between Pole and Lupset.* This work typifies
the struggle between medievalism and reform which was discussed
above. In the face of Henry VIII's "modernist" despotism, and in
response to the crises of the 1530's, Starkey was writing as a conserva-
tive humanist chronicling the failures of Tudor England and urging an
elected, limited monarchy along the lines of the English philosophy
characteristic of the later Middle Ages. Thus Starkey's thought, which
has been referred to as an improbable combination of medievalism and
Renaissance humanism,[26] represents a logical fusion of medieval theory
and a humanistic, neo-medieval reaction to the king.

  Starkey uses the anthropomorphic analogy to illustrate this idea of
membership or cooperation:

> Like as we say then every man's body to be strong, when every part can execute
> quickly and well his office determed by the order of nature; as the heart then is
> strong when he, as fountain of all naturale powers, ministereth them with due order
> to all other, and they then be strong when they be apt to receive their power of
> they [*sic*] heart, and can use it according to the order of nature, as, the eye to see, the
> year to hear, the foot to go, and hand to hold and reach; and so likewise of the rest.
> After such manner the strength of this politic body standeth in every part being able
> to do his office and duty. For this body hath his parts, which resemble also the parts
> of the body of man.[27]

Informing and altering the concept of cooperation, which implies an
equal commitment of all the members to the well-being of the whole
body, is the idea that both bodies politic and natural are unions of
elements which are unlike in form, function, and significance. In
particular, the analogy is used here to justify social inequality.[28] This
idea is in some respects in tension with the first since rather than com-
munality it suggests an independence of all the members of the body:

> But now, to keep this body knit togidder in unity, provision would be made by
> common law and authority that every part may exercise his office and duty—that is
> to say, every man in his craft and faculty to meddle with such things as pertaineth
> thereto, and intermeddle not with other. . . . Moreover, to all seditious persons
> that openly despise this order, unity, and concord whereby the parts of this body

26. E. M. W. Tillyard in his introduction to *A Dialogue between Reginald Pole and Thomas Lupset,* ed. K. M. Burton (London: Chatto and Windus, 1948), p. 3.
27. Starkey, *A Dialogue,* p. 57.
28. This we have seen as far back as Aristotle and St. Paul. In addition, von Gierke cites a telling comment from Aquinas: "Ordo autem maxime videtur in disparitate consistere" (*Summa Theologica,* I, q. 96, a. 3; von Gierke, *Political Theories,* p. 134).

are, as it were, with sinews and nerves knit togidder, perpetual banishment or rather, death, must be by law prescribed.[29]

All the parts are necessary, but they cannot perform the same function or be of equal importance. Therefore, as Nicholas Breton says, "if a Courtier, know thy place; if a Scholler plie thy booke; if a Souldier, look to thine honor; if a marchant, take thy fortune; if a farmer follow thy plough; if a beggar, fall to prayer."[30]

One corollary of this harmonized diversity is the notion that as a human body is not simply arms, legs, torso, and head but rather a particular ordering of those elements, so too the body politic has a specific system by which the features must be joined. The origins of this idea are to be found in the fourteenth-century response to papal imperialism within the Church. Rather than working with the Church's peaceful hierarchy, the popes were reaching all the way to the bottom in their efforts to control the Church. This prompted a response in terms of the anthropomorphic analogy in the *Defensor Pacis* of Marsilius of Padua which can stand as the classic defense of the organic and traditional structure:

> But now, with respect to the form of this body, which ought to consist in the proper order and position of its parts, it will be seen, on close examination, to be like a deformed monster. For if an animal's body had its individual members directly joined to its head, who would not regard it as monstrous and useless for the performance of its proper functions. For if the finger or the hand were joined directly to the head, it would not have its proper position, and hence it would not have its proper power, movement, and action. But this does not happen when the finger is joined to the hand, the hand to the arm, the arm to the shoulder, the shoulder to the neck, and the neck to the head, all by proper joints. For then the body is given its appropriate form, and the head can give to the other members, one through the other their proper individual powers in accordance with their nature and order, and thus they can perform their proper functions. And this form and procedure must be heeded in the ecclesiastic as well as in every civil regime. For the universal pastor or ruler cannot immediately inspect and direct the individual acts of all men in all provinces, so that if this inspection and direction are to be accomplished properly and adequately, he must have the assistance of special ministers and agents in proper order; only when the body of the church is thus ordered can it endure and grow. And this was the view held by the Teacher of the Gentiles in Ephesians, where he wrote as follows: "That we may grow up into him in all things, which is the head, even Christ; from whom the whole body fitly joined together and compacted by that

29. Starkey, *A Dialogue*, p. 146.
30. "A Murmurer," in *Works*, ed. Alexander Grosart (Edinburgh: Constable, 1879), 2 : 10.

which every joint supplieth, according to the effectual working in the measure of every part, maketh increase of the body."[31]

One can readily see how this organic conservatism opposing papal imperialism of the fourteenth century would be revived in the opposition to Henry, as well as in the official conservatism of the next generation. In addition, Starkey was facing a realm in which he believed the proportion of population in useful and ornamental walks of life to be radically unsound, with too many of the latter. Thus he too had recourse to the image of a body with just the proper proportions and structure:

> This beauty also standeth in the due proportion of the same parts togidder, so that one part ever be agreeable to another in form and fashion, quantity and number, as craftsmen and ploughmen in due number or proportion with other parts, according to the place, city or town. For if there be either too many or too few of one or the other, there is in the community a great deformity.[32]

This summary of the interpretations of the anthropomorphic analogy should make it clear to what extent the meanings assigned to the image in Renaissance England summed up the medieval and classical traditions behind it. In addition, it is interesting that the analogical technique associated with the image combined all those which preceded. We saw that in the classics the image of the body was idealized and rhetorical. St. Paul's institution of the *corpus mysticum* suggested ways in which the body could be actually and dogmatically genuine. In the medieval period, the analogy was realized in much more realistically corporeal terms at the same time as its actuality was believed and its potential for differentiation was increased. In Renaissance England, the analogy had all of these attributes. The idealized image for purposes of propaganda was at the same time a field for corporeal realism suggesting elaborate anatomies of the State and also a genuine image of the nature of world order—rather than a mere rhetorical device—to the Elizabethans. Without adding substantially to the content or even the style of the image, the writers in the English Renaissance realized new possibilities for it in poetic technique. We can now pass to this area.

31. *The Defender of Peace*, trans. Alan Gewirth (New York: Harper and Row, 1967), pp. 326–27.
32. Starkey, *A Dialogue*, p. 58.

2

The potentialities for the anthropomorphic analogy as a poetic trope can be readily seen as a kind of hierarchy, moving from the simplest to the most sophisticated poetic methods. At the simplest level, the analogy serves as an emblem or moral exemplum demonstrating some aspect of the organic theory of the State. The analogy here is generally static and pictorial, based upon a visual or conceptual similarity, but not strongly concerned with the real operation of either State or body. On the next level we find analogies on the basis of function: the poet accepts parts of the body in terms of their functions as fully as he understands those functions, and he uses them to delve into the actual functioning of the State. The more he concerns himself with real bodily functions, the more the poet sees life *sub specie corporis*. Thus at a higher level in the hierarchy, the body natural is reintroduced for a lifelike comment upon both the body politic and the idealized body which is supposedly analogous to the body politic. This reintroduction of the non-idealized natural body leads, at a still higher level, to the introduction of a person who is clothed in this natural body. His corporeal nature, and by extension his self and his destiny, are made analogous to the idealized body which is itself analogous to the State.

Once the analogy is personified by a single individual who contains within himself a natural body, an idealized, analogous body, and the body politic, this figure undergoes a multiplication of the self. As we have so often seen, the diversity of the human body, particularly once its different organs are made parallel to different aspects of the commonwealth, images forth a self which may be torn apart with internal dissension. If the individual is a king or a prince, this internal dissension is at once analogous to and the cause of a fragmentation in the State. The final extent of this multiplication produces a kind of infinite regress of analogous bodies: if the individual's body contains the State, it must contain smaller bodies, which contain smaller bodies, etc. These concepts of multiplication and infinite regress grew up along with the theological and political history of the analogy, and they are fertile grounds for metaphoric thought in English Renaissance literature.

The emblematic analogies are intrinsically static. Equations between parts of the anatomy and elements of the State are proposed but not developed. Most often these equations are purely pictorial: the body acts as a vertical measuring rod for the hierarchy of society. An early fifteenth-century poem, "The Descryvyng of Mannes Membres," illustrates this style. The poet's lesson is the need for cooperation within the polity. As is characteristic of the late medieval English point of view, the lesson of cooperation is stressed above that of leadership:[33]

> I likne a kingdom in good astate,
> To stalworthe man, myghty in hele.
> While non his lymes other hate,
> He is myghty, with a-nother to dele.
> If eche of his lymes with other debate,
> He waxeth syk, for flesch is frele.
> His enemys wayte erly and late,
> In his feblenesse, on hym to stele.

[121–28]

The structure of the commonwealth as it parallels the body in this poem is almost entirely a vertical picture of hierarchy: "The heued y likne to a kyng," "the nekke . . . to a Iustice," "mannys brest, / To presthod," "the shuldres and the bakebon / I likne to lordis," etc. Function of the bodily members is often quite blatantly ignored, as when the poet tells us that "Mannys leggis, likne y may / To all craftes that worche with handes" (57–8). The legs hold up the body just as the handicraftsmen support the commonwealth. The poet mixes his metaphor here because he is treating the body in relatively concrete terms and the commonwealth in vague and abstracted ones. The artisans "support" the body not with their legs but with their hands. But the poet is not concerned with the actual physical nature of each man's contribution to the State.

Even where the poet does attempt to add a functional parallel along side of the pictorial hierarchy, the workings of the State remain relatively static and emblematic, or they even ignore the concrete physical parallel:

> Now I lykne mannys brest,
> To presthod in good degre,
> Most in perile, lest in rest

33. Citations are to *Twenty-Six Political and Other Poems*, ed. J. Kail (London: Paul, Trench, Trübner, 1904), pp. 64–69.

> For besiness in spiritualte;
> In penaunce and in preyer prest;
> Meke of spirit in pouerte
> Holde hospytal to goddis gest,
> And fede the pore in charyte.

[25–32]

Again, pure physical hierarchy—and here even that is rather strained—triumphs over function to the extent that the poet makes no attempt to join the priesthood with the human breast, but obfuscates the analogy with eight lines describing the priesthood irrelevantly. Only "most in perile" seems vaguely connected with the breast, but "lest in rest" again seems irrelevant. A similar, though not quite so extreme, case involves the analogy of thighs and merchants. Physical form dictates this analogy, merchants being at the top of the common people, but the poet does manage to include the fact that "marchaundes in periles ride and gon, / Bryngen wynnyng, gold, and fee." Thus the commonwealth is either abstracted, or it is treated without any dynamic sense of the parallel.

When John Lydgate uses the analogy between the body and the state in *The Fall of Princes*, he considers the functioning of the body, but his images remain abstract, static, and emblematic. He makes the rather logical connection between judges and eyes:[34]

> Prudent iuges, as it is skele and riht,
> To punshe wrong and surfetis to redresse,
> In this ymage shal ocupie the siht:
> For loue or hate, bi doom oo rihtwisnesse,
> For freend or fo his iugementis dresse,
> So egali the lawes to susteene,
> In ther werkis that noon errour be seene.

[855–61]

This comparison is common in spite of another tradition, that justice is blind. Thus Lydgate discards one traditional emblem for a less common one. He does not elaborate the usefulness of eyes to judges, but merely bases his analogy upon the hierarchic importance of eyesight among the five senses. The visual reference in the stanza's final line acts only as a tiny flight of wit.

---

34. Citations are to *The Fall of Princes*, ed. H. Bergen, *E.E.T.S.*, orig. ser. vols. 121–24 (London: Oxford University Press, 1924).

In the stanza which directly follows, Lydgate makes the same vague use of physical shape which he had of function:

> Mid this ymage there is a bodi set
> An agregat of peeplis and degrees.
> Be parfit pes and vnyte I-knet
> Bi thestatis that gouerne comountees,—
> As meires, prouostes & burgeis in citees,
> Marchauntis also, which seeks sundri londis,
> With othir crafftis which lyuven bi ther hondis.

[862–68]

Seeing the torso as a kind of great grab bag, Lydgate hurls the third estate into it and realizes with that image a good sense of the close interconnection necessary among these people. But his presentation is almost exclusively pictorial; the torso has no inner anatomy which corresponds to the individuals who have been thrown into its bag, and of course "othir crafftis which lyuen bi ther hondis" produces again the familiar discrepancy between function and emblem.

An analogy truly based upon function is dynamic. Both the commonwealth and the body are envisioned in operation, and when the two operations are juxtaposed, the results are revealing in both directions. Each of the activities or officials in the commonwealth is declared to be like an organ in the idealized human body which is analogous to the State. In the case of the head and the sense organs, especially, the analogies are almost inevitable, since shape and function follow almost the same path. The head nearly always represents the king, for reasons of physical preeminence, mental capacities, or possession of the soul:

> Mihti pryncis for ther hih renoun,
> As most worthi shal ocupie the hed,
> With wit, memorie and eyen off resoun
> To keepe ther membris from myscheeff & dreed.

[841–44]

The head rules the body, stands on top of the body, and contains reason, much like the king in relation to the body politic.[35] The oppo-

35. When the heart is king, as in Starkey's *Dialogue*, the image of the idealized human body is equally functional, but the image of the State is even more concerned with dynamic social forces: "For like as all wit, reason and sense, feelings, life and all other natural power springeth out of the heart, so from the princes and rulers of the state cometh all laws, order and policy, all justice, virtue and honesty to the rest of this politic body" (Starkey, *A Dialogue*, p. 57). Starkey is so completely concerned with function

site ends of both bodies, the feet and the common people, are equally simple to equate both hierarchically and functionally. The feet hold up the body, they work the hardest, they move the body into battle, etc.

The functional analogies which lie between the highest and lowest parts of the body have required of their inventors a good deal more ingenuity to turn into convincing parallels. This ingenuity often produced a more lifelike sense of the functioning of both bodies, if only because of the author's need to stretch the meanings and implications of the analogy. "The Descryvyng of Mannes Membres" includes this analogy between ribs and lawyers:

> Mannys rybbes, y likne now—
> Flesch and skyn in body hydes,—
> To men of lawe is to alow,
> That kepes in loue bothe sydes.
> Rybbes, to resoun though they bow,
> So lawe doth: ofte in fauour bydes,
> Tyl ground be sought ere lawe doth grow,
> Ende in charite, that no man chydes.

[41–48]

Though the parallel itself is based more upon the logic of riddles than upon that of serious political thought, both bodies are understood in a complete and sophisticated way, since the functions of both must be drawn out at some length in order to make the analogy plausible.

John of Salisbury was especially adept at this elaborated functional analogy, as is apparent when he compares financial officers with the stomach and intestines,

which, if they become congested through excessive avidity, and retain too tenaciously their accumulations, generate innumerable and incurable diseases, so that through their ailment the whole body is threatened with destruction.[36]

Both anatomy and political organization have complete integrity. The parallel is farfetched, and the analogous human body remains idealized, but the corporeal image is striking, and the political lesson is subtle and sophisticated.

Up until this point in the hierarchy, the human body is largely

---

that he ignores the pictorial significance of the head in order to present the image of a commonwealth that exists as realistically in political and geographical terms as does the idealized body to which it is analogous.

36. *Policraticus*, 5.2, p. 65.

idealized. Whether static or dynamic, it remains a construct conjured up for rhetorical purposes and without any real identity as the physical part of a man. Thus in John's parallel above between the financial officer and the stomach, there is no suggestion that an actual financial officer uses his stomach in order to accomplish his duties. An actual human stomach has little or nothing to do with the analogy. Once a real body is introduced, the possibilities for a sophisticated metaphor are greatly enhanced. Of course it is impossible to draw this line too distinctly: the king, who is likened to the head, uses his own real head, and the common people, represented by the feet which "trauayle bothe in drye and weet, / . . . In het, in cold, in snow and slet" ("Descryvyng," 67,69), trudge along on their own feet.

In simple treatments of the analogy such as those discussed here, the natural body is often superimposed upon the idealized, analogous body by means of the repeated use of a single word, usually referring to an anatomical element, in a variety of real and idealized meanings. A revealing example is John of Salisbury's analogy of magistrates and the hands. The basic reason for the analogy is that the hands are the final tool in the execution of the ruler's will. In this sense both the soldiers and the magistrates are represented by the hands. But he goes on to elaborate the comparison by stressing the hands of these magistrates: "A magistrate should not only have continent hands but continent eyes as well. And the continence of rulers is praiseworthy when it is such that they not merely refrain their own hands from extortion and wrong, but restrain the hands of others as well." The repeated use of "hands" here, each time with a slightly different reference, begins to make the anatomical and political worlds interdependent. "Their own hands," which the rulers above are keeping from extortion, are simultaneously parts of their natural body and, in the terms of the metaphor, the magistrates themselves. The "hands of others" are of course those of the magistrates and officers in a literal sense, but the metaphoric implication is that each human being is a commonwealth in which personal magistrate-like power is centered in the hands. The passage goes on to connect the corruption of magistrates with thieves, who are notorious for working with their hands. Thus hands become the symbolic key to a social division among men.[37]

37. John indulges in the same kind of intellectual play uniting real corporeality with the idealized body analogous to the State in his treatment of the feet, which are analo-

The presence of a real as well as an idealized body leads us inevitably to the next stage in the hierarchy, the introduction of an actual person whose real body is described. We are already familiar with this phenomenon from the history of the metaphor, for this parallels the juxtaposition of the *corpus verum* of Christ with the ideas of *corpus politicum* and *corpus mysticum*. But Christ is certainly not the only figure who can be introduced into the analogy. At the simplest level, the person is the reader himself. The polemicist uses the corporeal analogy in order to strike the reader where it will hurt most, for the reader's failure to heed the argument will produce a "disease" in the body politic, and since he is himself a member of that body, the disease will seem to be in some part of his own body.

Most often the identity which is attached to the natural body is that of the monarch. John of Salisbury, for instance, describes Carthage as a kind of happy kingdom ruled by Dido, who "if she did not join with her own hands in the labor of the lower orders, yet with her eyes she superintended the work and gave to it the undivided attention of her mind."[38] We have here what is ostensibly a direct connection between Dido's natural body and the commonwealth, with the intervening step of the idealized analogous body left out. Yet by viewing the action of the commonwealth *sub specie corporis* and embodying that action in the person of the monarch, John reminds us of the emblematic and functional analogies to the various corporeal functions. The eyes, hands, and mind, which earlier are made to represent groups within the commonwealth, are given human character and a total form in the person of the queen.

Nicholas Breton's character sketch "A Murmurer" is a good example of political life viewed *sub specie corporis* and of the introduction of a composite character whose real body corresponds to the idealized, analogous body. Breton's basic premise about the commonwealth is

---

gous to the common people. When he says that considering the vast numbers of the common people, the commonwealth "exceeds in number of feet not only the eight-footed crab but even the centipede," he is turning the analogy back upon itself and presenting a new realization of the commonwealth as an actual animal organism. When he speaks of afflictions among the common people as "a sign and proof of the goutiness, so to speak, of the prince," he is uniting prince, subjects, and the abstract commonwealth into a single anthropomorphic organism and using his metaphor as a logical step in proving his political philosophy.

38. *Policraticus*, 6.22, p. 246.

the necessity of complete subordination of each part to the whole. To prove this he uses the image of the body:

> In the body of man, if the head ake, the heart is not well, if the Eye be hurt, the head is distempered, the heart is diseased, and all the body is the worse, if the finger bee hurt, the head will seeke to help it, the heart hath a feeling for it, the Eye will pittie it, and the feete will goe for ease for it; if the foote be hurt, the Head, Heart, and Hands will seeke for cure of it, while the Eye will be carefull to look to the dressing of it.

Breton thus rederives a commonwealth within the functional operations of the natural body. The murmurer, or rebel, whom Breton excoriates, becomes a composite figure embodying and personifying the ill health of a commonwealth which contains rebels. Just before comparing the healthy body with the well ordered community, Breton describes the murmurer as a physical wreck:

> Behold his Eyes, like a hogge, euer bent downewards as if he were looking into Hell: his cheekes like an Anathomie, where the fleshe from the bones doth fall, with fretting; his browes euer wrinkled with frownes, to shew the distemper of his vnquiet Braine; his lippes euer puld inward, as if Enuie would speake, and durst not; his Tongue, like the sting of a Serpent, which vttereth nothing but poison, his voice, like the hissing of an Adder, which maketh musique but for hell; his necke like a weake piller, wheron his head stands tottering, and readie to fall.[39]

This lively image of ill health carries over forcefully to the description of the healthy commonwealth as a healthy body. An unhealthy commonwealth becomes more than an abstraction; its body is identified with the body of the very murmurer who makes it unhealthy. When Breton tells us that "No more can the Counsell, the Eye of the common wealth bee disturbed; but the king will find it, and the Commonwealth will feel it," we cannot help but connect this disturbance with the murmurer's eye, "euer bent downewards as if he were looking into Hell." The murmurer is a fictive character whose form gives life to the commonwealth of which he is a part. Thus an unhealthy commonwealth becomes an actual living body which has been realized as a character.

The highest stages of the analogy, the multiplication of the self and the infinite regress of analogous bodies within bodies, are the logical culmination of the whole philosophical tradition, but they belong much more in the province of sophisticated literature than in that of

39. Breton, *Works*, 2:10.

polemicists like Starkey or Breton. Nonetheless, these highest stages have their conceptual source in the history of the political analogy. The multiplication of the self can be said to be both the basic impulse behind the human body analogy and the highest achievement of its sophisticated literary use. The starting point for almost all the political theorizing we have reviewed is the need to reconcile the desire for physical or ideological unity with the obvious diversity of man and of society. This holds true for Plato's organic theory, for Aristotle's notion of membership, for the mystical body in all its interpretations, and for the whole range of medieval and Renaissance concepts of papacy and monarchy. The human body was an apt image for containing these diversities. Once a real human being is clothed in this analogous human body, whether he be Christ or the king, his self is multiplied and diversified by a juxtaposition of his own natural body with the multiplicity of society for which that body is an analogue. The depiction of the king in English Renaissance literature becomes that of a man containing his own society within himself. This leviathan-like image, which might have been a comic absurdity, finds its source in the whole tradition of a multiple body, analogous in its various parts to society, and both idealized and real.

When we see a man as containing his whole society, we diversify and multiply that man. When we turn our gaze back to society, which contains men who contain societies within them, we begin to see an infinite regress of bodies within bodies. This vision of the world as a nest of Chinese boxes—in this case the box being the human body—is one of the most significant of the traditional ways to bridge unity and diversity. Otto von Gierke describes, for example, the system of the fourteenth-century abbot Engelbert of Volkersdorf:

> Universal nature shows a building-up towards Unity, so the *ordo totius communitatis publicae* shows an ever recurring 'subalternation' until a single point is reached: above every common weal stands a commoner: every lower end is means to a higher end: the sum total of this-worldly ends is means to another-worldly end: the 'felicity' of every narrower depends on that of some wider community, and thus in the last resort on the felicity of the Empire.[40]

In terms of the human body, this line of thought creates an image in which parts of the diversified and multiplied overall body are themselves personified as figures within the larger society. Because they are

40. *Political Theories*, p. 128.

personified, these figures within, which may correspond to individual organs (i.e., political functions) of the larger body, have whole bodies of their own. The ultimate stage in the multiplication of the self has been reached when the very particles of the self are themselves multiplied selves. Expressed thus epigrammatically, the principle may be confusing, but the whole hierarchy which is crowned by this technique of the infinite regress may be a key to the methods and meanings of some of the most important English Renaissance works treating the ruler and his society.

3

The narrative and imagistic structure of Ben Jonson's *Sejanus His Fall* illustrates the ways in which the body politic, the idealized analogous body, and the natural bodies of the rulers and subjects can be joined. At the most basic level the explicit political ideas which form the basis for the drama are traditionally hierarchical and treated emblematically. Sabinus, one of the normative, choric figures in the play, says, "No ill should force the subject undertake / Against the sovereign. . . . A good man should, and must / Sit rather down with loss, than rise unjust" (4.163);[41] and Sejanus himself, with uncharacteristic explicitness, expresses this traditional system in terms of the emblem which runs through the play:

> Rome, whose blood,
> Whose nerves, whose life, whose very frame relies
> On Caesar's strength.
>
> [3.128–30]

But Jonson is not so concerned with the abstraction of the State as with the individuals who comprise it, and thus he frequently joins the bodies and identities of these individuals. The characters' functions in the working of the State are often expressed in terms of their anatomy, so that their identity is reduced to the parts of their bodies which do the State's work. Agrippina speaks of the spying efforts of the emperor and his lieutenant: "Were all Tiberius' body stuck with eyes, . . .

---

41. Citations are to *Sejanus His Fall*, ed. W. F. Bolton (London: Benn, 1966). See also Christopher Ricks, "Sejanus and Dismemberment," *Modern Language Notes* 76 (1961): 301–08. This article provides an excellent catalogue of the corporeal images in the play but does not offer a coherent interpretation of them.

Yea, had Sejanus both his ears as long / As to my inmost closet, . . ."
and her son Nero impulsively announces, "'Twere best rip forth their
tongues, sear out their eyes, / When next they come" (4. 450. 477).
Silius taunts his accuser: "Employ your mercenary tongue" (3.177),
and the emperor orders Macro "to be our eye and ear to keep strict
watch" (3. 681). This is a cynical, "modern" version of the emblematic
and functional traditions in which the human body analogy was used.
If, for instance, John of Salisbury referred to the magistrates as the
hands, then it is possible, in such a world as that of *Sejanus*, to reduce
the actual magistrates to mere hands.[42]

At the same time the viper's nest of tyrannical power in Rome
seems to emanate from a single human body, while each individual who
collaborates with this power is reduced to only part of himself, that
organ whose work he does for the emperor or for Sejanus. Even the
courtiers, as described scornfully by Sabinus, are organs of the State's
body:

> We have no shift of faces, no cleft tongues,
> No soft, and glutinous bodies, that can stick,
> Like snails, on painted walls.
>
> [1.7–9]

The recurrent body imagery reduces the pretensions of the Roman
world in another, more familiar way, by emphasizing the purely
physical aspect of their lives. Man is little more than a beast, since in the
world of *Sejanus* he is only a collection of physical sensations. These
implications are generally reserved for the malefactors in the tragedy,
but everywhere the poetic fabric abounds in gratuitous anatomical
description. Silius describes the obsequiousness of Sejanus's toadies:

> ready to praise
> His lordship, if he spit, or but piss fair,
> Have an indifferent stool, or break wind well.
>
> [1.38–40]

Similarly Sejanus's conversation with the physician Eudemus about the
means of seducing Livia reduces sexual relationships not only to purely
physical love, but further, to pure physical processes:

> Why sir, I do not ask you of their urines,

42. This kind of reduction, as we shall see, is important to Shakespeare's technique in
Coriolanus.

Whose smells most violet, or whose siege is best?
Or who makes hardest faces on her stool?

[1.304–06]

By connecting the men in power to a single human body and by
stressing the physicality of the body, Jonson equates the State with this
body, seeing the State's fortunes in terms of anatomy or health. For this
reason the honest opposition to tyranny is rarely included in the body
imagery. Germanicus was "of a body as fair / as was his mind" (1. 126),
but significantly he is dead. Old Lepidus is asked, "What are the arts
. . . That have preserved thy hairs, to this white dye, / And kept so
reverent, and so dear a head, / Safe, on his comely shoulders" (4. 290–
93), but Lepidus is too old to have any effect on the State and is satisfied
with exhibiting Stoic detachment. Silius, who might be young and
powerful enough to accomplish something in fact says, "I want brain /
Or nostril to persuade me, . . ." (3. 247–48) so that he is excluded
from the body of the State.

The images of natural and metaphorical body are most tellingly
used for the forces of tyranny in the drama, and these images create a
tension between Tiberius and Sejanus. We have already seen some of
the ways in which the emperor's body is the body of the State. He is
referred to as "the face of the whole world" (Sejanus is the "second
face"); he asks Macro to be his eyes and ears; his body is all eyes as he
spies on Agrippina's family; his body is a kind of map on which we see
imperial decisions plotted, as is clear from Arruntius's reaction to the
emperor's seeming promotion of Agrippina's sons:

If this were true now! but the space, the space
Between the breast and lips—Tiberius' heart
Lies a thought farther, than another man's.

[3.96–98]

Tiberius's body, depraved both in its literal form and as an analogue
to the body of the State, is all that holds this State together. But the
metaphorical body of the emperor fails ultimately to hold the State
together because his literal body has been enthralled to Sejanus. This
physical enthrallment is partly sexual—Sejanus was "the noted pathic of
the time"—and partly stems from Sejanus's having saved the emperor's
life, an event described so as to emphasize the way in which Sejanus's
body held back disaster from the emperor's body:

> Only Sejanus, with his knees, hands, face,
> O'erhanging Caesar, did oppose himself
> To the remaining ruins, and was found
> In that so labouring posture, by the soldiers
> That came to succour him.
>
> [4.53–57]

Yet in the running of the State Sejanus's body cannot successfully substitute for the emperor's. Latiaris uses the physical trope to make this clear:

> the proud Sejanus!
> He that is all, gives Caesar leave
> To hide his ulcerous, and anointed face,
> With his bald crown at Rhodes, while Sejanus here stalks
> Upon the heads of the Romans.
>
> [4.172–76]

"His ulcerous, and anointed face" perfectly combines the two modes in which the body is being treated. The king is the anointed face of the body politic, but his natural face is ulcerous with diseases of immorality.

The State, as the whole allegorical tradition indicates, is a highly diverse and multiple body. By superimposing his body over the emperor's, Sejanus attempts to spread his body over the entire body politic, thus producing that multiplication of the self which we saw as one of the culminating stages of the human body analogy. He addresses Macro as "part of myself" (5. 347), and says to his supporters at the moment of what he takes to be his greatest triumph:

> I wish I could divide myself unto you;
> Or that it lay, within our narrow powers,
> To satisfy for so enlarged bounty.
>
> [5.282–84]

Fittingly, then, Sejanus's downfall takes the form of the ultimate extension of his body. The crowd dismembers his body, an act which culminates an image pattern that has run throughout the play. In the first act Arruntius says that if he thought Sejanus intended anything against Agrippina's family,

> My sword should cleave him down from head to heart,
> But I would find it out: and with my hand

> I'd hurl his panting brain about the air,
> In mites as small as atomi.
>
> [1.254–57]

When in the final act this desire is realized, though not through the agency of the good characters, the action proceeds through a series of dismemberments. At first the crowd tears at his body and strains its own body for love of Sejanus. They

> Make legs, kiss hands, and take a scattered hair
> From my lord's eminent shoulder! See Sanquinius!
> With his slow belly and his dropsy! look,
> What toiling haste he makes! here's another,
> Retarded with the gout, will be afore him!
>
> [5.453–57]

Hysterically they assemble to hear him; Arruntius says ironically, "is not he blest / That gets a seat in eye-reach of him? more, / That comes in ear, or tongue-reach? O, but most / Can claw his subtle elbow, or with a buzz / Fly-blow his ears" (5. 507–11). Up to this point Sejanus's body can be partially equated with the body politic, but as his downfall approaches, his body extends in other directions. Macro tells him, "Kick up thy heels in air, tear off thy robe, / Play with thy beard and nostrils" (5. 678–79). The mysterious disasters which befall his statues give a foretaste of this fragmentation, and after his doom is pronounced, the crowd first dismembers him by destroying his statues (5. 774–79).

The speech in which Terentius as a messenger describes the actual dismemberment of Sejanus is the culmination of the human body imagery:

> Sentence, by the Senate;
> To lose his head: which was no sooner off,
> But that, and th' unfortunate trunk were seized
> By the rude multitude; who not content
> With what the forward justice of the State,
> Officially had done, with violent rage
> Have rent it limb, from limb. A thousand heads,
> A thousand hands, ten thousand tongues, and voices,
> Employed at once in several acts of malice! . . .
> These mounting at his head, these at his face,
> These digging out his eyes, those with his brain,
> Sprinkling themselves, their houses, and their friends;
> Others are met, have ravished thence an arm,

> And deal small pieces of the flesh for favours;
> These with a thigh, this hath cut off his hands;
> And this his feet; these fingers, and these toes;
> That hath his liver, he his heart.

[5.808–28]

This speech chronicles the ultimate union of Sejanus and the body politic—to the extent that such a union is ever possible. The two bodies are united because in dismembering him, the crowd dismembers itself and, therefore, the body politic. For Sejanus has the same effect upon the State which the State has on him. He has dismembered the imperial power and the succession, and in the end his own downfall coincides with a complete fragmentation of the State. Even before the last moments, Tiberius has become confused and distracted, and the people do not know what he intends or what his orders are.

Finally, after the hero's death, his exiled wife Apicata dismembers herself. Then, as a sign that the State is not united even in its dismembering rampages, we are told that the crowd has had second thoughts:

> Part are so stupid, or so flexible,
> As they believe him innocent; all grieve:
> And some, whose hands yet reek with his warm blood,
> And grip the part which they did tear of him,
> Wish him collected, and created new.

[5.886–90]

But this cannot be. Sejanus vainly attempted to turn his body natural into the Roman body politic, and the two are only united in the fact that both are irrevocably dismembered.

4

We can begin to see in *Sejanus* that a vision of man in society making use of the human body analogy is likely to have a roughly hourglass-shaped structure. Society, seen as basically multiple and fragmented, is imaged forth by the diversity of the human body and at the same time unified by that image. The single body of society is analogous to or even identical with the body of the monarch, which is, in its ideal form, single and unified. But the monarch is himself fragmented by his public and private torments, and this fragmentation is in turn imaged forth by a diversification and multiplication of his own body, a process which makes him all the more analogous to the multiple body of the State. Since the action generally produces a confrontation between the ruler and the society, the hourglass is joined at its two broad ends, with the multiplicities of the ruler and of his society each trying to impose a unity upon the body politic. Nowhere are these images and actions more fully developed than in *Coriolanus*.

The kernel of the corporeal analogy in *Coriolanus* is the fable of the belly, which Menenius uses to pacify the plebeians, and Shakespeare's individualistic treatment of this ancient fable may be a key to his methods. This story, whose earliest appearance is in the second book of Livy's *History of Rome*, has throughout its history followed closely along the lines taken by all the analogies of commonwealth and natural body. The belly, idle and useless, takes in all the body's nourishment while the other members, who are busy performing their various functions, receive nothing. They rebel and, in some versions, prevent the belly from receiving nourishment. Soon each member discovers that he is incapable of existing without the belly, since it not only takes in but also disseminates the food. The belly always stands for some seemingly useless element of society, and the moral is not only that the nobles, or senators, or clergy, are indispensable but also that the amputation of any one part of the body politic is fatal to all the others.

The version in Livy's *History*, which was translated by Philemon Holland in 1600 and doubtless available to Shakespeare, is a rather more elaborate tale than that of Plutarch. Livy postulates a parliament taking place at the time of the body's creation. He emphasizes the functions of all the members of the body, and consequently suggests that the members oppose the belly because it seems to have no function. The description of the open rebellion clearly indicates the extent of Livy's interest in the human body as a functional image of the State's workings:

> They mutinied and conspired together in this wise, That neither the hands should reach and convey the food to the mouth, nor the mouth receive it as it came, ne yet the teeth grind and chew the same.

Similarly, when the lesson is learned and the belly's purposes demonstrated, they too reflect Livy's interest in organic functions within body and State:

> Then was it well seen, that even the very belly also did no smal service, but fed the other parts, as it received food it selfe: seeing that by working and concocting the meat throughlie, it digesteth, and distributeth by the veines into all parts, that fresh and perfect blood whereby we live, we like, and have our full strength.

What does not concern Livy may be more interesting than what does. In describing the mutiny, he offers some sense of a commonwealth of individuals, but none of the individuals is humanized. Consequently, neither the overall body nor the individuals comprising it seem particularly human. In addition, Livy does not go to great lengths to establish parallels between the body politic and the idealized analogous body. Anatomical functions are described, but not given political equivalents. In Holland's translation there is, however, a linguistic attempt to connect the body politic with the metaphorical body, and particularly with the bodies of the very citizens who provoke the narration of the story:

> Comparing herewith, and making his application, to wit, how like this intestine, and inward sedition of the bodie, was to the full stomacke of the Commons, which they had taken and borne against the Senatours, he turned quite the peoples hearts.[43]

The puns are not elaborated metaphorically here, but they can take part in a complicated allegorical system, as we shall see in *Coriolanus*. "The full stomacke of the Commons," and to a lesser extent their "intestine" and "hearts," combine individual anatomy with the universal. The language begins to hint that each of the citizens is himself an anatomized commonwealth within which there can be just such a battle between stomach and heart as is to be seen in the body politic.

The version in Plutarch, translated by Sir Thomas North, and Shakespeare's principal source, is with respect to anatomical and political function much simpler than Livy's. The members in Plutarch's fable do not, in fact, go on strike. The anatomical functions are not particularly elaborated. All that is said about the rest of the body is that it "dyd labour paynefully, and was very carefull to satisfie the appetites and desires of the bodie." Nor is the belly's function, when finally put forth, specified beyond that of general nourishment. The human body

---

43. *The Romane History written by Titus Livius of Padua*, trans. Philemon Holland (London, 1600), p. 65.

and the commonwealth do not interpenetrate so as to form a lifelike picture, except by a *double entendre* such as "for matters being well digested and their counsells thoroughly examined. . . ."[44] The only development of the fable beyond Livy is in the characterization of the belly. Whereas in Livy none of the parts of the body actually speaks, here the belly addresses the members and tells them the moral of the fable. It is Plutarch who is responsible for having the belly laugh at the folly of the other members. Thus Plutarch personifies the belly against the background of a very undifferentiated body politic.

Plutarch and Livy are doubtless the most important sources of the fable in *Coriolanus*. But it is interesting to compare them with a version purportedly told to John of Salisbury by Pope Hadrian IV. John of Salisbury's version differentiates the parts of the body and creates a community around them by stressing the separate anatomical functions with more realization of human character than we saw in Livy. First each function is made very specific:

> the eyes waxed dimme, the feete could not support the bodie, the armes waxed lasie, the tongue faltered, and could not lay open the matter; therefore they all with one accord desired the advice of the Heart.[45]

Here specific function is combined with something like human characterization. None of these actions as described goes beyond what is totally applicable to parts of the anatomy, yet each is an emblem of a disintegrated personality, which in turn stands for the disintegration of the collective personality of the commonwealth. Compared with Livy's "the whole bodie besides, pined, wasted, and fel into an extreme consumption," this description seems particularly humanized. Further, the use of the heart as the center of reason marks one of the few times in which the functional breakdown of the body politic is actually utilized in the plot of the fable.[46]

---

44. In *Shakespeare's Plutarch*, ed. C. F. Tucker Brooke (New York: Haskell, 1966), 2:145–46.

45. In William Camden, *Remaines Concerning Britaine* (London, 1614), p. 265.

46. The fable has a rather different burden in "The Descryvyng of Mannes Membres," as in this case the members are surfeiting with excess food and drink, and they beg the mouth—rather then the stomach—to stop eating. Thus the moral of the necessity of the belly and of the cooperation among the members is lost, and the poet has a difficult time finding a different moral; but the allegorical style of his tale is still interesting. This version reaches an extreme of communal bickering among the members, who are very lively even though they are not individually characterized. The poet is aware of both

Shakespeare borrows something from all the techniques with which the fable has been told, and he adapts them to the dramatic structure of *Coriolanus*. He approaches his fable in two different ways: the body as a whole is fully developed but remains merely the classical emblem of the idealized human form analogous to the body politic, while the belly steps out of the emblem with personality and character. The First Citizen anatomizes the body as a whole:[47]

> The kingly crowned head, the vigilant eye,
> The counsellor heart, the arm our soldier,
> Our steed the leg, the tongue our trumpeter.
>
> [1.1.114–16]

These are the traditional analogies expressed with the traditional images, and the same kind of language is used by the belly himself when he speaks of sending the nourishment "through the rivers of your blood, / Even to the court, the heart, to th' seat o' th' brain."

But whenever the belly is described, either in terms of its function, or in analogies, or as a character, it is realized as a whole person rather than a mere mechanical part. Even the terms which Menenius and the First Citizen apply to the belly show a wide range not seen elsewhere: "cupboarding the viand," "cormorant," "sink o' th' body," "the storehouse and the shop / Of the whole body." Shakespeare sticks to the actual anatomical facts, but into them he injects such a range of references that indeed the belly seems to be a human being. He also turns the belly into a tangible character type. The belly indulgently smiles at the members' folly but is also capable of tauntingly responding to them. "Your most grave Belly was deliberate, / Not rash like his accusers," and he speaks in an extremely elegant, senatorial style. In fact, the belly is a character very much like Menenius, and within this vignette which opens the tragedy we find the key to both the personality and the prevailing sentiment of the play's normative character.

---

animation and function, and the very rhythm of quoted outbursts suggests the hectic pace of political activities among the members of a commonwealth. Then, when after the period of fasting the stomach is dying of deprivation and shouts nastily to the mouth, " 'Vnbynde thyn handes, are they faste? / Stere, and lete the mylle grynde, ' " the new layers of the metaphor, particularly in the suggestion that the mouth has hands, give a further sense of the members as separate human beings with bodies of their own. *Twenty-Six Political and Other Poems*, ed. Kail, pp. 123–24.

47. Citations are to *The Tragedy of Coriolanus*, ed. John Dover Wilson (Cambridge, Eng.: Cambridge University Press, 1969).

This doubleness in the fable of the belly corresponds to Shakespeare's vision of the commonwealth in *Coriolanus*. Shakespeare's plebeians are but slightly characterized, and they are differentiated from each other only in the emblematic terms corresponding to those of the traditional metaphorical body. Consequently throughout the tragedy the images tend to turn the plebeians into a single body. The senatorial party, particularly the hero, is not only characterized but is also given its own internal anatomy. Thus Coriolanus, though only a part of the body politic, is seen in terms of a complex and multiple body of his own. Shakespeare treats the belly in a similar fashion. When Menenius tells us that he "may make the Belly smile / As well as speak," he emphasizes not only the lifelike quality of this particular organ but also the fact that the organ may have organs of its own.

The confrontation between the belly and the rest of the body—or between Coriolanus and the commonwealth—is not simply between one part of the body and all the others but, on an ideological level, between two different visions of corporeal wholeness. By giving the belly life and a body of its own, Shakespeare makes use of the infinite regress of analogous bodies. Thus the real struggle between Coriolanus and the plebeians can be seen in imagistic terms as that between the plebeian's organic social theory, in which each man is a "member" of a larger body, and Coriolanus's solipsistic theory, in which each man, and particularly the emperor, is a whole social world within himself.

The basic image of the body politic in *Coriolanus* is of multiplicity and fragmentation. Not only are there great differences between the plebeians and the patricians, but there are even greater differences within each group. Coriolanus never hesitates to refer to the people as a diverse, fragmented mass: "Get you home, you fragments," he says in the first scene, and later he calls them "the mutable, rank-scented meiny" (3.1.66). But even without the hero's bias, their own actions proclaim their multiplicity. At the heart of the narrative is the moment when the people change their minds about approving the election of Coriolanus. Having just accepted him, the Second Citizen announces that he "will deny him: / I'll have five hundred voices of that sound," to which the First Citizen answers, "I twice five hundred, and their friends to piece 'em" (2. 3. 209–11). Significantly the individual citizen disagrees with himself as much as he disagrees with others, as is clear from the Third Citizen's later rationalization: "Though we willingly consented to his banishment, yet it was against our will" (4. 4. 145). The change of heart against Coriolanus, accompanied here as else-where by large numbers, leads to a further multiplicity of points of view. Sicinius and Brutus induce the actual reversal by telling the citizens to pretend that the tribunes had forced them into the original acceptance: "Say you chose him / More after our commandment than as guided / By your own true affections" (2. 3. 228–30). Thus both tribunes and citizens have come to contain the two opposite points of view within themselves.

This fragmentation of the multitude is often expressed in terms of a human body. Such a designation as "the many-headed multitude," which Coriolanus is said to have given the plebeians, is an obvious case, almost too traditional to warrant special comment, but other instances are less inevitable. Brutus describes the popularity which Coriolanus enjoys with the crowd: "All tongues speak of him . . . leads filled and ridges horsed / With variable complexions" (2. 1. 202–09). In the hero's own references to the crowd, the body imagery also tends to combine with the imagery of fragmentation. At the beginning he looks forward to the war as a purgation for the numerous and clamoring hordes: "We shall ha' means to vent / Our musty superfluity" (1. 1. 224–25). The image comes from digestion: Coriolanus is describing the crowd's multiplicity as something like stomach gas or the excess of a humour within a larger organic body.[48] The insistence upon numbers, which are often used to tally up the membership of the crowd, as in the groups of five hundreds quoted above or the tallying of votes at the beginning of 3.3, is also joined with parts of the body when Coriolanus defies the threats of the tribunes:

> Within thine eyes sat twenty thousand deaths,
> In thy hands clutched as many millions, in
> Thy lying tongue both numbers, I would say
> "Thou liest."

[3.3.70–73]

The individual body suggested by "eyes," "hands," "tongue," as contrasted with the large numbers, is very typical of the relation be-tween multiples and corporeal units in the play. The body organs are

48. John Dover Wilson suggests as a source North's references to "mutinous and seditious persones" as the city's "superfluous ill humors." Shakespeare characteristically brings the body image to life by speaking of processes rather than of permanent states.

those of a single being, but their power is vast and multiple. This relationship is realized in the narrative itself by the connection between the crowd and the tribunes, who do in fact unite twenty thousand deaths in one body. With the riot of the final killing, the multiple murderer shoots forth its single doom, the destruction of Coriolanus.

The multiplicity of the crowd is both enlarged and contained by references to the body of a vast and multiple monster, a technique always associated with images of an unhealthy or malformed body politic. In *Coriolanus* the crowd is seen as "multiplying spawn," either many animals or a single complex monster. The animal imagery is thus a kind of corporeal imagery. As a monster the crowd is often said to have many heads: "The beast / With many heads butts me away" (4. 1. 1–2). Shakespeare alludes to a classic emblem of the commonwealth: the head is traditionally the source of direction and leadership, so that the beast with many heads has too many leaders and therefore no leadership. At the same time that the monster is leading itself in all directions at once and multiplying diffusely, it is contained by the fact that its principal and most detrimental action is directed against itself. The movement of the crowd in the tragedy, as it destroys its own peace and the commonwealth's safety, illustrates this self-defeat, which Coriolanus pinpoints at the very beginning:

> You cry against the noble Senate, who
> (Under the gods) keep you in awe, which else
> Would feed on one another.
>
> [1.1.186–88]

By seeing the plebeians in terms of their bodies, Shakespeare uses the idea of physical form to contain their diversity and lead toward single-ness. The various powers of the people are frequently given expression in terms of parts of the body. The First Citizen tells Menenius at the beginning, "They say poor suitors have strong breaths: they shall know we have strong arms too" (1. 1. 49–50). And Menenius soon replies, "For the dearth, / The gods, not the patricians, make it, and / Your knees to them (not arms) must help" (1. 1. 71–73). Shakespeare re-derives the hierarchic analogy of parts of the human body and neces-sary functions in the commonwealth. The plebs not only have many heads, i.e., confused leadership, but also arms, physical power, knees, spiritual power, and, most importantly, voices, elective power.

Throughout the election campaign, the people's approval is always referred to as "voices," so that after the banishment debacle, Cominius is able to taunt the people with "You're goodly things, you voices" (4. 6. 146), an accusation which reduces them to the single anatomical part which corresponds to the role they played.[49]

This structuring of public function by anatomy is epitomized in Brutus's reaction to the imminent naming of Coriolanus as consul:

> Let's to the Capitol,
> And carry with us ears and eyes for th' time,
> But hearts for the event.
>
> [2.1.265–67]

The contrast between the senses, which merely record things as they happen, and the heart, which rules without necessarily being guided by the senses, defines the essential fragmentation in the world view of the people and their tribunes. The body image, which has throughout its whole tradition been a sign of harmony, emphasizes the fragmentation of the body whose heart and senses do not work together.

Shakespeare's image pattern suggests in a variety of ways that the people are all part of a single body. Apart from several references to the "common body" or "the body of the weal," he creates this image of the single body by drawing upon the tradition which turns people in a commonwealth into functional anatomical members of one metaphorical body. Once he has made use of the tradition, though, he is free to explore a wide range of its implications. Thus the First Citizen says quite straightforwardly to Coriolanus: "He shall well know / The noble tribunes are the people's mouths, / And we their hands" (3. 1. 269–71). The functions of speaking and executing commands are associated with mouth and hands in this traditional image of the hierarchical society unified in a single body. But earlier in the same scene Coriolanus uses just the same picture with a different force when he calls the tribunes "the tongues o' th' common mouth" (3. 1. 22). The body image is still true to function: the people are, as we have seen, voices, and the tribunes are the spokesmen of the general voice. But Coriolanus uses the physicality of the image to turn this single body into something like a monster or a disgusting creature with a "common

---

49. Note the connection between *votum* and *vox*, also the phrase *vox populi* and the French *voix*.

mouth," a suggestion which refers back to the "strong breaths" which these poor suitors have.

Shakespeare stretches the traditional functions within the commonwealth's body as well as their moral implications. Thus the Second Officer says:

> He hath so planted his honours in their eyes and his actions in their hearts that for their tongues to be silent and not to confess so much were a kind of ingrateful injury.
>
> [2.2.27–30]

The public functions of different parts of the body are multiplied not for ornamental effect but rather in order to emphasize the singleness of this body. Though the organs mentioned here can all be properly understood as belonging to each plebeian rather than to all of them collectively, the force of the image creates an imaginary physiological process by which a certain kind of implantation in the eye and another in the heart lead to a reflex action of the tongue. The completeness of the system, even though it is miniature, reinforces the image of a single anatomized body politic.

As the processes become more elaborate and draw upon more anatomical analogies, the idea of the single body becomes even stronger, Coriolanus berates the tribunes:

> Are these your herd?
> Must these have voices, that can yield them now,
> And straight disclaim their tongues? What are your offices?
> You being their mouths, why rule you not their teeth?
>
> [3.1.33–36]

The plebeians are made into a single body, part human, part monster, with its own internal anatomy which mirrors their action in the whole tragedy. The citizens themselves have recognized this:

> Ingratitude is monstrous [says the Third Citizen] and for the multitude to be ingrateful were to make a monster of the multitude; of the which we being members, should bring ourselves to be monstrous members.
>
> [2.2.9–13]

The whole course of the tragedy, both in action and imagery, is in some sense contained in these words.

The converse of the multiple commonwealth made single is the single individual made multiple, and this latter transformation informs not only the imagery but also the action of the tragedy. Shakespeare multiplies single individuals either by use of actual numbers or by a tendency to build out of them complex and multiple organisms which are fundamentally their own bodies. "Which of you / But is four Volsces," says the hero exultantly to his men. Frequently this multiplicity is suggested by presenting a single individual as a complex unit capable of subdivision. This subdivision is usually along physical lines. The different organs, when separated, are also capable of confronting each other. The process is the mirror image of that described above, in which the commonwealth was seen as a single being with its inevitable subdivisions imaged forth by separate anatomical organs. Thus at the hero's banishment, he chides the tearful Menenius saying, "Thy tears are salter than a younger man's / And venomous to thine eyes" (4. 1. 22). Shortly thereafter, Menenius subdivides himself still further:

> If I could shake off but one seven years
> From these old arms and legs, by the good gods,
> I'ld with thee every foot.
>
> [4.1.56–58]

Aufidius is also capable of being subdivided, as is apparent from the Servingman's description of his alliance with Coriolanus:

> Our general is cut i' th' middle and but one half of what he was yesterday, for the other has half by the entreaty and grant of the whole table.
>
> [4.5.203–05]

Likewise Volumnia is seen as a complex, subdivided organism. She says of herself, "Anger's my meat; I sup upon myself, / and so shall starve with feeding" (4. 2. 50–51), an image which keeps the idea of a single and a multiple body in endless regeneration. Menenius makes the same point about her in his exultation over her triumph: "This Volumnia / Is worth of consuls, senators, patricians, / A city full" (5. 4. 52–54).

These subdivisions of single individuals are part of the image and thought patterns of the tragedy. But the subdividing of the hero himself is the nexus of the structure. Throughout the history of the hero's military campaigns, his victories have been readable as wounds on his body. Menenius asks Volumnia where her son is wounded:

> *Volumnia.* I' th' shoulder and i' th' left arm: there will be large cicatrices to show the

people, when he shall stand for his place. He received in the repulse of Tarquin seven hurts i' th' body.
Menenius. One i' th' neck, and two i' th' thigh—there's nine that I know.
Volumnia. He had before this last expedition twenty–five wounds upon him.
Menenius. Now it's twenty-seven: every gash was an enemy's grave.

[2.1.145–54]

Here and in the whole crisis concerning Coriolanus's display of his wounds to the common people, Shakespeare suggests that his body is an extension of the State. He himself equates his service to the State with drops of blood shed, and Aufidius's servingmen are able to identify him by reading this same body:

What an arm he has! he turned me about with his finger and his thumb, as one would set a top.
Nay, I knew by his face that there was something in him.

[4.5.155–58]

But this very breadth and multiplicity makes Coriolanus unable to hold himself together, to keep serving the best interests of himself, his class, the commonwealth, and his women. As Sicinius says, "He cannot temp'rately transport his honours / From where he should begin and end, but will / Lose those he hath won" (2. 1. 221–23). This description of what is to follow is very astute, and the word "temp'rately" applies specifically to his vast and multiple body. When Coriolanus turns against the plebeians and then against Rome, he is directly attacking the body politic and trying to substitute his own body natural. This movement, thematically implied by all of the imagery around the hero, crystallizes the treatment of the body allegory in the drama, juxtaposing a real body with the abstract body, and placing them in violent opposition. Sicinius expresses this bluntly:

Where is this viper
That would depopulate the city and
Be every man himself?

[3.1.262–64]

From then on Coriolanus is constantly attempting to kill the body politic as it has existed and to substitute his own.

The hero's union with Aufidius, intended to strengthen his body, turns out to be impossible because the spirits of the two generals are too vast and diverse to fit in one body: "He and Aufidius can no more atone / Than violent'st contraries" (4. 6. 73–74). But in Coriolanus's Roman campaign, his body is one with his soldiers, it seems, and quite capable of murdering the body politic. Menenius says, "Not a hair upon a soldier's head / Which will not prove a whip" (4. 6. 134–35), and later, "He is able to pierce a corselet with his eye, talks like a knell, and his hum is a battery" (5. 4. 19–21). Coriolanus's body and the body of his army are one, but in his confrontation with the multiple and yet anthropomorphic body politic, it is his body, not theirs which is killed.

In this final confrontation we can come to understand Shakespeare's purposes in his whole use of the human body allegory. Each of the two great forces in the play has its own powerful tendency toward disharmony. The multiplicity of the body image itself demonstrates this tendency, but the disharmony is more than an image, as the Third Citizen himself understands, when replying to the accusation of being the "many-headed multitude":

> We have been called so of many; not that our heads are some brown, some black, some abram, some bald, but that our wits are so diversely coloured: and truly I think, if all our wits were to issue out of one skull, they would fly east, west, north, south.
>
> [2.3.17–22]

In fact all their wits are issuing out of one skull; they are an organism with a single body and yet too multiple and diverse to be a single form. Coriolanus, too, flies in too many directions to be able to temper his body. The whole body politic dies not only because the plebeians and Coriolanus are each without harmony but also because there does not seem to be room for both of them in one body. Shakespeare is redefining the concept of commonwealth, and his insistence on the body image reminds us that it must include all the functions.

In an important sense the parallels between the two forces are as great as the differences. When the two parties discuss the health of the body politic, it is clear that each is trying to be the whole commonwealth and that neither can exist without the other. Coriolanus feels that the illness of the body politic is to be cured by excluding the votes of the plebeians:

> [You that] wish
> To jump a body with a dangerous physic
> That's sure of death without it—at once pluck out
> The multitudinous tongue; let them not lick
> The sweet which is their poison.
>
> [3.1.153–57]

Later in the same scene Menenius argues with the tribunes over the same disease in the body politic, but the tribunes of course feel that it is Coriolanus who must be amputated. Brutus says that mild medicine—less than banishment—would be "very poisonous / Where the disease is violent" (3. 1. 220–21), and Sicinius says, "He's a disease that must be cut away," to which Menenius replies, "O he's a limb that has but a disease; / Mortal, to cut off; to cure it, easy" (293–95). Menenius is right, both politically and anatomically. Neither extreme can recognize that it is part of the same body; a disease is not a separate entity which can be cut off, but rather it reposes in a limb which cannot be removed without spite to the whole body. The same disaster would result from the amputation which Coriolanus suggests.

Yet as we saw in connection with the fable of the belly, the confrontation is fundamentally between two different visions of man and society: a traditional, organic theory held by the people, which lends itself to the corporeal image, and the solipsistic image of an internalized body politic with an infinite regress of human bodies. When, near the end of the tragedy, Menenius attempts to excuse Coriolanus's obduracy by describing the emperor's bodily processes, the speech stands as a kind of counterpoise to the fable of the belly:

> He was not taken well; he had not dined:
> The veins unfilled, our blood is cold, and then
> We pout upon the morning, are unapt
> To give or to forgive; but when we have stuffed
> These pipes and these conveyances of our blood
> With wine and feeding, we have suppler souls
> Than in our priest-like fasts: therefore I'll watch him
> Till he be dieted to my request.
>
> [5.1.50–57]

Coriolanus's own anatomy becomes the field on which the war of the commonwealth must be fought.

In *Coriolanus* we see what is perhaps the most complete Shakespearean version of the analogue between the human body and the commonwealth, but the image is by no means confined to that work. As Caroline Spurgeon points out, insurrection in the State Shakespeare frequently saw as a disease of the body politic, and quite often this diseased body politic is expressed anthropomorphically.[50] Shakespeare

---

50. *Shakespeare's Imagery and What It Tells Us* (Cambridge, Eng.: Cambridge University Press, 1966), p. 160.

was particularly fascinated by the connection between the war within the individual body and the fragmentation of a commonwealth in a state of rebellion. In *King John*, for example, Salisbury laments the "infection of the time" in traditionally physical and medical terms only to have Lewis return with praise that is couched in terms of the troubles and tempests within Salisbury's own body:[51]

> A noble temper dost thou show in this;
> A great affection wrastling in thy bosom
> Doth make an earthquake of nobility:
> O, what a noble combat thou hast fought
> Between compulsion and a brave respect!
> Let me wipe off this honourable dew,
> That silverly doth progress on thy cheeks. . . .
> But this effusion of such manly drops,
> This shower, blown up by tempest of the soul,
> Startles mine eyes.
>
> [5.2.40–51]

Once insurrection is proposed to Macbeth[52] he must "bend up / Each corporal agent to this terrible feat" (1. 7. 80–81); and in the same situation Brutus meditates with the classic version of an internal struggle mirroring insurrection in the body politic:[53]

> Between the acting of a dreadful thing
> And the first motion, all the interim is
> Like a phantasma, or a hideous dream:
> The genius and the mortal instruments
> Are then in council; and the state of man,
> Like to a little kingdom, suffers then
> The nature of the insurrection.
>
> [2.1.63–69]

Outside of *Coriolanus*, perhaps the most continuous use of the analogy between body and commonwealth is to be found in the Lancastrian tetralogy.[54] The progress of these four plays demonstrates a

51. Citations are to *King John*, ed. John Dover Wilson (Cambridge, Mass.: Harvard University Press, 1959).

52. Citation is to *Macbeth*, ed. Kenneth Muir (Cambridge, Mass.: Harvard University Press, 1959).

53. Citation is to *Julius Caesar*, ed. T. S. Dorsch (Cambridge, Mass.: Harvard University Press, 1958).

54. For an excellent treatment of this general area, see Joel Dorius, "A Little More than a Little" in *Shakespeare the Histories*, ed. E. M. Waith (Englewood Cliffs: Prentice–Hall, 1965), pp. 113–32.

whole range of attitudes toward the meaning and the poetic use of the analogy. The world of *Richard II* is medieval not only in its ideals but also in the relatively emblematic style of its metaphors and analogies for the State. Under Richard's reign, England is an organic body which is ailing and a garden which is untended. The trimming and dressing recommended by the gardener are medicinal acts, which Richard, as doctor attending his country's body, has specifically decided against: "Let's purge this choler without letting blood: / This we prescribe, though no physician; / Deep malice makes too deep incision" (1. 1. 153–54).[55]

But this body of the land is not meant to be a natural human body, despite the association of Richard's own physical condition with England's disease when Gaunt tells the king, "Thy deathbed is no lesser than thy land," and when Richard realizes that the disasters of his reign can be contained within the "hollow crown" that is at once a symbol of his kingship and a part of his anatomy.[56] His final soliloquy represents his attempt to construct a new, purer, and safer kingdom entirely within himself:

> I have been studying how I may compare
> This prison where I live unto the world:
> And for because the world is populous,
> And here is not a creature but myself,
> I cannot do it. Yet I'll hammer it out:
> My brain I'll prove the female to my soul,
> My soul the father, and these two beget
> A generation of still-breeding thoughts;
> And these same thoughts people this little world,
> In humors like the people of this world,
> For no thought is contented.
>
> [5.5.1–11][57]

---

55. Citations are to *Richard II*, ed. Peter Ure (Cambridge, Mass.: Harvard University Press, 1956).

56. The "hollow crown / That rounds the mortal temples of a King" is an image remarkably rich in metaphoric reverberations. Both "crown" and "temples" covertly suggest the intimate relations between Richard (either as individual or as king) and the land he governs. By juxtaposing Gaunt's earlier accusation, "A thousand flatterers sit within thy crown, / Whose compass is no bigger than thy head" (2.1.100–01), we begin to see ways in which *Richard II* is partly an internal morality play.

57. Thus here the internal morality play takes over Richard's conscious life as he retreats from an area where natural bodies (whether personal, political, or geographical) predominate.

The metaphor remains abstract. Richard's body is joined with the body of his kingdom, but in keeping with the hero's medieval world view, the body natural is largely excluded from the analogy.

The deposition of Richard brings on the chatotic, "modern" world of the *Henry IV* plays, and in that world the analogy with the body takes on a newly physical meaning at the same time as it retains an emblematic relation to the state.[58] King Henry and Warwick can still speak in the old medieval imagery:

> *King.* Then you perceive the body of our kingdom
> How foul it is, what rank diseases grow,
> And with what danger, near the heart of it.
>
> *Warwick.* It is but as a body yet distemper'd,
> Which to his former strength may be restor'd
> With good advice and little medicine.
>
> [3.1.38–43]

But such idealized images are overshadowed in the Lancastrian world by palpably, even grossly physical versions of the body. We need no gardener in *Henry IV* to describe the kingdom's sickness when each of the individuals who comprise the problem himself contains a disordered body. Falstaff's body hardly needs to be anatomized. In the first part, he is merely fat, a condition which the Prince can interpret as self-indulgent and cowardly, while Sir John himself sees it as greater humanity: "more flesh . . . therefore more frailty." By Part Two, Sir John's body has become considerably less attractive. His urine portends more diseases than the doctor can imagine, and age has taken its toll, as the Chief Justice points out:

> Have you not a moist eye, a dry hand, a yellow cheek, a white beard, a decreasing leg, an increasing belly? Is not your voice broken, your wind short, your chin double, your wit single, and every part about you blasted with antiquity? And will you yet call yourself young?
>
> [1.2.179–84]

Falstaff is not alone in being physically disordered. Hotspur is drunk with choler, and interest in rebellion has deprived him of "stomach, pleasure, and . . . golden sleep." King Henry's blood is too cold.

---

58. Citations are to *The First Part of King Henry IV*, ed. A. R. Humphreys (Cambridge, Mass.: Harvard University Press, 1960), and *The Second Part of Henry IV*, ed. A. R. Humphreys (Cambridge, Mass.: Harvard University Press, 1966).

Northumberland is sick. Falstaff's recruits are physical wrecks. Even poor Bardolph's face is pockmarked.

England's body is as troubled by insurrection as is Rome's in *Coriolanus*: men like King Henry, Hotspur, and Falstaff try to impose their own natural bodies upon the body politic. The triumph of Prince Hal over these attempts can be seen in part as the union of a healthy, tempered (perhaps over-tempered) natural body with the idealized body politic. Even Falstaff recognizes this in a quite elaborate anatomical conceit:

> A good sherris-sack hath a twofold operation in it. It ascends me into the brain, dries me there all the foolish and dull and crudy vapours which environ it, makes it apprehensive, quick, forgetive, full of nimble, fiery, and delectable shapes, which delivered o'er to the voice, the tongue, which is the birth, becomes excellent wit. The second property of your excellent sherris is the warming of the blood, which before, cold and settled, left the liver white and pale, which is the badge of pusillanimity and cowardice; but the sherris warms it, and makes it course from the inwards to the parts' extremes. It illumineth the face, which, as a beacon, gives warning to all the rest of this little kingdom, man, to arm; and then the vital commoners, and inland petty spirits, muster me all to their captain, the heart; who, great and puffed up with this retinue, doth any deed of courage; and this valour comes of sherris, so that skill in the weapon is nothing without sack, for that sets it a-work, and learning a mere hoard of gold kept by a devil, till sack commences it and sets it in act and use. Hereof comes it that Prince Harry is valiant; for the cold blood he did naturally inherit of his father he hath like lean, sterile, and bare land manured, husbanded, and tilled, with excellent endeavour of drinking good and good store of fertile sherris, that he is become very hot and valiant.
>
> [4.3.94–121]

The old knight brings together human anatomy, the metaphorical body politic, and the actual government of the country, recalling the gardening images of *Richard II*.

The new king describes his own body in a great cosmological image united with the familiar emblematic terms of the body politic:

> The tide of blood in me
> Hath proudly flow'd in vanity till now.
> Now doth it turn, and ebb back to the sea,
> Where it shall mingle with the state of floods,
> And flow henceforth in formal Majesty.
> Now call we our high court of parliament,
> And let us choose such limbs of noble counsel
> That the great body of our state may go

> In equal rank with the best govern'd nation.
>
> [5.2.129–37]

Finally, at the opening of *Henry V*, the Archbishop of Canterbury can see Henry's body as a newly redeemed Eden:[59]

> The breath no sooner left his father's body
> But that his wildness, mortified in him,
> Seemed to die too; yea, at that very moment
> Consideration like an angel came
> And whipped th' offending Adam out of him,
> Leaving his body as a paradise
> T' envelop and contain celestial spirits.
>
> [1.1.25–31]

By the end of the tetralogy, not only is order restored to the body politic and health to the body natural, but in addition, the style of the analogy has recaptured some of the emblematic quality of the more medieval *Richard II*.

5

As an afterword to this chapter it is worth pointing out that the analogy between the human body and the State, despite its traditional associations with that organic world picture that died with the advent of Copernicus, Machiavelli, and Montaigne, did continue in a new form. Perhaps the most famous work of all in which this idea figures is the mid-seventeenth-century *Leviathan* of Thomas Hobbes. This work and its implications for literature are beyond the chronological bounds of this study, but a brief reference to some of Hobbes's mutations of these familiar patterns may set the patterns themselves in clearer light.

The title page of *Leviathan* shows a picture of a huge king whose body is made up of a crowd of individuals all looking toward the king's head. This is the Leviathan, the king of the proud in Job. The inscription is a quotation from Job: "Non est potestas super terram quae comparetur ei." For Hobbes this king of the proud, whose body is the proud, represents the commonwealth. There could be no more literally anthropomorphic representation. Yet we are not to under-

---

59. Citation is to *Henry V*, ed. John Walter (Cambridge, Mass.: Harvard University Press, 1960).

stand from this that Hobbes sees the commonwealth as an organic being. Far from viewing the state as animate, Hobbes barely sees man as an organic being. Man is above all a mechanism, and the State is an analogous artificial mechanism. So he begins his work:[60]

> Nature, the art whereby God hath made and governs the world, is by the *art* of man, as in many other things, so in this also imitated, that it can make an artificial animal. For seeing life is but a motion of limbs, the beginning whereof is in some principal part within; why may we not say that all automata . . . have an artificial life? . . . For by art is created that great LEVIATHAN called a COMMONWEALTH, or STATE, in Latin CIVITAS, which is but an artificial man.
>
> [p. 5]

Hobbes, like so many before him, enumerates the functions of the State in analogy to those of the body, but with rather a different spirit:

> the *sovereignty* is an artificial soul, as giving life and motion to the whole body; the magistrates, and other officers of judicature and execution, artificial joints; reward and punishment, by which fastened to the seat of the sovereignty every joint and member is moved to perform his duty, are the nerves, that do the same in the body natural; the wealth and riches of all the particular members are the strength.
>
> [p. 5]

Despite the abstractness of the title page picture, Hobbes's body is an actual working machine, and his commonwealth is an actual political machine. The analogy is best drawn in the chapter enumerating the ills of a commonwealth and comparing them with physical ills. A commonwealth can be weak because the king was forced to make compromises in his absolutism in order to gain power; this is analogous to having children who are sickly or break out in scabs because of diseased conception. A passion for democracy, where individuals abhor just the absolute power which they require in their government, is like hydrophobia, "as he that is so bitten, has a continual torment of thirst, and yet abhorreth water"(p. 214). Separation and equality of spiritual power and temporal power are analogous to epilepsy, in which unnatural spirits obstruct the normal power of the soul in the brain. These parallels are not purely devices of wit; Hobbes genuinely believes in an essential identity between the body politic and the body natural.

Though the analogy does not run continuously through *Leviathan*, still the reference to the human body as the original type of all automata

60. Citations are to *Leviathan*, ed. Michael Oakeshott (Oxford: Clarendon Press, n. d.)

is crucial to Hobbes's creation. John of Salisbury juxtaposed Dido's natural body with the body politic, and Shakespeare juxtaposed that of Coriolanus. Hobbes, by treating both bodies in shockingly physical terms of anatomy and disease, involves the reader's own body, forcing him to view it as a machine and then creating a very natural transition to the familiar elements of the State's machine. Perhaps the perfect example is the analogy of blood and money. Unthinkable before Hobbes's time, this analogy confronts the reader with the two substances that mean the most to his actual, mechanical life.

The times and politics have changed, and with them the specific analogies drawn, but the metaphor remains the same. The human body and the State are both cosmic constructions: if man's body is the image of God, then politics represents an attempt to repeat the process at one further remove by creating the State in the image of man. The analogy can be pure propaganda or mental gymnastics, but Hobbes's medical elaborations or Shakespeare's depiction of political heroes can make use of the analogy to transform the State into a flesh and blood being and to unite man with his political role.

3

The Human Body, Esthetics,

and the Constructions of Man

In the light of another tradition in which the human body was allegorized, Hobbes's mechanical approach was not nearly so alien to the thought of the Middle Ages and the Renaissance as it may have appeared in connection with the metaphor of the commonwealth. The cosmic analogy was inspired by notions about the fabric of the human body; the political analogy was inspired by notions about its processes. The subject of this chapter is that strand of analogies which was inspired by the shape and structure of the human body. These arithmetic and geometric ideas, originally mere tools for graphic artists, were ultimately invested with cosmic significance by natural philosophers. From numbers, the study of the body as an artifact moved to geometric shapes and thence by comparison to man-made shapes like buildings and temples. This chapter will follow the histories of the abstract numerical and geometric tradition, and of architectural speculation, proceeding then to consider a number of literary images and traditions which grew out of this philosophical analogy.

1

It is of course impossible to know when men started measuring their own bodies and to what purpose, but it seems likely that the Egyptians had a fully developed, if somewhat limited canon of human proportions, and that this may have been brought over from the esthetic theories of still earlier cultures.[1] The measurement of the human body, of course, need have nothing to do with a microcosmic metaphor. For the Egyptians, and quite possibly the Greeks and the Byzantines, anthropometry was a science derived from observation of the body and put into practice for depiction of the body. Thus the nature of these systems and variations among them may reflect interestingly on prevalent esthetic principles, but since they are exclusively concerned with the human body as an esthetic object, they are outside the domain of this study. Erwin Panofsky makes a useful distinction between anthropometry as a means of determining esthetic norm and as proof of a harmonistic reading of the cosmos. The former he associates with the rational Aristotelian tradition and the latter with Neoplatonism and mysticism. He feels that by and large they do not function well together, that philosophically derived systems of measurement either do not make for lively representation or are not in fact put into practice. As his stated interest is the history of style, he emphasizes the normative esthetic tradition and as a result has a tendency to stereotype the philosophic tradition.

To study the allegorical view of the human body as an esthetic object is to trace one derivation of a vision of the cosmos as a *discordia concors*. Harmonized diversity has been an essential feature in all the metaphoric treatments of the body, but in none of the traditions is that moral lesson drawn so directly as it is here. Philosophers who attempt to grasp the wholeness of a diverse cosmos in something like physical terms have a quite natural recourse to the corporeal microcosm, whose diversity is apparently so well harmonized by nature. Estheticians bridging the gap between physical representations and philosophical conclusions imbue the concrete bases of diversity and unity with cosmic or moral significance. Architects come to see their goal as the building of a microcosm at third remove from the cosmos, and they unify their buildings either by literally copying the body (which stands between the building and the cosmos), or by abstractly emulating its harmonic laws. All these traditions, which concentrate on producing harmony, transform the allegorized human body into a relatively static and homogeneous image. Poets using the image attempt to

1. See Erwin Panofsky, "The History of the Theory of Human Proportions as a Reflection of the History of Styles" in *Meaning in the Visual Arts* (Garden City: Doubleday, 1955), pp. 55–108.

return to its original connection with human life, to reinvest the body with life and personality, and to find in it new sources of multiplicity which the natural or god-given corporeal form can harmonize and unify.

Though the human body has been studied and measured as subject and object for artists since the beginning of time, its esthetics only begin to be interpreted through metaphor and allegory in the high Middle Ages. A unique combination of ideas and preoccupations during the twelfth century gave birth to a tradition of interpreting the body's esthetics which grows and alters through the Italian Renaissance but never seems to lose all contact with its origins.

Perhaps the most important context in which to understand the esthetic allegory of the human body in the Middle Ages is that of contemplation. In the contemplative system characteristic of the school of Chartres in the twelfth century, there are six progressive stages turning one from the self to God and to the deepest mysteries of the Trinity. We are concerned here with the first three stages, which involve contemplation of real objects in the world: first, the direct observation of objects by means of the senses; second, the use of the intelligence to determine the scientific structure, principles, and causes of objects; and third, the use of the imagination to fashion allegorical significations for objects.[2] The human body is one of the prime objects of observation, and once the body is applied to this system, each stage of contemplation yields a particular vision of the body. Direct observation is akin to straightforward esthetic perception and description of the body, the savoring of the body's beauty and perfection in and of itself, a subject largely outside our current interest. The scientific or technical contemplation of the body attempts to understand God's creation by comprehending its physical laws; and the allegorical contemplation of the body attempts to grasp the physical cosmos through a mystical vision of wholeness uniting its apparent diversity. These two types of contemplation form the basis for the esthetic metaphor of the human body, both in the Middle Ages and as passed on to the Renaissance.

2. This system is to be found in the works of Hugh and Richard of St. Victor, both members of the twelfth-century school of Chartres. See, for example, Hugh of St. Victor, *De Modo Dicendi*, in *Patrologia Latina*, ed. Migne (Paris: Garnier, 1879), 176: 877–80.

The technical vision of the body's esthetics, at least in the Middle Ages, tends to derive from a combination of Platonism and science. This unlikely union, associated particularly with Chartres in the twelfth century, gives rise to a scientific interest which is directed at an understanding not so much of the body in itself as of the scientific principles of animate nature. In the platonic commentary of William of Conches, for instance, the creation is seen in simultaneously biblical, platonic, and practical terms. Creation itself, as in the *Timaeus*, is distinguished from ornamentation. Creation is the making of primordial matter, while ornamentation involves the separating and distinguishing of matter into its infinite variations. In platonic terms it is not possible to conceptualize existence before the creation, but only before the ornamentation. Such a shift in the *terminus a quo* turns the contemplation away from the *quidditas* of the cosmos and toward its infinite variety.[3] This is perhaps the keynote of the highly influential "nature" poetry of the twelfth century, for example, the works of Bernard Silvestris and Alanus de Insulis. The endless variety of nature, described in poetic terms which Chaucer and Spenser will borrow directly from Alanus, is the world's essential quality.

Once the emphasis in contemplation of the world is upon its physical ornamentation and diversity, the world is felt to be in tension between evident multiplicity and necessary unity, much as was dramatized by the political metaphor discussed in the previous chapter. Again the human body appears as the perfect vehicle for a metaphor expressing both unity and diversity. The body, as we saw in the first chapter, is the cosmos in mininature at the same time as it is in itself one of the principal works of God in the cosmos; thus, it can best teach the laws of the physical cosmos. In this platonic and scientific tradition, the lesson which the human body teaches is mathematical and geometric. Whether it is the diversity or the unity which is being celebrated, God is seen as the divine geometrician, mathematician, and architect, as is perhaps most apparent in a passage from *De Planctu Naturae* of Alanus de Insulis:

[Deus] tanquam mundi elegans architectus, tanquam aureae fabricae faber aurarius, velut stupendi artificii artificiosus artifex, tamquam admirandi operis opifex . . . mundialis regiae admirabilem speciem fabricavit.[4]

3. See Guillaume de Conches, *Gloses sur le Timée*, ed. Parent, Publications de l'Institut d'Etudes médiévales d'Ottawa (Ottawa, 1938), p. 160.
4. *De Planctu Naturae* in *Patrologia Latina*, ed. Migne (Paris: Garnier, 1855), Vol.

Yet despite this emphasis upon the diversity of God's plenty, the scientific tradition of contemplation tends to see the body as an image of unity. This unity of the physical cosmos can be grasped only through an understanding of proportion. God is truly the great geometrician, not so much for His creativity, as for the perfect proportioning of the whole creation, and the human body is the quintessential example of the art of proportion. In the high Middle Ages this point of view remained rather abstract. A mathematical working out of the body's proportions is less characteristic of this scientific view of the body's esthetics than it is of the cosmological, allegorical view to be discussed below, and only in the Italian Renaissance are all these strands truly connected. Thus proportion was seen as a key unlocking the meanings of the world's diversity, even in the twelfth century when the men who were extolling proportion were not attempting to derive it mathematically.

To Alanus de Insulis, the body is perfection only in the sense that it is an abstract unification of diversity and resolution of tension. Thus his description of Dame Nature in *De Planctu Naturae* consists of a blazon enumerating the perfections of her body, with no special scientific or allegorical significance except that each feature is the harmonization of potential extremes. Later in the work he has Nature identify herself in terms which can stand as an introduction to the esthetic vision of body and cosmos, a vision which the later Middle Ages and the Renaissance will imbue with concrete qualities:

> Ego sum illa quae ad exemplarem mundanae machinae similitudinem hominis exemplavi naturam, ut in eo velut in speculo ipsius mundi inscripta natura appareat. Sicut enim quattuor elementorum concors discordia, unica pluralitas, consonantia dissonans, consensus dissentiens mundialis regiae structuras conciliat, sic quattuor complexionum compar disparitas, inequalis aequalitas, deformis conformitas, divisa identitas aedificium corporis humani compaginat.[5]

210:453. "Like a splendid world's architect, like a goldsmith working in gold, like the skilful artisan of a stupendous production, like the industrious workman of a wonderful work, He fashioned the marvelous form of His earthly palace" (*The Complaint of Nature*, trans. Douglas M. Moffatt [New York: Henry Holt, 1908], p. 43).

5. Ibid., 443. "I am she who have fashioned the form and eminence of man into the likeness of the original mundane mechanism, that in him, as in a mirror of the world itself, combined nature may appear. For just as, of the four elements, the concordant discord, the single plurality, the dissonant consonance, the dissenting agreement, produce the structures of the palace of earth, so, of four ingredients, the similar unsimilarity, the unequal equality, the unconformed conformity, the separate identity, firmly erect the building of the human body" (Moffatt, p. 25).

The vision of the body as a union of all these opposites lays the groundwork for a more truly scientific derivation of the *discordia concors*.

The allegorical method, whether in contemplation or in scriptural interpretation, expresses a paradoxically greater interest in the actuality of objects in the world than does the scientific method described above. The allegorists attempted to attain the invisible world by contemplation of the visible; hence they felt they must fully accept the visible world and minutely scrutinize it in order to make this leap possible. Thus while the scientific tradition saw a tension between the variety of created nature and the unity of the divine creative spirit, the allegorical tradition identified the tension as between the multiple and complex workings of the individual created object and the unity offered by the object's harmonious placing in the cosmic order. The human body is significant for the allegorical tradition because its workings are most multiple and complex, and because its harmonious placing in the cosmos was most assured. According to this point of view, man is internally multiple and diverse but unified on the outside in his divinely ordained place in the cosmos.

The tendency of the allegorical method is not the abstract idea of proportion but rather the search for specific principles which could unite the form of the body with that of the cosmos. The most basic of these is number itself. Edgar de Bruyne has well expressed the general significance of number in nature to the esthetics of the Middle Ages:

> Le nombre est, en effet, à la base de l'esthétique musicale du Moyen-Age qui est avant tout une esthétique littérale et formelle. La proportion preside à la fois aux formes sonores et aux formes visibles. Elle est le principe, au moins théorique, de toute "composition." Elle doit donc se retrouver aussi bien dans l'homme que dans l'église. Mais dans la nature aussi bien que dans l'art le nombre a une valeur symbolique, révélatrice de significations cachées et de correspondances mystérieuses entre choses d'origine et d'espèces diverses.[6]

Perhaps the most important assertion for our purposes is that the allegorical esthetic of the Middle Ages was "littérale et formelle." When applied to the human body, this literalness combined with the allegorical propensities resulted in an interest in the measurement of the body, and in an allegorical interpretation of that measurement.[7]

6. *Etudes d'esthétique médiévale* (Bruges: De Tempel, 1946), 2:343–44.
7. It should be pointed out that numerology of the ecstatic sort associated with Renaissance Neoplatonism may have originated in medieval traditions, but the medieval variety was never pushed to the intellectual limits characteristic of the Renaissance, particularly with respect to the human body.

Medieval systems of measurement demonstrate two kinds of allegorical reading. The Gothic system was not concerned in any way with the organic structure of the body, but measured and reproduced the human form entirely in terms of geometric shapes contained within the body. The more flexible Byzantine system reduced the body to a single, rather large module, approximately one-ninth of the body's height. In contrast to classical systems of measurement, which were fractional and expressible only in terms of the body itself, the Byzantine module could be equated directly or proportionally with a system for measuring the whole cosmos.

The two tendencies, geometric and modular, combine when we investigate the philosophical principles behind the medieval allegorical system. In both cases the emphasis is upon external unity rather than internal diversity, for both systems delineate unchanging principles which do not vary from man to man. The canons of measurement for the artist do not account for perspective or even for the changes brought about by the movement of the body. These are the pictorial equivalents of the philosophical propensity for essences deriving from concrete specifics which is so characteristic of the medieval allegorical system.[8]

This abstract reading of the concrete data of man's body is perhaps clearest in the Middle Ages in the work of St. Hildegard of Bingen, a thirteenth-century mystic whose visions are described in her *Liber Divinum Operum*.[9] Her thought has elements of both the Byzantine and the Gothic systems: she sees man's body in modular terms, inscribing it proportionally in the circle of the cosmos, and she also sees it as containing geometric shapes which have abstract numerological significance. In Hildegard's visions both the cosmos and the human body are divided into a series of threes, occasionally giving place to important twos. The universe is made up of three concentric spheres, the outer extending from the top of the firmament to the clouds, the

8. Apropos of the medieval system, Panofsky (*Meaning*, p. 77) describes the esthetic canon of measurement belonging to the "Brethren of Purity," an early medieval scholarly sect: "Forming part of a 'harmonistic' cosmology, it was not supposed to furnish a method for the pictorial rendering of the human figure, but was intended to give insight into a vast harmony that unifies all parts of the cosmos by numerical and musical correspondences. Hence, the data transmitted here do not apply to the adult but to the newborn child, a being who is of only secondary significance for the representational arts but plays a fundamental role in cosmological and astrological thinking."

9. *Patrologia Latina*, ed. Migne (Paris: Garnier, 1855), 197:739–1037.

middle from the clouds to the earth, the inner the earth. These are equal divisions, and they correspond to equal divisions within man's body, that is, to his head and torso, with the demarcation points being the base of the throat and the navel. The outer sphere is itself divided in three equal parts of fire, ether, and air. And these correspond to an equal division of the head, with the base of the forehead and of the nose as demarcation points.

The limbs are rather an embarrassment to Hildegard's system. At one point they are said to be analogous to the four winds, though this involves a break in the visual metaphor, and at another point they are related to water, which, being within the earth, is part of the innermost circle. This measurement would imply that the whole body can be evenly divided into three at the throat and the navel, which is empirically false. As far back as the *Timaeus* the limbs have been an image of the mortal diversity—rather than the divine essence and unity—of man. Hence their incompatibility with Hildegard's system is a key to its emphasis upon cosmic unity over human multiplicity.

Hildegard argues for this cosmic unity by suggesting that each section of the body partakes of its analogy in the cosmos. This is seen most clearly in the tripartite division of the outer sphere. The brain is connected with the planets which reside in the zone of fire (Saturn, Jupiter, Mars), while the eyes are obviously connected with the sun and moon which reside in the ether, and the inner third, part of which is called heavy or strong air, is connected in a rather farfetched way with the teeth. The torso has similar analogies: the breast as the seat of life connected with that part of the atmosphere which is supposed to sustain animal life, and the belly with the earth itself, surrounded by rocks just as the belly is surrounded by ribs. Further, the limbs, whether connected with wind or water, clearly partake of the qualities of motion.

Although these analogies begin to suggest differences among the organs of the body, they are fixed and fated, concerned not with any possible differences among individuals, but merely rendering precise the universal condition of man. Their essential feature is equality, a state which is of course unalterable. The religious and ethical conclusions drawn are inevitably concerned with the perfect proportioning of God's universe.

Hildegard's geometric ideas are equally idealized in their philosophical implications. She sees man as a square within the circle of the cosmos, a particularly pregnant relation involving mysterious analogies such as the impossiblity of squaring the circle and the irrationality of the relation between the two shapes. The idea of the square, for its very multiplicity, has a great range of analogy. For one thing, the body was seen as being made up of several squares, thus a multiple unit rather than a single described circle. More importantly, the four-sidedness of a square gave rise to connections with the whole numerological tradition. *Homo quadratus* is linked with countless fours in the cosmos, in astronomy, in meteorology, in the elements, in arithmetic, in the New Testament. Nonetheless, the evenness of the four lines in the square of man's body suggests, as we saw earlier, a static perfection and an equality which do not admit of variations among men and tend to deemphasize the physical basis of the square in the anatomy. The only allegory in which the corporeal form of the square is crucial is that which connects man as a square with the image of the crucified Christ. It is interesting to note that this image is not in accord with the conventional position of the crucifixion, but rather with the more cosmological Christ crucified, a position in which His limbs point in opposite directions toward the four corners of the earth. Here, then, the square is fully realized as a metaphor with both physical and metaphysical or mystical properties.

In general, Hildegard's canon was not in any sense a practical set of rules for graphic artists attempting to reproduce man as an individual. Yet the idea that measurement itself can be a key to the microcosm is by no means a blind alley in literary study, for the literal equivalence possible in such thought as this can be extremely rich material for metaphor, especially in traditions that borrow heavily on Neoplatonism and mysticism.

2

The philosophical preoccupations of the twelfth and thirteenth centuries may form the speculative background for the esthetic allegory of the human body, but the real flowering of the idea in both theory and practice comes in the Italian Renaissance. Universal harmony and the derivation of man's place in the cosmos are still, in the fifteenth century, to be found in mathematics, measurement, and proportion of the human body. The important difference is that this study of the body has become practical in both implication and application: the estheticians use the human body to measure the world, and because of the aptness of that measurement they can construct buildings on the basis of it. Thus Alberti in *De Re Aedificatoria* idealizes beauty as a state of harmony and perfect proportion to which nothing can be added or subtracted except for the worse; and this perfection he images forth in corporeal terms by suggesting that its essence is numerical, and that these numbers and proportions are a kind of key to the cosmos.[10]

The measurement of God through the cosmos and through the human body which we associated with the school of Chartres in the twelfth century becomes more practical in the Italian Renaissance when the relations among these entities, in numerical terms, become themselves the object of study. The science of proportion, intrinsically the study of relationship, becomes the prime focus when it is felt that man cannot imitate the divine order or the cosmos directly since these entities are too vast to be reconceived or reproduced. Rather, man must imitate them in smaller, proportional replicas. Since the human body is God's own smaller, proportional replica, it becomes a focal point for the study of esthetician or architect. The emphasis may still be on the unity rather than the diversity, but even when it is, diversity seems to have been more exhaustively taken into account than it was earlier.

As the esthetics of the Renaissance are primarily practical, they will perhaps become clearest in terms of the actual architecture. But before passing on to that subject it will be useful to suggest some of the ways in which Renaissance estheticians viewed the body as a fruitful ground for abstract speculation. In fact, the rational tradition of the Renaissance, according to which man's body is a measuring stick for either the natural or the man-made world, brings together the theoretical and practical concerns of earlier times. It was a time of profound interpenetration between the realms of practical graphic artist and speculative natural philosopher. Consequently a very close relation could develop between practical measurement of the human body and cosmic philosophical meanings which were attributed to the results of that measurement. The idea of the microcosm could grow directly out of the

10. See *Ten Books on Architecture*, ed. Rykwert (London: Tiranti, 1955), p. 140.

practical details of human representation and lead to a practical or speculative measurement of the world.

An excellent capsule form of the movement from pure human proportions to the measurement of the world is to be found in the *Trattato dell' arte della pittura* of Giovanni Paolo Lomazzo. The theory is straightforward and purely numerical:

> From the proportions of man's body (the most absolute of all God's creatures) is that measure taken which is called Brachium, wherewith all things are most exactly measured, being drawne from the similitude of a mans Arme, which is the third part of his length and breadth, and the Arme containeth 3 heads or spans. . . . There are also two other kindes of measures in mans body used by the Geographers, the one a foote, and the other a Pase, drawne likewise from the foote and pase of a man. These were first invented to measure the earth withall; because it was troublesome to bowe downe the arme in measuring thereof.[11]

He goes on to extend the system of measurement in both directions, and at each point there is a parallel to part of the body. In itself the system of measurement by feet, paces, etc., may seem to make the world anthropomorphic only in the most trivial and circumstantial way. But this is the path which esthetic theorists trod. From the measurement of the body they passed either directly to the measurement of man's works, or, more commonly, to shapes which could be described by these measurements, and thence to man's works.[12]

About the geometric shapes of the human body much has been written, both in primary sources and in modern critical commentary. Most of the theorizing about these shapes is connected with the rational Renaissance tradition which sees the body as a source of measurements and proportions. The squares, circles, and triangles which the body describes, rather than being directly linked with similar shapes in the cosmos and therefore directly microcosmic, are deduced from observation of the body and lead to physical comparisons with the man-made

11. Giovanni Paolo Lomazzo, *Tracte Containing the Artes of Curious Paintings, Caruinge, Buildinge*, trans. Richard Haydock (London, 1598), p. 108.
12. Another path between measurement of man's body and the cosmos was musical, based upon the idea that man's proportion was in a perfect musical series. Thus Francesco Giorgi (see below, note 17) compares man's corporeal harmony to that of a harp and so catalogues it. On the same subject see Athanasius Kircher, *Musurgia Universalis* (Rome, 1650), 2:410. This progression via musical forms from man's measurement to the world's is, of course, included in the famous stanza describing the House of Alma, where the geometric shapes themselves produce the "goodly diapase."

world. The geometric forms are produced by contortions of the body which alter its outline. If the legs are extended to their most extreme angle and the arms held at a forty-five degree angle from the chest, then the outline of the body is a circle whose center is the genitals. If the legs are together and the arms extended to their highest possible angle, then the outline of the body is an equilateral triangle. If all four limbs are extended at the most extreme possible angle, then the outline of the body is a square.[13] This kind of geometric derivation differs significantly from that which finds the forms within the stationary body. In that tradition the head is a circle (or occasionally a triangle) set atop a series of squares, consisting of the chest, the belly, the forelegs, and the lower legs. But this is characteristic of the more mystical, medieval vision of St. Hildegard. It is easy to see how this latter view of the body, which presupposes no movement or distortion of any kind and which depends exclusively on unchanging anatomical proportions would be associated more with the metaphysical than with the practical tradition.

As far as physical analogies to geometric shapes are concerned, the most basic truth derived from the presence of these geometrical shapes in the body is the notion of the microcosm itself, the idea that man's body contains everything in the universe and therefore contains all possible shapes. In *Haec Homo*, a commentary on woman as natural man (notice the pun on gender in the title) which is much influenced by a reading of Spenser, William Austin moralizes the body in this way:

> But whether this building (for the form) were square; like a castle, or cornered like a triangle: or round; like a tower: or, like a Roman H. according to most of our modern aedifices, is partly questionable. To this, must be answered; that it is made in all the *Geometricall* proportions that are, or can be imagined: For as all *Numbers* and *proportions*, for measure (both of *inches, spannes, digitis, cubits,* feet, &c.) are derived from the members, and dimensions of the humane body: so is also the body answerable to *all proportions, buildings, and figures,* that are. Not onely answerable (I say) to the *whole world*, (of which it is an *epitome*) but for the most part, to every particular *figure, character, building,* and fabrick in the world.[14]

It is interesting to see that here, as elsewhere, the body acts as a bridge between the abstract and presumably god-given geometrical shapes on the one hand and man's creation ("character, building, and fabrick") on

13. Sir Kenneth Clark suggests that the body perfectly inscribed in a square looks more like that of a gorilla than of a man. See *The Nude* (New York: Pantheon, 1956), p. 38.
14. William Austin, *Haec Homo* (London, 1637), pp. 75–76.

the other. The body is in the unique position of being analogous to both, containing considerable diversity at the same time as it is an image of cosmic unity.[15]

When the geometric shapes of the human body are allegorized beyond the simple assertion of a microcosm, the morals drawn generally relate to those shapes as they are found in mathematics or in cosmology. In *De Divina Proportione*, Luca Pacioli sees the body as both describing and containing geometric shapes. All these shapes are moralized in terms of their geometric properties. For Pacioli the most important relationship within the shape of the body is that between the head and the torso. This he explains in terms of the traditional associations of the head with the king, God, etc., and he refers to it as the ruling part of the body when the body is seen as citadel. Thus the head and the torso are made in the shapes of the "two most principal figures without which it is impossible to create anything, namely that figure whose circumference is perfectly circular and which has the largest possible content. . . . The other is the square."[16] The geometric properties of the circle, which contains more space than any other form, and the square, which is perfectly even, are crucial in seeing the body not in the light of any specific philosophical ideas but rather as the summit of perfections.

Pacioli sees the body not only as analogous to the findings of geometry but also as something of an inspiration leading to the discovery of its laws. He explains that lines joining the top corners of the torso with the crown of the head would describe an equilateral triangle. This fact, he says, led Euclid to use as his basic principle, upon which all subsequent books are built, the idea of constructing an equilateral triangle upon a given line. Thus the body's perfection leads us to perfections in the abstract mathematical realm.

The more theological reading of the shapes is also concerned with

15. It ought to be pointed out that some kinds of relations between the body and moralized geometric shapes I have not felt to be quite pertinent to this study. In many cases, particularly in Pythagorean and other numerological traditions, geometric shapes are associated with the body and interpreted mystically or philosophically but have, in fact, nothing to do with the literal form of the body. When, for example, the body is seen as a circle because God is a circle and man imitates God, no metaphor has been made out of physical fact, since God's circularity is merely an abstraction by which the abstraction of man's circularity is then derived.

16. In *Quellenschriften für Kunstgeschichte*, ed. Winterberg, n.s. 2 (Vienna: Graeser, 1896): 297.

perfections but of a more abstract and divine sort. In the *De Harmonia Mundi* of Francesco Giorgi the circle is the essential figure, exclusively the circle of the outstretched body.[17] The circle of the body is analogous to a cosmic circle, which, in this work, is a very uneasy compromise between abstract and concrete. Giorgi attempts to set up a Christian hierarchy on a circular basis, with the Word at one extremity and man at another, and all that which is created by the Word in the middle. This seems more like a straight line than a circle until we realize that man imitates the Word, so that the extremes at which these two stand must be in a continuous line. But if man in general is a point or a series of points on the circle, his body forms a different and analogous circle. Again it is a geometric form of perfection, but the perfection consists in the ways in which it imitates the higher circle. These imitations are invariably more philosophical than physical, and the further they move in that direction the less they are attached to a concrete notion of the human body as describing geometric forms.

The geometric description of the human body in Spenser's House of Alma is so clearly an epitome of the traditional esthetic allegory that it may suggest the nature of that tradition better than any longer text. At the same time, it leads in directions not envisaged by medieval and Renaissance estheticians:[18]

> The frame thereof seemed partly circulare,
>   And part triangulare, O worke diuine;
>   Those two the first and last proportions are,
>   Th' one imperfect, mortall, foeminine;
>   The other immortall, perfect, masculine,
>   And twixt them both a quadrate was the base,
>   Proportioned equally by seuen and nine;
>   Nine was the circle set in heauens place,
> All which compacted made a goodly diapase.
>
> [2.9.22]

The stanza in many respects typifies all the hunger for abstraction and unity which we have associated with the tradition. The method seems to be a most abstract version of the second degree of contemplation: a mechanical view of the body dividing it into three shapes, aimed not so

17. Francesco Giorgi, *De Harmonia Mundi* (Paris, 1544), p. 182.
18. Citations are to Edmund Spenser, *Poetical Works*, ed. J. C. Smith (Oxford: Clarendon Press, 1961).

much at deriving anatomical diversity as at abstracting and unifying the creative principle behind the construct. The third, or allegorical stage of contemplation, apparent in the parallel adjectives of the fourth and fifth lines, is also at its most abstract, based as it seems to be on the abstract and Neoplatonic significations of the geometric forms rather than the anatomical properties of the parts of the body which are formed in the three shapes.

This abstract quality of the stanza goes almost far enough to suggest that the body is itself the merest excuse for the vision of spiritual (and incorporeal) harmony which Spenser chooses to find in the human condition. This, I think, is a limited view of the stanza but not an incorrect one, and it has the sanction of a long history of critical comment. Sir Kenelm Digby's "Observations," whose near contemporaneity with the poem make them a starting point, suggest an understanding of the "frame" as an allegory for the human condition, with direct correspondence between its physical features on the one hand and the elements of man's spirit and of the cosmos on the other. The circle is the soul and the triangle is the body, not because of any physical feature of either soul or body, but because of the meaning of the two geometric shapes:

> By the Triangular Figure he very aptly designes the body: for as the Circle is of all other Figures the most perfect and most capacious: so the Triangle is most imperfect, and includes least space.[19]

Digby seems to despise the body, particularly for just those multiple qualities which the present study has documented. "Man's soul is of [simple substances] the noblest (being dignified by hypostaticall Union above all other intellectuall substances) and his elementated body, of [compound substances] the most low and contemptible."[20] This point of view leads him to include as much soul and as little body as possible in his reading of the lines. Thus he connects the shape of Alma's "frame" with geometry, astrology, cosmology, music, and moral action. The closest he arrives at the physical body is to suggest connections between the triangle and the three dimensions (longitude, latitude, and profundity) of the body, and connections between the

19. In *The Works of Edmund Spenser, a Variorum Edition*, ed. Greenlaw *et al.* (Baltimore: Johns Hopkins Press, 1932), 2:473.
20. Ibid., 2:475.

"quadrate" and the four elements, but these are quite clearly the very weakest links in his reading.

The researches of such later interpreters as Vincent Hopper and Alastair Fowler[21] have continued to see the "frame" as less body than soul. Seven and nine are, quite logically, seen as the numbers respectively of body and soul, and Fowler does make reference to Macrobius's *Commentary on the Dream of Scipio*, in which the physical body is catalogued in terms of many groups of seven.[22] But this is as close to a physical body as Fowler comes. He composes one of his nines, supposedly representative of the soul, out of Francesco Giorgi's novenary consisting of the five external senses and the four internal senses, even though the senses are in Spenserian terms parts of the body rather than of the soul. The much vexed quadrate Fowler also interprets in exclusively abstract and mathematical terms, with Digby's references to the four elements of the microcosm dismissed. When Fowler proposes to harmonize the "frame" by means of the arithmetic mean eight, which he derives mathematically via the quadrate and philosophically via his other preoccupations in the stanza, he is ignoring the patterns of this particular section of the poem, inspired by the physical form of man.

Of course the whole history of the esthetic allegory serves to demonstrate that Spenser was writing in a tradition always preoccupied with abstraction and unity, tending to leap from a few physical facts to a harmonistic reading of man and the cosmos with little intervening sense of the concreteness or complexity of the human body or human life. Even the more rational Renaissance tradition as it appears in this stanza is largely abstract. The microcosmic idea implied by the variety of geometric shapes is purely mathematical, and the numbers refer only to an external rather than an organic measurement of the body's form.

This description of the human body epitomizes the tradition by remaining abstract, but it transcends and revivifies the tradition by the ways in which the concreteness and complexity of man's form and man's life are suggested within it. Some of these are obvious but still worth pointing out in order to suggest the limitations of the purely

21. Vincent Hopper, "Spenser's House of Temperance," *PMLA* 55 (1940): 958–67; Alastair Fowler, *Spenser and the Numbers of Time* (London: Routledge and Kegan Paul, 1964), pp. 260–89.

22. Macrobius, *Commentary on the Dream of Scipio*, trans. W. H. Stahl (New York: Columbia University Press, 1952), pp. 115–17.

numerological view. Spenser's construction is, after all, an accurately described body with circular head, triangular outstretched legs, and rectangular torso in between. The human torso is, in fact, proportioned by seven and nine, and Spenser's triangle is imperfect because the two legs do not have a base. At the same time, the construct is a viable architectural form: E.W. Naylor includes a picture of a building constructed along the same lines.[23]

The uniqueness of Spenser's contribution lies not so much in justaposing the abstract and concrete as in uniting the two just as body and soul are united. Despite all the references to the Pythagoreans and the Neoplatonists, the ultimate source here both of Spenser's thought and of its explication may well be Plato's *Timaeus*.[24] As was suggested in the first chapter, Plato saw the body as a corporeal soul; far from being at odds with the soul and made of completely different matter, the body contains each part of the soul in a fit physical habitation. In the same way Spenser's House of Temperance does not polarize body and soul, for in the temperate man the body is a "worke divine" and is not separable from the soul.

The "frame" under discussion in this stanza is the body, and thus the primary meaning of the three shapes is anatomical: the head at one end, the spread legs at the other, and the torso between. But these three parts of the body contain just those parts of the soul which are characterized by the abstract readings of the three geometric shapes. The head contains the highest and most perfect form of the soul, the legs are associated with generation, perhaps concupiscence and certainly with the earth,[25] and the torso, finally, contains the basis of our ability to stay alive, standing therefore in analogous relation to the foundation of a piece of architecture.

This body inscribes a miniature cosmos while being inscribed by the circle of the true cosmos. Its own perfect circle, the head, contains immortal elements, and its quadrate contains the nine of cosmic spheres,

---

23. Cited in *Variorum*, ed. Greenlaw, 2:485.

24. Ellrodt, in *Neoplatonism in the Poetry of Spenser* (Geneva: Droz, 1960), p. 55, notes that "the not impossible influence of the *Timaeus* is not sufficiently established . . . but [it] may have reached Spenser through medieval channels." He does concede that Spenser's nearer sources, e.g., Alanus de Insulis, Jean de Meun, and Bartholomaeus Anglicus, were steeped in the *Timaeus*.

25. Not in Plato but in the works of medieval mysticism, e.g., St. Hildegard of Bingen.

while the torso also contains the seven of corporeal members.[26] On the other hand, the outstretched body is also a circle which fits into the nine of the nine orbs in the next to the last line and makes the "goodly diapase." It is important to see that these circular perfections are not limited to the head, which would thereby lose its corporeality and become pure soul. The soul is contained within this body not simply in emblematic or visual terms but rather as part of the whole plan of the body.

Spenser's "goodly frame," then, is a complete container including body and soul, all the basic geometric shapes, man and cosmos, etc., and the stanza argues fervently for an essential harmony among these diversities. Yet the poetics of the stanza introduce a sense of precarious diversity which sets the whole tradition in a new light. An actual construction consisting of a circle supported by a rectangle which is in turn supported by two legs of an equilateral triangle would be highly precarious. An emphasis upon opposites in the early part of the stanza ("first," "last"; "imperfect, mortall, foeminine," "immortall, perfect, masculine,") gives way to the even more tense relationship between seven and nine, a ratio with an unresolvable decimal. Both the opposites and the seven and nine are, of course, intended basically to demonstrate *discordia concors*, but the onrush of terms and descriptives in the stanza allows the impression of potential discord to be in some respects as strong as the harmony.

The last two lines fittingly rederive the harmony by moving from internal shapes to the image of man's outstretched body, which describes the circle of the cosmos. Spenser is suggesting that the place of man in the cosmos is perfect, harmonious, and unified like the "circle set in heavens place," but that the life of man, suggested by his internal dimensions and shapes, is a highly precarious balance. This distinction has been implicit throughout the tradition. When Vitruvius and St. Hildegard see man as a square inscribed in the cosmic circle, they are in fact viewing internal man as falling short of the perfection with which God has placed him in the cosmos. This contrast becomes even stronger when a number of squares or a variety of shapes is seen to be contained in the body while the external outline remains circular. Spenser is alluding to the same contrast in the two references to "nine" in the

26. See Macrobius, *Commentary*, pp. 115–17.

stanza, the first being a complex internal measurement and the second a traditional image of cosmic perfection. It is because these two nines can be reconciled that the temperate body makes the "goodly diapase."

In this precariousness and diversity implied by the stanza, Spenser's image of the body becomes an image of man's life. This is a dynamic body capable of moving from temperance to intemperance and back. This movement is made possible because the body is such a delicate balance of opposing forces and because different parts of the body, with different functions and different kinds of soul, can gain or lose control. The fact that the body is microcosmic and all-embracing speaks gloriously for the harmony of the universe but, Spenser is suggesting, it also means that man's life consists of a particularly difficult struggle to contain his own internal diversity. The human body is an image of external unity and internal diversity.

3

The construction of Spenser's House of Alma takes us beyond the geometric shapes of the body and into the subject of architecture. Throughout the history of the esthetic analogy, the idea of the human body as a building has offered a broader sense of the individual life than has been suggested by geometric shapes. In the medieval period the analogy is largely abstract and rhetorical. The platonic school of Chartres saw man's works as the lowest term in a hierarchy surmounted by the works of nature, and above all the works of God. William of Conches in his commentary on the *Timaeus* explains:

> Opus ergo creatoris contrahit ex suo artifice perpetuo subsistere, opus vero naturae per prolem subsequentem, opus vero hominis omnino transire.[27]

The works of nature are an attempt to imitate the divine idea, and in a parallel way, the works of man are an attempt to imitate the idea in the mind of the human creator. The human body, which subsists "per prolem subsequentem" rather than "perpetuo," is considered a work of nature, and therefore capable of bridging the gap between the divine

---

27. Guillaume de Conches, *Gloses*, p. 148. "Therefore the work of the creator effects things through his skill to last forever; the work of nature continues in fact through the succession of offspring; and the work of man is in truth altogether transitory."

idea of God and the transient idea of a human creator. Cosmic order consists of a great chain of imitations with man's body as the nexus.

The concrete details of the parallels between the human body and architecture and their allegorization do not, in the Middle Ages, form a rich and complex system. In the same centuries when the political allegory of the body was being restricted to the body of Christ, the architectural analogy was limited to the cruciform church with its corporeal associations. Just as the human body was the greatest work of nature, the church was the greatest work of man; and the Gothic church was frequently seen anthropomorphically, whether from a scientific or from an allegorical point of view. The general outline of this parallel is quite straightforward and can be seen in the *Gesta Abbatum Trudonensium* in a description of the abbey church of St. Trond:

> Nam habebat, et adhuc habere cernitur, cancellum, qui et sanctuarium, pro capite et collo, chorum stallatum pro pectoralibus, crucem, ad utraque latera ipsius chori duabus manicis duabus alis versus meridiem et septentrionem expansam, pro coxis et cruribus.[28]

Despite the anatomical generality of this passage it must be remembered that the Gothic church was a universal human symbol only as a result of its more basic application to the crucified body of Christ.

Through this union of man's body with that of the crucified Christ many allegories were possible. The frequent rock imagery of Peter's epistles, for instance, with rocks referring to Christ, to man, and to Peter in particular, was applied to the church building so that it became a kind of leviathan, and its physical similarities to the microcosmic human body were the more eagerly sought out. Consequently the church was not only the image of Christ crucified: since it was anthropomorphic and since man's body is a microcosm, the church became the image of Christian humanity crucified, just in that position in which the various parts of the body mirror the shape of the church.[29] Finally, different types of buildings could be made to represent different parts of

---

28. Cited in Georg Weise, "Die Ehemalige Abteikirche von St. Trond," *Zeitschrift für Geschichte der Architektur* 4 (1910–11): 126. "For it had, and still can be seen to have, a chancel which together with the sanctuary stands as head and neck; a choir with stalls as the chest; a cross on both sides of this same choir like two sleeves or two wings extended toward the north and south, and these are like the hips and legs."

29. This is an esthetic expression of St. Paul's *corpus mysticum*. See chapter 2.

the Christian truth. Honorius of Autun in *De Gemma Animae*[30] first derives round churches from circular man and rectangular churches from squared man, then explains the two types: "They are cross shaped to show that the Christians are crucified in the world; or they are circular to symbolize eternity without end based on love."

The unity and simplicity of human life as it appears in the medieval architectural analogy with the body become transformed in the Italian Renaissance into a multiplicity of derivations, parallels, and allegories. We saw that in the Middle Ages the analogy was derived as part of a great chain of imitation. This is no less true of the Renaissance, but the nature and methods of that imitation became the subject of exhaustive study. The estheticians of the Italian Renaissance derived the analogy through the scientific study of measurement and proportion by which works of architecture could be simulacra of the body.

The *De Architectura* of Vitruvius is the ultimate source for this scientific derivation of the analogy. A document of unique significance for the whole development of technique and esthetics in Renaissance engineering, it was perhaps even more important for the philosophical basis which it gave to the study of buildings in the humanist circles of Renaissance Italy. One of the cornerstones of this philosophical base is Vitruvius's frequently reiterated parallel between architecture and the form of the human body. Vitruvius derived the analogy between the human body and architecture by assuming the need for symmetry and being led by that assumption to the study of proportion:

> The planning of temples depends upon symmetry: and the method of this architects must diligently apprehend. It arises from proportion (which in Greek is called *analogia*). Proportion consists in taking a fixed module, in each case, both for the parts of a building and for the whole, by which the method of symmetry was put into practice. For without symmetry and proportion no temple can have a regular plan; that is, it must have an exact proportion worked out after the fashion of the members of a finely shaped human body.[31]

Man's body is the key to architecture for reasons both of its simple, unified external features and of its internal complexity. The unity of its features, in this case the fact that the body with outstretched limbs can describe a perfect circle or square, proves the body is so perfectly pro-

30. In *Patrologia Latina*, ed. Migne (Paris: Garnier, 1895), 172: 590.
31. Vitruvius, *De Architectura*, 3:1, trans. Frank Granger (Cambridge, Mass.: Harvard University Press, 1955), 1:159.

portioned that it must stand as the basis for man's constructions. The internal complexity is captured in Vitruvius's modular system of measurement. The human body is a paradigm of proportion because it is a totality each and all of whose parts can be expressed in terms of simple fractions of the total. His proportional canon is unlike that of the Egyptians, who reduced everything to multiples of a basic unit which was itself without physical significance. Nor is it like the Greek canon, which was based on the relation of each part of the body to the part to which it was attached. Vitruvius declares that each anatomical section has a meaningful proportion only in terms of the total:

> The face from the chin to the top of the forehead and the roots of the hair is a tenth part; also the palm of the hand from the wrist to the top of the middle finger is as much; the head from the chin to the crown, an eighth part; from the top of the breast with the bottom of the neck to the roots of the hair, a sixth part; from the middle of the breast to the crown a fourth part.[32]

Thus in the tradition that follows Vitruvius the individual parts of the body are scrutinized, but they remain largely subordinate to the total image. Perhaps the most significant aspect of this derivation by proportion is the style of thought which it presupposes. "It arises from proportion," says Vitruvius, "(which in Greek is called *analogia*)." It is no coincidence that this term can apply to both the system of proportioning and its ultimate cosmological goal. The same style of thought which scrutinizes the mathematical relations among the parts of the body scrutinizes the relations among the members of God's universal set. And, conversely, if the world can be subdivided so that man, the Creator, and His temples are at once separated and unified by analogy, so too man himself can be separated, unified, and allegorized by the subdivision of his body.

The analogy of mathematical proportion between man's body and architecture as conceived by Vitruvius had an enormous influence on both theory and practice in the Renaissance. Both the geometric harmony and the modular measuring system came down to the Renaissance estheticians as a concrete image of harmonized diversity in the cosmos. Yet though Vitruvius's derivation of the analogy remains the basic one, many of his followers understand his derivation in more diverse terms which are meant to explain a more diversified style of

32. Ibid.

architecture than Vitruvius imagined. In Francesco Giorgi's memorandum describing the architecture of San Francesco della Vigna, he discusses the grounding of the proportional method by which he will proceed:

> When God wished to instruct Moses concerning the form and proportion of the tabernacle which he had to build, He gave him as model the fabric of the world and said (as it is written in Exodus 25) "And look that thou make them after their pattern, which was shewed thee in the mount." By this pattern was meant, according to all the interpreters, the fabric of the world. And rightly so, because it was necessary that the particular place should resemble His universe, not in size, of which He has no need, nor in delight, but in proportion, which He wills should not be only in the material places, in which He dwells, but particularly in us of whom Paul says, writing to the Corinthians: "Ye are the Temple of God."[33]

A tortured piece of logic, but very characteristic of the allegorical style of thought in sixteenth-century Italy.

Here multiplicity begins to play a part in the derivation of the analogy. God's world, which is His true monument, is infinite in variety and glory, as is its pinnacle, man. The elements of this variety and glory cannot possibly be reproduced in a man-made monument to God. It is possible, however, to scrutinize each element within this variety and reproduce it on an infinitely smaller scale while keeping the proportion among them constant. The body is again seen as "elementated," to use Sir Kenelm Digby's term of disparagement.

The actual substance of the parallels drawn between man's body and his buildings could vary depending upon the extent to which the corporeal canon of measurement was taken seriously. Parallel proportions lead to parallel form, which leads to parallel character. At the one extreme we find the lengthy catalogue in the chapter of Lomazzo's *Trattato* entitled "Howe the Measures of ships, temples, and other things were first drawn from the imitation of mans bodie." These parallels are related to series of measurements in units derived from the proportions of the body. Thus Lomazzo says of arches: "some of the ancient have likewise drawne their plat-forme from the trunke of mans body, . . . the thicknesse whereof is just a third part, adding moreover hereunto the space betwixt the throat-pit and the nose, with

33. Reprinted in Rudolf Wittkower, *Architectural Principles in the Age of Humanism* (London: Gollancz, 1967), pp. 155–57.

the same thicknesse, as may appeare in the arches of Titus, Septimius."[34] Each building imitates a whole series of structurally discontinuous parts of the human body. Theaters, for instance, are derived from the oval of the head, the oval formed by "the bendings of his hands," and various other oval contortions of the body. Round temples are round in recognition of the circle which the outstretched body describes, but their height is one and a half times their diameter in recognition of a completely unrelated feature of the body. Thus in Lomazzo's case, the analogy between body and building is abstract and farfetched. The body is a reference book of architectural materials, but the architect is not expected to reproduce faithfully the relation among the entries in the reference book. He has, in a sense, captured the diversity without imposing the unity.

The next step logically is the reproduction of the body's system in some fashion that mirrors the relative placing of each element within the body. The cross shaped church and the centralized church of the Renaissance are best adapted to this parallel. The basic symbolism which gave rise to the cross shaped church led also to the idea of imitating the body which died on the cross. But the relation of the cross shaped church to the human body had more than merely ceremonial or commemorative significance. For those explaining Renaissance church architecture, the analogy with the human body was a way to give both external unity and internal coherence to architectural forms which could seem excessively multiple and flamboyant to conservative contemporaries.

In Francesco di Giorgio Martini's *Trattato di architettura civile e militare*, the human body is in fact inscribed in the familiar pattern of a centralized church in order to demonstrate the form's essential unity inside and out.[35] The diversity is maintained, but the image of the inscribed human body contains it. This differs interestingly from the same parallel as drawn by Lomazzo. Lomazzo structures the "crosse temple" by placing man in a variety of different positions within it.

34. Lomazzo, *Tracte*, p. 111.
35. Cited in Wittkower, *Architectural Principles*, p. 11. Francesco di Giorgio Martini (1439–1501), architect, engineer, painter, and sculptor, is to be distinguished from Francesco Giorgi (or Zorzi, or Giorgio), a sixteenth-century Venetian friar who was the author of *De Harmonia Mundi* and the memorandum for San Francesco della Vigna.

The height of the nave is proportional to an upright man, the length to a supine man, the breadth to the ribs, which, since they are two-tenths of the body, require that the roof contain five diameters of the vault, and he adds many other irrelevant parallels. This formal explanation, rather than viewing the body and its analogue in complete and coherent terms, uses it rhetorically, transforming it wittily into a series of alternative poses. Martini's treatise, on the other hand, considers the natural form of the body, the diversity subservient to the unity.

The allegorization or moralization of these parallels between man's body and architecture represents an internalized and psychological version of that traditional *discordia concors* of which the body has always been an image. Since the perfectly proportioned church is an *aemulatio* of the human body, which is in turn a miniature of the cosmos, the individual human being beholding that church experiences an internal, almost involuntary sense of the rightness of God's whole creation. Rudolf Wittkower has aptly described this process:

> It is, according to Alberti, an inborn sense that makes us aware of harmony; he maintains, in other words, that the perception of harmony through the senses is possible by virtue of the affinity of our souls. This implied that if a church has been built in accordance with essential mathematical harmonies, we react instinctively; an inner sense tells us, even without rational analysis, when the building we are in partakes of the vital force which lies behind all matter and binds the universe together. Without such sympathy between the microcosm of man and the macrocosm of God, prayer cannot be effective.[36]

By concentrating upon the psychology of the observer, Alberti introduces a human experience which completes the familiar progression from the human body through an analogous, larger entity—in this case the church building—back to the nature of human life. According to this vision, man's life requires a synthesis of the senses which is man's only means of knowing God. The church building is a man-made leviathan requiring all human skills in its construction and necessitating complementary skills in the observer. Thus the observer becomes in himself an image of *discordia concors*, for all his varied capacities and senses are individually reached as he reads the church, which is a reading of his own body, in turn a replica of the cosmos.[37] As we

36. Ibid., p. 27.
37. Wittkower offers two relevant citations on the subject of the viewer's total involvement of the senses. From Alberti: "The numbers by which the agreement of sounds affects our ears with delight, are the very same which please our eyes and our

approach a literature with emblematic corporeal buildings, it will become clear that the psychology of the observer is an important locus for that play of diversities which can ultimately be traced back to the image of the human body.

A more concrete allegorization introduces the form and character of a specific human life. In the Italian Renaissance, as earlier, this specific form and life was generally that of Christ, though the nature of the imitation was likely to be somewhat more mathematically intricate than it had been earlier. For those who sought to imbue that parallel with a Christian allegory, the function of the body was to distinguish elements of the Christian story and then to unite them. When the body was seen in terms of its total symmetry rather than its individual proportions, the message of unity and uniformity alone is drawn from the allegory. Thus Palladio in his *Quattro Libri dell' Architettura* rederives and Christianizes the Vitruvian concept of symmetry and lays great emphasis upon a circular form of church derived from the circles within the body. The circle is of course the ultimate expression of perfection in unity, and Palladio uses the parallel to evoke the non-elementated features of Christianity: "The infinite essence, the uniformity, and the justice of God."[38] By its very nature such an allegorical approach does little to enrich the interrelations of the body and the work of architecture or to enable both to shed interesting light on the Christian principle behind them.

A further step is taken when the familiar cosmological allegory is introduced into the relation between the human body and the church building. Thus Gianozzo Manetti in his life of Pope Nicholas V, after demonstrating the anthropomorphic nature of a church which Nicholas built, argues for the aptness of this shape in terms of man's place in the cosmos:

> Si itaque huius Templi figura humano corpori instar fuisset, ceu supra potuisse videtus, nimirum ipsum nobilissimam speciem sortiturum fuisse constat, cum formam hominis ceteris omnibus et animatarum et inanimatarum rerum figuris longe praelatum esse non ignoremus; eam quippe et similitudinem totius Mundi fabricatam fuisse nonnulli doctissimi Viri putaverunt.[39]

---

minds." And from Francesco Giorgi: "The proportions of the voices are harmonies for the ears; those of the measurements are harmonies for the eyes." Ibid., pp. 110, 113.

38. *The Four Books of Architecture*, ed. A. K. Placzek (New York: Dover, 1965), p. 82.

39. In *Rerum Italicarum Scriptores*, ed. Muratori (Florence, 1723), 2:937. "If, therefore, the form of this temple was a likeness for the human body, just as has been dem-

Here we see in general terms that the parallel of the church to man's body acts as a key to unlock the whole world, for by copying the body, the church can attain some of its microcosmic quality.[40]

The story of Christ is by its very nature likely to stress unity rather than diversity. Perhaps the only place outside of imaginative literature where we can see a richly and specifically developed parallel with mortal life is in Vitruvius's own derivation of the three orders of columns. And despite its chronological position it would be well to close this historical survey by a description of his progression from proportions to form to character in the order of columns. The earliest of these orders, the Doric, was derived on the simple proportional basis of man's feet being one-sixth of his height. When later men created the Ionic column, they moved from mere proportion to anthropomorphic form. To the one-to-six type of column they added a more feminine type and went further in copying man's form:

> Under the base they placed a convex moulding as if a shoe; at the capital they put volutes, like graceful curling hair, hanging over right and left. And arranging cymatia and festoons in place of hair, they ornamented the front, and, over all the trunk (i.e., of the shaft), they let fluting fall, like the folds of matronly robes; thus

onstrated above, then doubtless it is certain that that body would be chosen as the noblest possible form since we know that the form of man is greatly preferred to all other forms, both of animate and of inanimate objects. Indeed many most learned men have thought it was in fact made as a likeness of the whole world."

40. The cross-shaped church was not the only image of the cosmos that was also seen as an image of man. The ark, which was by its very nature a microcosm, had been built in proportions parallel to those of the human body. The body was divided into three hundred minutes, and Lomazzo, speaking in a tradition that goes back to Augustine and Origen, explains that "unto each minute they made that kinde of Cubite answere, by which Moses measured the Arke. For as mans body consisteth of three hundred minutes in length, fiftie in breadth, and thirtie in thicknesse: So was the Arke 300 Cubites long, 50 broade, and thirtie thicke or high" (pp. 111–12). This proportional relationship was moralized to the point where Francesco Giorgi endowed the ark with human anatomy and personality.He draws parallels between the various apertures of the ark and the body; and in the opposition between the higher, good openings and the lower, bad ones, he sees the essential tension in man. Thus as with the image of Christ crucified, the physical microcosm is a key to spiritual truth. See also Manetti (*Rerum*, ed. Muratori, 2:938), who suggests the exhaustiveness of the ark in containing both the entire animal world and, by proportion, the human body. See Donne, "The First Anniversary," ll. 318–20, in *Works*, ed. Grierson (Oxford: Clarendon Press, 1966), 1:241: "Shee, who if those great Doctors truly said / That the arke to mans proportions was made, / Had been a type for that."

they proceeded to the invention of columns in two manners; one manlike in appearance, bare, unadorned; the other feminine.[41]

The Corinthian column, according to Vitruvius, not only copies human proportion and form but also goes on to characterize a particular individual: "the slight figure of a maiden; because girls are represented with slighted dimensions because of their tender age, and admit of more graceful effects in ornament."[42] Vitruvius relates how Corinthian capitals originated in the floral decoration which adorned the tomb of a dead maiden of Corinth. Because of the placing of the dead girl's favorite goblets, and the way in which the acanthus gradually grew out of them, an extremely pleasing set of proportions and decoration came into being as a natural commemoration for the girl. Thus Corinthian columns imitated her maidenly form as they characterized her particular fate.

4

The Corinthian maiden whose shape and character were captured in the Corinthian column is probably as close to a living human being as we are likely to find, outside of imaginative literature, in the tradition of allegorizing the human body esthetically. The emphasis upon concord rather than discord within the tradition tends to exclude vivid human life and character, and when poets take up the metaphor it falls to them to redress the balance between *discors* and *concors* and to find somewhere in the tension between the two the beat of real life. The fascination with the plentifulness and variety of nature, the mathematical complexity of created objects, the multiplicity of sophisticated architecture, the elaborateness of an observer's responses to an architectural work—these are facets of the tradition which poets will elaborate.

Much architectural poetry is purely mechanical or purely elegiac, but some works juxtapose a building, real or ideal, with its inhabitants, specific or generic, such that the human body, treated metaphorically, bridges the gap between house and man. Two poetic genres seem par-

---

41. Vitruvius, *De Architectura*, 4.1; 1:209.
42. Ibid.

ticularly relevant: the house poem, which by describing an ideal country house extols its lord; and the castle of the body, in which the human body is turned directly into a work of architecture or a citadel and then often attacked by opposing forces.

The country house poem is not necessarily concerned with the human body. In the classical form of this tradition in Horace, Martial, Statius, and Sidonius Apollinaris, the house and its master are closely connected, but in purely moral rather than physical terms. The fact that these poems extol country retreats assumes paramount importance (none of the classical or Renaissance house poems eulogizes a palace or town house), and moralized pastoral description surrounds the architectural description. The physical side of these poems is likely to consist of natural beauty moralized so as to suggest peace and contentment of soul.

The Jonsonian tradition, which stems from "To Penshurst," treats these country houses more nearly as images of the entire lives and times of their inhabitants. Poems like "To Penshurst," Carew's "To My Friend G. N. from Wrest," and Herrick's "A Panegyrick to Sir Lewis Pemberton" show a whole social milieu in action and often treat this milieu quite directly in the metaphoric terms of the four walls that surround it. The ultimate ancestor of this trope is Homer's description of the house and gardens of King Alcinous in the *Odyssey*.[43] That this heavily idealized and allegorized dwelling is inhabited by someone whose name means "strength of mind" touches both the anthropomorphic country house tradition and the castle of the body, for Homer is in some sense describing *mens sana in corpore sano*.

Once the work of architecture has been turned into a man-made cosmos, the analogy between the physical form of the house and that of its inhabitant may or may not follow. Herrick is not very concerned with physical description, and Jonson and Carew, though they describe the houses at some length, only begin to suggest the possible connections between house and body. The reason that the poets do not elaborate the metaphor here seems to relate to the original purpose of the encomia. Penshurst and Wrest are praised above all for their simplicity, and it is not consistent to use such an elegantly elaborated metaphor as this in the service of such simplicity. It was left, then, to

43. See D. C. Allen, *Image and Meaning* (Baltimore: Johns Hopkins Press, 1960), pp. 119–21.

the peculiarly self-contradicting mind of Andrew Marvell to praise simplicity by the complicated use of an elegant metaphor.

In the light of the propensities toward abstraction and unity which we have seen throughout the tradition, "Upon Appleton House" is particularly interesting because the vision of architecture in that poem is charged throughout with the physicality and complexity of human life. The poem appears to emanate from a consciousness which is struggling to find man's place in the miniature or the greater cosmos, and this struggle is often expressed by the variety of ways in which the universe, or Appleton House in particular, is anthropomorphized.

The poem ultimately questions its own premises and methods, but this anthropomorphic quality is most straightforward in the early stanzas:[44]

> Humility alone designs
> Those short but admirable lines,
> By which, ungirt and unconstrained,
> Things greater are in less contained.
> Let others vainly strive t' immure
> The circle in the quadrature!
> These holy mathematics can
> In every figure equal man.
>
>   [41–48]

The "holy mathematics," which Marvell anthropomorphizes in the last two lines, includes all of the poem's concerns. We have seen, for instance, that the square in the circle was a commonplace vision of regular but imperfect man harmoniously placed in a perfect cosmos. By reversing the figure, Marvell calls attention to the abstractness of the geometry and its futility, since squaring the circle has proved impossible. But then in the last line he swings the pendulum to the opposite extreme, dismisses the abstraction, and declares that this geometric vision of man's place in the cosmos is entirely anthropomorphic.

The "holy mathematics" also refers to the condition of Appleton House, where "things greater are in less contained." That the inhabitants are transcendently great while the house is limited (though beautiful) forms a parallel to the perfect circle which is contained by the less

44. Citations are to Andrew Marvell, *The Selected Poetry*, ed. Frank Kermode (New York: New American Library, 1967).

perfect but regular square. Appleton House succeeds in squaring the circle. In addition, "things greater are in less contained" is a definition of microcosm; since "microcosm" was a Renaissance commonplace term for man, the "things greater" once more "In every figure equal man."

The tendency toward anthropomorphization is not always so obvious as in the sixth stanza, and yet throughout the early part of the poem, the idea of perfect architectural proportioning is derived corporeally. The example of the animals is used tellingly:

> Why should of all things man unruled
> Such unproportioned dwellings build?
> The beasts are by their dens expressed,
> And birds contrive an equal nest;
> The low-roofed tortoises do dwell
> In cases fit of tortoise-shell.
> No creature loves an empty space;
> Their bodies measure out their place.
>
> [9–16]

Marvell defines the proportion of a dwelling as the aptness of its size and shape to the body of its resident. Tortoises are a special case of this apt relation. Since the tortoise's house is his own body, it stands as an image, both in terms of geometry and of materials, of the joining of man's body with his house.

The moralization of the architecture itself suggests ways in which the plan of the house depended upon the physical form of its inhabitants, a form which is seen in moral terms. Marvell praises Appleton House for being

> Of that more sober age and mind,
> When larger sized men did stoop
> To enter at a narrow loop;
> And practicing, in doors so strait,
> To strain themselves through Heaven's gate.
>
> [28–32]

Doors here stand in a special relation to the shape and size of the men who go through them. Marvell's ideal involves a physical constraint: if the door is several sizes too small for the large man, his size will be all the more expanded if he is able to fit through it. This trope goes back to Aeneas's entrance into the narrow portals of Evander's palace. In stooping to enter, the hero scorns riches and makes himself "dignum deo."[45] Architectural simplicity is a type of the entrance into heaven, whose gate is famed for narrowness and whose petitioners are famed for breadth. In these lines, then, the physical forms of man and buildings are juxtaposed and measured against each other.

Several stanzas later, Marvell takes up this vein again:

> So honor better lowness bears,
> Than that unwonted greatness wears;
> Height with a certain grace does bend,
> But low things clownishly ascend.
>
> [57–60]

Here he has gone even further. In these lines men and buildings are inextricable from each other, and both are seen in basically physical terms. There is a kind of contradiction—and Marvell is nothing if not contradictory—between the tortoises, whose shells are exactly the right size, and the people like Romulus and the "larger sized men," whose shells, though physically akin, are even smaller than they are. That both of these states are idealized must be attributed to the special quality of Appleton House, which is at once the exactly fitting tortoiseshell made of Fairfax's body and also the modest country residence too small to contain his greatness and therefore showing it off all the more.

The "Fairfacian" anthropomorphization of Appleton House may seem both easy and unquestionably moral, but the poet, in his struggle to find man's place in the cosmos, casts both these propositions into doubt. At the very opening of the poem, Marvell takes the anthropomorphic metaphor to its ultimate complexity describing architectural complexity, when he refers to the "foreign architect,"

> Who of his great design in pain
> Did for a model vault his brain,
> Whose columns should so high be raised
> To arch the brows that on them gazed.
>
> [5–8]

These lines are a précis of the psychological tradition which was associated above with the writings of Alberti. Human complexity enters the poem via the Promethean overreaching of an architect with too many ingenious faculties. The building comes to have too much

45. See *Aeneid*, ed. T. E. Page (London: Macmillan, 1962), 8. 362–68.

complexity and multiplicity in just the way the architect's brain did. And as in Alberti's writings, the building demands of the viewer complicated emotional response which is in some sense a complementary or mirror image of the building itself.

Complexity of corporeal form is again associated with discord in the descriptions of the nunnery. This earlier form of Appleton House is also anthropomorphized, but it seems to have the body more of a monster than of a man. The nun's speech to Isabella emanates from the voice of this monster. At the end of the speech we are told that "The nun's smooth tongue has sucked her in." The double use of "tongue" emphasizes its anatomical status, and Nun Appleton seems united with the persona of the nun as a body which has spoken these words and sucked in the virgin Thwaites. Thus the complexities of man seem in the first half of the poem to be irreconcilable with the unity and simplicity of the "holy mathematics."

Unity and simplicity are further threatened by a process which Marvell sees as the converse of anthropomorphization: the metamorphosis of people into objects. This process can be applied to Appleton House, which occasionally turns man into architecture ("A stately frontispiece of poor / Adorns without the open door") and has the power to include real people among its appointments ("Nor less the rooms within commends / Daily new furniture of friends"). But these attest more to the richly varied possibilities of the house than to its potential for disharmony. When applied to the nunnery, this objectification places greater emphasis upon a multiplicity which is tainted. The nun wants to give all of her artwork Isabella's shape:

> Some of your features, as we sewed,
> Through every shrine should be bestowed:
> And in one beauty we would take
> Enough a thousand saints to make.
>
> [133–36]

At the same time as the nun is transforming Isabella's body into artifacts, she is turning the unity and simplicity of the girl into the forms of a thousand synthetic saints. This kind of objectification and complexity is much like the work of the foreign architect.

But as has been said, the poem is a struggle to find man's place in the cosmos, and unity and harmony are not so easily triumphant as the first parts of the poem may suggest. The metaphoric method of the poem is metamorphosis, and metamorphosis is by its very nature complex and multiple. Once the poet is himself included in the metamorphoses, we are deliberately left without a reference point. Form seems to become meaningless because of its very changeability. The poet is trapped in the nature he is describing:

> The oak-leaves me embroider all,
> Between which caterpillars crawl;
> And ivy, with familiar trails,
> Me licks, and clasps, and curls, and hales.
>
> [587–90]

Once the poet comes to accept this loss of self, it is apparent that this change represents the good converse of anthropomorphization, in contrast to the nun's desire to synthesize Isabella. The poet's willingness to accept his loss of identity is a personalized version of the readiness of Appleton House itself to accept nature, even though the house itself is a man-made artifact.

Nature as accepted by the poet and the house is full of complexity and multiplicity:

> 'Tis not, what once it was, the world,
> But a rude heap together hurled;
> All negligently overthrown,
> Gulfs, deserts, precipices, stone.
> Your lesser world contains the same,
> But in more decent order tame;
> You Heaven's center, Nature's lap
> And Paradise's only map.
>
> [761–68]

Thus to the extent that Appleton House is a microcosm—quite apart from its anthropomorphism—it represents only an effort to return to unfallen order and simplicity, and it must accept the fact that despite its glories it still contains the multiplicity of the world. The gardens of Appleton House are at once images of an unfallen simplicity and also of the extremely fallen world which precipitated the construction of the ark, as they are a place "where all creatures might have shares, / Although in armies, not in pairs" (487–88). This image of the ark is a particularly telling compromise between unity and diversity because it calls up the multiplicity of God's plenty and at the same time the harmony and regularity of His plan for repopulating the earth. At the same time, of course, the ark was traditionally associated with the proportions and dimensions of the human body.[46]

Through the patterns of metamorphoses in the poem, the house becomes a mirror for the multiple and yet unified nature which it accepts. Marvell speaks tellingly of the river, whose mirrorlike quality recapitulates that synthesis of forms which the poet himself felt:

> And its yet muddy back doth lick
> Till as a crystal mirror slick;
> Where all things gaze themselves, and doubt
> If they be in it or without.
>
> [635–38]

We see here the image of visual anthropomorphism offered by the mirror: at the same time as the natural bodies lose their form in the flowing stream, they find in the water replications of their form so accurate that the objective body cannot be distinguished from the mirror image. This image is itself microcosmic.

"Upon Appleton House" is a series of microcosms which share similar forms. At the very end of the poem, just after Marvell has suggested that this house is an unfallen microcosm, we see that the overarching metaphoric parallel is between man's body and that of the piece of the cosmos which Appleton House represents:

> How tortoise-like, but not so slow,
> These rational amphibii go!
> Let's in; for the dark hemisphere
> Does now like one of them appear.
>
> [773–76]

The salmon fishers' form is like the animals', and, specifically, like that animal which has become the prototype of the natural house, the tortoise. The canoes are the fishermen's tortoise shells. Consequently, the canoes resemble the men, and the men are well shod or housed within them just as Fairfax is well housed in Appleton House.

But man's body resembles more than a tortoise shell and a canoe. It also resembles "the dark hemisphere," the whole cosmos, as night falls upon Appleton House. Marvell finds the true complexity of man's condition in man's power to accept the diversity and in the mental power which enables him in this acceptance to transform himself into

---

46. See above, n. 40.

the different images of the cosmos which he accepts. Appleton House itself is only the most consummate of these acceptances and transformations; the poet who is describing it is engaged in another version of the same complex effort. The human body is a significant form because it appears to be so rigid and unique. When slavishly copied, it typifies the hubris of man imitating nature. But when accepted as a microcosm and a moral exemplum, it is an image of unity and harmony; and when it loses itself in nature, as the poet does, it is an image of the acceptance of diversity.

5

The house poem attempts to capture the complexity and harmony of a single person in architectural terms. The castle of the body makes use of a combination of architectural, political, and anatomical images to illustrate the complexity and harmony of man's overall moral condition. The analogy between man's mortal existence and a castle, tabernacle, or citadel seems to be among those imaginative ideas which are common to nearly every tradition of thought. Our current interest in matters which are specifically corporeal and architectural will tend to restrict consideration here to certain versions of the metaphor that demonstrate the range available to medieval and Renaissance poets and to Spenser in particular.

Perhaps the most significant source of the analogy, more influential even than Plato's *Timaeus*, is the Bible. In the rhetoric of the New Testament, especially in the Epistles, where the apostles are studiously attempting to convert the concrete realities of Old Testament political and military life into moral maxims of the New Dispensation, this analogy, whose very essence is to bridge concrete and abstract, has one of its flowerings.

Three basic strands of the analogy come to light in scriptural sources, and although they are rarely joined in the Bible, they remain the essential contents of the metaphor. The grounding for the analogy comes from the image of mortal life as a dwelling in a tabernacle of clay. Thus Peter says in his second epistle, "Yea, I think it is meet as long as I am in this tabernacle, to stir you up by putting you in remembrance; Knowing that shortly I must put off this my tabernacle" (2 Pet. 1: 13, 14). Here the image is only on the verge of being realized: the tabernacle is not quite the body nor is it quite an architectural form; rather it exchanges the abstraction "mortal life" for another word which amounts to an abstraction. But one of Peter's sources, the speech of Eliphaz to Job, at once takes the metaphor in both directions: "Behold, he put no trust in his servants; and his angels he charged with folly: How much less in them that dwell in houses of clay, whose foundation is the dust, which are crushed before the moth?" (Job 4: 18, 19). From the "house of clay" comes the natural corollary that mortal life is a preparation for life in a heavenly house, as we see in Second Corinthians: "For we know that if our earthly house of this tabernacle were dissolved, we have a building of God, an house not made with hands, eternal in the heavens" (2 Cor. 5: 1). This strand of the analogy emphasizes the dichotomy between body and soul—though they may be triumphantly joined in the virtuous man—and moralizes the earthly building materials of his body.

The second strand is concerned with the warfare which the devil wages against the virtuous man, as we see in Ephesians: "For we wrestle not against flesh and blood but against principalities, against powers, against the rulers of the darkness of this world, against spiritual wickedness in high places" (Eph. 6: 12). Poets later join the tabernacle, which becomes a citadel, and the devil's siege, but the combined image is not present in Scripture.

The third strand is the concrete realization in the human body of faculties or abstract qualities, and it is joined with the deveil's war in a number of places in Scripture. Perhaps the most elaborated instance is the continuation of the text from Ephesians quoted above:

> Wherefore take unto you the whole armour of God, that ye may be able to withstand in the evil day, and having done all, to stand. Stand therefore having your loins girt about with truth, and having on the breastplate of righteousness; And your feet shod with the preparation of the gospel of peace; Above all taking the shield of faith, wherewith ye shall be able to quench all the fiery darts of the wicked. And take the helmet of salvation and the sword of the spirit, which is the word of God.
>
> [6:12–17]

These incipient metaphors are tremendously important, first because as major sources of the allegorical tradition of scripture interpretation they relate directly to medieval and Renaissance fashions of allegory, and, second, because they approach a point where the human body is abstracted and allegorized. St. Paul's metaphor is, of course, in perfect harmony with a scorn for the body, as these Christian virtues are specifically coverings for the weak willed body; but when we consider the conflating effects of many other traditions which allegorize the human body, it is not such a great leap from "the breastplate of righteousness" to the idea that righteousness resides in the breast itself.

As was suggested in discussing the shape of Alma's castle, the castle of the body has two concrete forms, the anatomical and the architectural. It also has two abstract forms: it can be the embodiment of abstract qualities, like the righteousness, peace, faith, and salvation of St. Paul's metaphor, or it can simply contain human faculties, like wit or will. One basic version which borrows from all of these possibilities without building a complete system on any level, is the twelfth-century *Chasteau d'Amour* of Robeit Grosseteste, a poetic dream vision of the Virgin.[47] The title refers to the body of the Virgin Mary, and the allegory treats of abstract perfection. There is no dearth of concrete detail, but it is all architectural. The castle is built on a rock in the sea and has four towers, seven barbicans, and three bailiffs. The allegorical lines are drawn directly between architectural features and abstractions which are rather more like pure qualities than like human faculties. The base of the castle is belief, the middle sweetness, and the top love. The towers are the four cardinal virtues, which can be seen in the light of human faculties, but they are realized in abstract rather than psychological terms.

The bailiffs come closest to joining the different metaphoric strands. They alone are in some sense human, and it will become clear that the more sophisticated the allegory the more likely that the castle has human inhabitants. Grosseteste's bailiffs also begin to join human faculties and concrete anatomy. The "innemayste bayli" he glosses as "holy maydenhod," the "myddyl bayli" as "holy chastite," and the "otmast bayle" as "hoole spousayle." Even without the hindsight afforded by *The Faerie Queene*, we can see that these are qualities which are resident in the body and which, at least in the case of "holy maydenhod," have something like real anatomical equivalents. The ordering of the bailiffs joins physical levels (at least in the case of "maydenhod") with chronological states and with layers of perfection. In this sense Grosseteste's "chasteau" is a body as we have understood "body"

47. Ed. M. Cooke (London: Asher, 1852).

in this study, but by and large it is merely a convenient container which can combine a multiple tapestry of virtues with a single human being, the Virgin Mary. It is significant because it begins to illustrate, as far back as the twelfth century, a style of metaphoric thought which envisions a play of abstractions and faculties dramatically set within the body of a composite individual. Grosseteste's "Chasteau"—and the other body–castles that follow—are interesting because they represent the most obvious instances of a literary trope which is buried in the substrata of the most sophisticated Renaissance allegories: the seemingly independent narrative world which is, in fact, internalized within a composite character.

Despite the lack of complex corporeality, Grosseteste's castle is also important because the body acts as an allegorical container, single and multiple at the same time. The particular tradition in which Grosseteste is writing lends to the House of Alma or Bunyan's Mansoul the peculiar force of an emblem, a unity of imagistic expression with a traditional message and a traditional style for the message. Part of this style is the gloss, for none of Grosseteste's concrete images is at all explicable without a gloss, and this didactic style conveys an intensity and expressness of purpose to moral allegory which comes to be associated with the human body as a container. The special multiplicity and singleness already evident in Grosseteste's work also enable the traditional attacks by the devil to result simultaneously from the moral feebleness of the individual man and from the ever recurring fall of the whole race.

A somewhat more coherently structured version of the castle realizes the human body in form, but sees it more in terms of abstract faculties than of concrete anatomy. Perhaps the best example is the Castle of Kynde in Passus Ten of *Piers Plowman*. The castle is "of kynde" only in the sense that nature made it; it is called "Caro," "as muche as to mene as man with his soule." It is man's body built by nature to house Anima, the soul. This castle is almost entirely abstract. The few concrete details image forth a kind of feudal society, but there is no concreteness to the anatomy. Twice the poet mentions man's being in the image of God, but this image seems to be one of psychological processes, or, in a somewhat more concrete form, a microcosmic reduction of the world. The "castle of kynde" is fundamentally a realization of man's faculties played against a background of feudal cooperation:[48]

> Ac the cunstable of the castel, that kepith hem alle,
> Is a wys knight with alle, Sire Inwyt he hatte;
> And hath fyve faire sones be his furste wyf:
> Sire Se-wel, and Sey-wel, and Here-wel the hende,
> Sire Werche-wel-with-thin-hond, a wight man of strengthe,
> And Sire Godefrey Go-wel, grete lordis alle.
>
> [10.16–21]

Human perfection is constantly in process, balancing dynamic forces that must work among themselves, but at the same time the poet's allegorical man is a unified creation with emblematic forces. This combination of forces and qualities is evident from the very origins of the castle: "Of erthe and eir it is mad, medlit togideris; / With wynd and with watir, wittyliche enjoynede" (10. 3–4). This is an elementated man with the points of junction among the various elements wittily— but not completely—covered.

The framework of the body and of the medieval citadel affords the poet not only the combination of multiplicity and singleness which Grosseteste utilized but also that kind of eternally shifting, precarious balance associated with any collection of individuals in a political context. This becomes particularly clear when the poet attempts to place these abstract faculties in concrete anatomical terms:

> That is *Anima*, that overal in the body wandrith,
> Ac in the herte is hire hom, heighest of alle. . . .
> Inwyt in the hevid is, and an help to the soule,
> For thorugh his connyng is kept *Caro & Anima*
> In rewele and in resoun, but reccheles it make.
> He eggith eighe sight and heryng to gode;
> Of good speche and connyng he is the begynnere;
> In manis brayn is he most and mightiest to knowe—
> There is his bour bremest, but yif blod it make.
> For whan blood is bremere thanne brayn, than is Inwit bounde,
> And ek wantoun and wilde withoute any resoun.
>
> [10.44–54]

At the same time, then, as the body provides an architectural framework, the relations among the multiple features have more in common with

---

48. Citations are to *Piers Plowman*, ed. T. A. Knott and D. C. Fowler (Baltimore: Johns Hopkins Press, 1952).

the political allegory discussed in the last chapter. Consequently it is clear that with the emphasis upon human faculty rather than anatomy the allegory shifts from architecture to social organization, and the message is more social than moral.[49]

In contrast to these rather abstract versions of the body–castle metaphor, we can consider the totally anatomical type of metaphor. This genre is in some sense the least metaphoric. Characteristically the subject is the body itself, described, idealized, and explained in fanciful terms. The purpose here is likely to be less scientific than devotional: we are not, for example, told the principle behind eyesight so much as the glory of it and the inevitability that God's design should take this particular physical form. Throughout the history of this approach to the subject of the human body, most of which is not metaphoric, there has been a tendency to explain or idealize in terms of a covert castle metaphor. Thus when Plato describes the hierarchy of functions in the body, he quite naturally resorts to the image of a castle:

> That part of the soul, then, which is of a manly spirit and ambitious of victory they housed nearer to the head, between the midriff and the neck, that it might join with it in restraining by force the desires, whenever these should not willingly consent to obey the word of command from the citadel.[50]

Similarly Lactantius, who idealizes the body at inordinate length in *De Opificio Dei* without producing an extended metaphor, sees anatomy partly as a series of self-protections. He says of the eyes, "Are not the very edges of the eyebrows equipped with short hairs, with ramparts as it were, a protection for the eyes lest anything fall upon them from above?"[51]

Du Bartas idealizes the body in the sixth day of his *Première Sepmaine*, recurrently using the image of the castle or building. Much of this idealization is in fact without any continuous microcosmic metaphor for the body. The description of the nose, for example, is witty and elegant but says nothing that an anatomist of the same time might not have said in his lectures at the Sorbonne:[52]

49. See also the description of "Castrum humani corporis" in Roberta Douglas Cornelius, *The Figurative Castle* (Bryn Mawr: Bryn Mawr College, 1930), pp. 17–18.

50. *Timaeus*, ed. Cornford 70a, pp. 286–87.

51. In *Minor Works*, trans. Mary Francis McDonald (Washington: Catholic University of America Press, 1965), p. 30.

52. Citations are to *The Works of Guillaume de Salluste, sieur Du Bartas*, ed. Urban Tigner Holmes *et al.* (Chapel Hill: University of North Carolina Press, 1935).

Le nez est un conduit qui reprend et redonne
L'esprit dont nous vivons, le nez est un tuyau
Par qui l'os espongeux de l'humide cerveau
Hume la douce odeur, le nez est la goutière
Par qui les excremens de pesante matiere
S'evacuent en bas.

[1.6.542–47]

And the description of the voice mechanism is metaphoric, but in a purely decorative and unelaborated way:

Nostre langue est l'archet, nostre esprit le sonneur,
Nos dents les nerfs batus, le creux de nos narines
Le creux de l'instrument d'où ces odes divines
Prenent leur plus bel air.

[1.6.592–95]

But the metaphor of the castle or citadel Du Bartas does use consistently and to some purpose. Du Bartas draws from his use of the metaphor a conception of God as the supreme organizer and designer, of the world as a perfectly organized creation, and of man's body as a flawless machine ready for use. For him, man's world is essentially a series of buildings, real or allegorical. He invites the reader to view the "cité du monde" thus:

Si vous desirez les beaux amphitheatres
Les arsenals, les arcs, les temples, les theatres,
Les colosses, les ports, les cirques, les rempars,
Qu'on void superbement dans nostre ville espars,
Venez avecques moy.

[1.6.5–9]

Again and again God is described as a maker of mechanisms, "l'ingénieux maçon" or "architecte divin, ouvrier plus qu' admirable." Man's body is a microcosm because everything in God's world is an effective machine and man's body the most encompassing and efficient of them all. The four elements are building materials, and the creation an act of literal construction: "tu prins de la poussiere, / La colas, la pressas, l'embellis de ta main, / Et d'un informe corps formas le corps humain" (1.6.490–92).

As a citadel man's body is perfectly orgainzed. Dangers are present, but the anatomy—or architecture—is such that they are kept in check. The head rules the citadel and all its members lest they become unruly, and the ear is wound in coils so as to transport dangerous messages from the outside world slowly enough to allow reason to work upon them. Most of the dangers imagined are indeed external, for there is little suggestion that the members of this body might ever be in disharmony. With the eyes as sentinels, the teeth as warders, the stomach as cook, etc., this citadel has little to fear in case of siege. But the effect of Du Bartas's image is more like that of a ghost town than of a citadel. Very few parts of the anatomy are allegorized as persons, though some may have human power. The metaphor serves to universalize this picture of the human condition, with the result that the body is an empty shell which contains no human specificity, but is merely the mechanical principle which keeps life going on a moral and Christian plane.

Phineas Fletcher's *The Purple Island*, probably the most exhaustive poetic treatment of the human body ever composed, is in fact more a pure idealization than a continuous metaphor. Nevertheless, we can see that its overall form falls generally into the citadel plan. The poem is an expansion into twelve long cantos of what Spenser usually treats in two, i.e., an allegorical core (House of Holiness, House of Temperance, etc.) and the fight to defend it. Only the first five cantos are concerned with the single human body, and that metaphor is laid aside during the fight and not brought back even after the battle is successfully concluded.

Insofar as the body is allegorized consistently in Fletcher's poem, it is seen as a geographical place, and though Fletcher uses the all-inclusive properties of this vague metaphor rather than limiting himself to a citadel, he still treats the island primarily as a fortified city. Within these fortifications, certain areas, like the heart, are castles within a castle, especially well fortified:

> Flankt with two severall walls—for more defence—
> Betwixt them ever flows a wheyish moat;
> In whose soft waves, and circling profluence
> This citie, like an isle, might safely float.
>
> [4.16]

The terms for most parts of the island are geographical, for in this very general category Fletcher can include cosmic, political, and architectural metaphors, holding in an unblended state all three strands. Within the geographical metaphor there are mountains, rivers, cities.

These can be analogous to a cosmos; their relations can be characterized by the kind of politics which parallels that of the well-ordered human body; and the man-made structures are castles made from individual parts of the body. Thus at the same time this geographical place is a whole universe and a replica of another greater one, which can of course be either heaven, if this is an island, or God, if this is a man (2.3). It is held together by political harmony: the cartilages and bones are "in one league combin'd" (2.6); the spleen is a benevolent despot like the belly in Menenius's fable (3.19); the "heart–city" is "leagu'd to the neighbour towns with sure and friendly bands" (4.2); and the body as a whole is divided from top to bottom "in three regiments, . . . Ord'-ring in peace and warre their governments / With loving concord and with mutuall aid" (2.14).

Fletcher's island is closest to the citadel images of Spenser and Du Bartas, whom Fletcher acknowledges as masters. Like Grosseteste's "Chasteau," the island is a container for a vast number of abstract ideals, but these are personified only in the later cantos and have no bodily reference at all. They are part of a lengthy cast of virtues realized as human beings, but these beings are largely bodiless and uncharacterized. The faculties of a sentient being which were the principal concern in the Castle of Kynde are also present here, but only dimly corporealized. Thus the three divisions of the brain, which Fletcher copies closely from Spenser, have little to do with the physical structure of their house. Primarily this is a mechanical human body, created by a God not unlike that of Du Bartas. The foundation is strong, the upper parts are secure, and all of the systems are geographically, politically, or architecturally logical.

Together these three strands, emphasizing abstract qualities, human faculties, and concrete building elements, add up to virtually all the metaphoric techniques and purposes which have animated the body–castle analogy. Before treating Spenser's House of Alma, where a fusion is realized, it will be worth looking at some other castles which approach the quality of Spenser's syntheses. The element most conspicuously lacking in the castles treated so far is the dynamic juxtaposition of human beings with the body–castle. This corresponds, in terms of the political analogy, to the introduction of a personified and corporealized monarch juxtaposed with the abstract body of the State. The presence of these characters has much the same effect as did the humanized version of the political image: the abstraction of the body–castle is revivified by the fullness and complexity which surrounds the introduction of real human personality and destiny. Once characters are introduced, the moral emblem is enlivened and viewed in the light of a particular character's life. The abstract faculties are set in motion, and the idealized machine is turned on and run by characters rather than mere mechanisms.

The appearance of an antagonist represents one of the most traditional means of introducing personality and complexity into the abstract corporeal emblem of man's condition. One of the seminal texts for this image is the *Psychomachia* of Prudentius. For later allegorists like Spenser and Bunyan, Prudentius provided the essential framework of a struggle within the individual human being which at the same time mirrors a struggle in the human race. Prudentius is not primarily an allegorizer of the human body. He leaves no doubt, in his introduction, that the virtues are warring against the vices within the body, but the correspondences between a place of war and the human body are by no means constantly drawn. The body is a battlefield and a house of clay, and the human faculties are inhabitants of the house: "We are abundantly rich in servants born in the house if we know through the mystic symbol what is the power of three hundred with eighteen more."[53] Nonetheless, Prudentius is not writing an anatomy. In fact, the victory over the vices is celebrated by the building of a holy temple, presumably the New Jerusalem, which has no anatomical analogies whatever and is nothing like Spenser's anthropomorphic "goodly frame." But Prudentius' composite individual is very much a single person, a newborn corporeal soul who grows older and wiser, and this forms the real framework for the elaborated personalized body–castle.

At the other chronological extreme from Prudentius we find the kingdom of Logistilla in *Orlando Furioso*. Ariosto makes use of the single and yet multiple allegorical container—here more a castle than a body—and truly personalizes the particles of his overall allegorical image. Thus he speaks of the sins which are besetting the castle (in this case actually Alcina's rather than Logistilla's city):[54]

53. *Works*, trans. H. J. Thomson (London: Heinemann, 1949), pp. 56–57.

54. Citations are to Lodovico Ariosto, *Orlando Furioso*, ed. Dino Provenzal (Milan: Rizzoli, 1955).

> Chi senza freno in s'un destrier galoppa,
> chi lento va con l'asino o col bue,
> altre salisce ad un centauro in groppa,
> struzzoli molti han sotto, aquile e grue; . . .
> Di questi il capitano si vedea
> aver gonfiato il ventre, e'l viso grasso.

[6.62–63]

But Logistilla's castle itself is a composite, bodylike figure, containing, for example, the four cardinal virtues who are personalized as Andronica, Fronesia, Dicilla, and Sofrosina. The jewels, the stones, the gardens of the castle are all particles of the multiple castle image which Ariosto separates into faculties so that each in turn can confront Ruggiero and bear upon his particular need for peace and virtue after the courtly love passions of Alcina's house.

Of greatest interest is Ariosto's description of the glorious, mirrorlike gems of the walls, which have exactly that power which a vision of the body–castle gives to Guyon or Arthur:

> Quel che più fa che lor si inchina e cede
> ogn' altra gemma, è che, mirando in esse,
> l'uom sin in mezzo all'anima si vede;
> vede suoi vizii e sue virtudi espresse . . .
> fassi, mirando allo specchio lucente
> se stesso, conoscendosi, prudente.

[10.59]

The House of Alma is also a mirror, as is any body–castle, for the man who looks at it from the outside and beholds himself. But Ariosto has reduced this physical analogy to the mirror itself. The gems of the walls are anthropomorphic in that they reflect the body and soul of the viewer.

For the current study, which concentrates upon English letters, the Logistilla episode is perhaps most interesting because of the way in which Sir John Harington moralized it in "A Brief Allegorie of Orlando Furioso," which is appended to his translation. This essay offers remarkable insights into the understanding of allegory in the 1590's, and may suggest how the poet of the time expected his allegories to be read.

Harington places particular emphasis upon the literal and concrete side of Ariosto's allegorical or metaphorical representations. Thus, after allegorizing the various beasts upon which the sins are riding when

they beset Alcina's city, he severely denigrates the abstract method of
interpretation:

> I needed not so curiously to have sought for such a hidden meaning in them, when as
> the verie things themselves are so untemperately used by many, that they keepe
> them from vertues and more honorable actions: How many men give themselves
> so extremely to these hunters, haukes, hounds, and horses, that they cannot scarse
> affoord an houre to the studie of wisdome and temperance?

For Harington, and I would add, others of his time, the concrete or in
this case corporeal side of allegories has an absolute reality. Consequent-
ly it is very telling that Harington interprets the whole episode of Alcina
and Logistilla as composite in a single human body:

> When this perfection was lost, and that the same great rebellion was made, to the
> overthrow of that quiet and setled state, the heart became so weake, as it was not
> able to indure the continuall assaults of the passions that assayled it, and in the end
> was content to take part with them against the reasonable part of the minde. And
> now every part of the body engenders such seeds of concupiscence, that nature is
> becoming a bastard sister to reason, and usurps that government that is due onely
> to her, and leaveth her only one castle, which was so strongly situated that it was
> impregnable: so that now reason is retired as it were to her principall fortresse,
> to the head, the rest of this kingdom being possessed (by Alcyna) by pleasure and
> fond delights.[55]

In this interpretation are contained all the strands of the body–castle:
the faculties, the anatomy, the separation of functions among parts of
the body, the castle, the political organization, and above all the vision
of a multitude of beings and experiences in the unifying light of a single
human body which belongs to a composite character. That Spenser or
Ariosto should have had such a vision proves only that it was available
to geniuses; that Sir John Harington should have readily turned uncon-
genial material into this farfetched interpretation proves that all these
strands of thought were truly current in the late sixteenth century.

6

Spenser's House of Alma culminates the tradition of the body–castle.
It includes scriptural strands: the tenement of clay, the siege undertaken
by the devil, the concrete versions of abstraction. Like Grosseteste's

55. Sir John Harington, *Orlando Furioso in English Heroical Verse* (London, 1591), pp.
408, 409.

Chasteau d'Amour it has emblematic force, using the body as a metaphoric container and placing it in Guyon's path. On the human side, it is concerned both with physical anatomy and with abstract faculties; and on the architectural side, it is both a building and a politically organized citadel. It contains the static devotional qualities which we found in Du Bartas at the same time as it multiplies the dynamic dimensions of Prudentius and Ariosto by including both a siege and a visit, and by actually documenting the process which leads from this anthropomorphic and emblematic mirror to the education of the observer.

One special quality of Alma lies in the interplay between the architectural and human strands of the metaphor. This interplay produces actual human beings as inhabitants rather than mere machines and functions as in other body–castles. The frame is itself a building with tower, beacons, portcullis, portal making up the face, then halls, cauldrons, bellows, ducts, etc., making up the trunk. But unlike other castles of the body, each part of Alma's "building" is inhabited by real human beings. Thus an anatomical element itself may be architectural but its function is anthropomorphized. The mouth is a barbican, but the tongue is a porter and the teeth are warders; the stomach is a great dining hall, but it is inhabited by Diet and Appetite. Abstractions take human form.

Yet Spenser's Alma is not a culmination of the traditional merely because it contains so many familiar elements. It is perhaps the most acutely presented version of *discordia concors* in all of Renaissance literature; the simultaneous possibilities of the human body for unity and fragmentation are both stretched to their utmost. From the twenty-second stanza we drew the conclusion that Spenser was using geometric terms to contrast the unity and perfection of man's place in God's cosmic design with the tension and multiplicity of his internal life. This contrast epitomizes the whole canto. Spenser brings life and complexity to the abstract emblem of the body by enlivening all the traditional sources of corporeal unity and harmony and by contrasting each one with an image of complexity which is personalized and human.

The opening of the canto expresses the philosophic basis of this technique most succinctly:

> Of all Gods workes, which do this world adorne,
>   There is no one more faire and excellent,
>   Then is mans body both for powre and forme,

Whiles it is kept in sober gouernment;
But none then it, more fowle and indecent,
Distempred through misrule and passions bace:
It growes a Monster, and incontinent
Doth loose his dignitie and natiue grace.

[2.9.1]

Spenser keeps strictly within the physical terms of the body, for it acts as a kind of litmus paper on which one can read the virtue or vice of the inhabitant. Other castles of the body tended to idealize the body as an intrinsic moral paragon, but then demonstrated that it could become utterly ruined if given over to the devil. Spenser makes this point as well, but for him the ideal and the debased are bound tightly together. Maleger's crew, the active force that threatens Alma, may well be external, but in the marrow of Alma's body there exist the powers both to submit and to conquer. Spenser's microcosmic elements are simultaneous: the negative possibilities are always tied directly to the idealization itself.

Spenser tends to establish the traditional unities associated with the body–castle and then to diversify them and call them into question. One of these basic unities derives from the notion that the human body is a complete microcosm, holding all the variety of the cosmos in the organic unity of its external outline. This idea we have seen throughout the esthetic tradition, whether applied to numbers, shapes, buildings, works of nature, or moral values. Spenser arrays and interprets the concrete details of the human body to make it as all-inclusive a mirror of the world in harmony as is possible. Borrowing from the political tradition, he extends the body's microcosmic harmony further than the mere image of a castle, for the well ordered commonwealth includes representatives of all classes of individuals. When the body or castle or commonwealth is then morally idealized, the microcosm extends still further into a realm of abstract principles. Other castles of the body which we have viewed went this far in creating a microcosm. But Spenser goes considerably further by attempting to be totally inclusive and at the same time restricting his treatment of these inclusive elements to the allegorical structure dictated by the body and the citadel.

One of the ways in which Spenser's body image is all-embracing is in its inclusion of history and geography. Spenser uses simile and comparison—often negative—to include the world of experience within the bones of the body. Thus the sins attack "As when a swarme of Gnats at euentide / Out of the fennes of Allan do arise" (16). The whole scene in the marshy countryside is subsumed into the experience of Alma. Yet more corporeal is the frequent connection of the body's building materials with substances from the world: "of things like to that *Aegyptian* slime" (21) he says of the "castle wall," and the forehead is made of "Stone more of valew, and more smooth and fine, / Than Iet or Marble far from Ireland brought" (24). The fens and Irish marble are clearly of another order from all other comparisons which have appeared in earlier body–castles. The romance style which tends to allude only to things distant or imaginary is itself so individualistic that the very narrowness of its concerns excludes a true microcosmic effect. It is for this reason that Spenser includes the more familiar elements.

This immediacy is not achieved merely by isolated references to places and happenings around the corner from the sixteenth-century reader. The whole House of Alma represents a breach of the high style of romance not because it is more straightforward than, say, Mammon's cave, but because it is in a sense so simpleminded. This is exactly Spenser's rhetorical ploy. The House of Alma shocks us because unlike most of the poem, its wooden allegory lifts the witty, decorative cover from the poetic works. This obviousness of the allegory is meant to parallel the obviousness in our own experience of the human body itself. Just before the two knights meet their partners, we are told of their wonder at the castle, "For neuer had they seene so straunge a sight" (33). Spenser is mocking them, for there is no sight less strange and more often seen than our bodies. But the elaborate romanticizing which has characterized other treatments of the body–castle defeats the most basic element of the body, its commonness and familiarity. If the poet then includes nothing but classical or biblical towers, citadels, and moral expressions, he is leaving out a great deal, even the majority of the cosmos, in his microcosm. Spenser includes this familiar element both by his homely references and more significantly by means of an emblematic allegorical technique which must to his readers have smacked very much of the native folk tradition.

Spenser further includes the native element in his microcosm by allowing Alma's brain to encompass, among other things, all of history. As Spenser points out, the knowledge of history makes the individual man older than the oldest man in history. By characterizing the extreme age of Eumnestes and by connecting him with far removed historical figures, the poet draws the remotest ages into his corporeal microcosm, while his insistence upon the physical effect of age, the worm- and canker-eaten books, etc., keeps the historical element within the concrete bounds of the physical picture which he is painting. But the less remote stretches of history are more significant. The chronicle of British history, though it passes far out of the corporeal metaphor and may have been inserted here for lack of a better place, is still logically contained within Alma's brain.

All of these microcosmic elements seem intended to demonstrate the containment and unification of diversity in the image of the body. Yet this very universality can on occasion be an image of excess and potential discord, as in the description of Phantastes' chamber:

> His chamber was dispainted all within,
>> With sundry colours, in the which were writ
>> Infinite shapes of things dispersed thin;
>> Some such as in the world were neuer yit,
>> Ne can deuized be of mortall wit;
>> Some daily seene, and knowen by their names,
>> Such as in idle fantasies doe flit:
>> Infernall Hags, *Centaurs*, feendes, *Hippodames*,
> Apes, Lions, Aegles, Owles, fooles, louers, children, Dames.
>
> And all the chamber filled was with flyes,
>> Which buzzed all about, and made such sound,
>> That they encombred all mens eares and eyes,
>> Like many swarmes of Bees assembled round,
>> After their hiues with honny do abound:
>> All those were idle thoughts and fantasies,
>> Deuices, dreames, opinions unsound,
>> Shews, visions, sooth-sayes, and prophesies;
> And all that fained is, as leasings, tales, and lies.

[50–1]

The inclusiveness of these stanzas is a direct response to the idea of the body as harmonious microcosm. Spenser crowds into one small chamber of the body an exaggerated and epitomized version of the whole tradition of *homo omnis creatura*, and the crowding is itself a telling indication that the discords may have a greater potential force than the concord.

Spenser's ambiguity about the reality and corporeality of this menagerie produces a subtler kind of discord in these stanzas. The strategy of the lines, particularly in the series ending the first stanza, leads us to accept the figures as much as we accepted other objective descriptions in the House of Alma, but the longer series at the end of the second stanza annihilates the poet's own corporeal vividness. Multiplicity and tension enter Spenser's abstract and unified corporeal container by way of images which the poet makes distinctly incorporeal, whatever bodily vividness they may have potentially. This is like the contrast between the circle and the square within it, as described in the twenty-second stanza. The divinely ordered human body with all its corporeal effects is complete and perfect in its harmonization of the microcosm. The complexities and confusions of mortal life are the contents of the body as allegorical container. They are intrinsically bodiless—since "body" is either divine or natural and therefore perfect in itself—but they form the discord within the body's concord.

The all-embracing quality of the historical microcosm can also introduce discord by suggesting specific references which are not in keeping with an idealized and harmonious vision of the body. Spenser introduces an allusion to the Tower of Babel in a passage of fervent idealization:

> . . . all so faire, and fensible withall,
> Not built of bricke, ne yet of stone and lime,
> But of things like to that *Aegyptian* slime,
> Whereof king *Nine* whilome built Babell towre;
> But O great pitty, that no lenger time
> So goodly workemanship should not endure:
> Soone it must turne to earth; no earthly thing is sure.
>
> [21]

Like the fancies in Phantastes' chamber, the Tower of Babel is intrinsically incorporeal. It is, however, the paradigm of bad architecture, and thus casts an aura of doubt over the architectural perfection which Spenser is describing. In addition, the Tower is an emblem of multiplicity since God's punishment for the builders' pride was to render them completely fragmented. In the implied reference to the builders of Babel we can see a counterpoise to the image of Alma as a complete and harmonious mechanism of political organization. The poet develops the same contrast between the natural body—or natural work of architecture—which is perfect, and the life of man which is as fragmented as the Tower's builders. But here the negative message is subtly integrated. Spenser is able to hold both the ideal and the debased in suspension by withholding judgment on the Tower of Babel and pretending an innocence about its implications with the mere suggestion that as a great work of biblical antiquity it must be glorious.

The *sic transit* afterthought is both a separate and parallel comment on the moral implications of the body, and a clever union of the body and the Tower of Babel. It is here that Spenser draws on the tradition of the house of clay which is beautiful but not enduring. Yet the implications of Babel do not stop here. With the single reference some stanzas later to the "bablers of folly" against whom the tongue stands on guard, Spenser judges his earlier image. Then, still later, the Tower of Babel is transformed to holiness in a description of the head that "likest is vnto that heauenly towre, / That God hath built for his owne blessed bowre" (47).

In the traditional image of the unified and harmonious human body, the *discordia concors* is achieved not only by the completeness of the microcosm but also because the form of the body is uniquely perfect. This is the principle behind most of the esthetic tradition: the assumption that God is the Divine Artist, Whose work is worth studying and copying as the summit of perfections. In most of the body–castles this idealization is the principal message, whether the poet stresses the multiplicity of the elements unified or merely idealizes the unity. In the House of Alma this kind of unity always results from the tempering of multiples or opposites which are diversely characterized. The wondrous marble from Ireland, for instance, which appears on the face, is at first part of a pure idealization of the body, yet over it "was cast a wandring vine, / Enchaced with a wanton yuie twine" (24). This reference, presumably to a moustache (reminding us that only the soul is feminine), casts immediate doubt on the perfect idealization, but immediately we are told that the nose is "Neither vnseemly short nor yet exceeding long," so that its moderation seems to temper the extremes.

Spenser's most characteristic image of *discordia concors* in the body's form is the creation of a many faceted but perfectly working machine. The whole castle is one of these machines, but it is broken down into many individual sets of processes which illustrate the harmonization of discord in action. The temperate man is allowed a multiplicity of impulses, capacities, and needs, but these multiples are pointed in identical or complementary directions. The potential discord may be as slight as the variety of jobs involved in the digestive system:

> The maister Cooke was cald *Concoction*,
>   A carefull man, and full of comely guise:
>   The kitchin Clerke, that hight *Digestion*,
>   Did order all th'Achates in seemely wise, . . .
>   The rest had seuerall offices assind,
>   Some to remoue the scum, as it did rise;
>   Others to beare the same away did mind;
>   And others it to vse according to his kind.
>
> [31]

Such a description as this is open to a wide range of simultaneous readings. It is a picture of an anatomical process; it is an idealization of our god-given bodies; it is an emblem of good social behavior; it is a celebration of cosmic order; and finally it is a prescription for individual moral behavior.

At another part of the digestive tract, there seems to be a much greater contrast contained within the system:

> And in the midst of all
> There placed was a caudron wide and tall,
> Vpon a mighty furnace, burning whot,
> More whot, then *Aetn'* or flaming *Mongiball*:
> For day and night it brent, ne ceased not,
> So long as any thing it in the caudron got.
>
> But to delay the heat, least by mischaunce
> It might breake out, and set the whole on fire,
> There added was by goodly ordinaunce,
> An huge great paire of bellowes, which did styre
> Continually, and cooling breath inspyre.
>
> [29–30]

This tension between the stomach and the lungs is a clear example of morality read on a corporeal plane. The complementary quality of these forces forms an abstract picture of balance within God's vision of man's life. At the same time it has wide implications in Spenser's definition of temperance. The fires of the stomach are clearly hellish in their potential. Yet this potential is not rejected or excluded from the divine plan. Rather the potential is equalized—though significantly not overcome—by the cooling force of the lungs. The discords are harmonized, but the harmony remains precarious.

The traditional corporeal harmony is questioned even beyond this point. We have remarked that throughout the history of the body–castle the most elaborate poetic effects tended to include personified and characterized members of the anatomy. Spenser makes more use of these figures than any of his predecessors, but with a special purpose. Most of the simple idealization of the body is imaged forth by architecture, machines, or at most very unspecified human characters. The closer Spenser comes to particularized human beings, the more he is concerned with the dangers and multiplicities of mortal life. Here, in contrast to the perfectly working machine, we have glimpses of a world of micro-individuals engaged in multiple and separate actions. Thus, for example, Spenser describes the Affections:

> Diuerse delights they found themselues to please;
>> Some song in sweet consort, some laught for ioy,
>> Some plaid with strawes, some idly sat at ease;
>> But other some could not abide to toy,
>> All pleasaunce was to them griefe and annoy:
>> This found, that found, the third for shame did blush,
>> Another seemed enuious, or coy,
>> Another in her teeth did gnaw a rush:
> But at these straungers presence euery one did hush.

[35]

None of these actions is particularly reprehensible and some are even pleasant. But the force of the poet's disapprobation comes down upon them for their very diversity, their mutual irrelevance, and their purposelessness. The series of independent terms, like those describing the fancies in the brain, is the perfect contrast to the overorganized structural allegory of Alma's virtuous parts.

The siege of Alma, in which external, or partially external, forces of evil are imposing upon her, is described in much the same way:

> Vile caytiue wretches, ragged, rude, deformd,
> All threatning death, all in straunge manner armd,
> Some with vnweldy clubs, some with long speares,
> Some rusty kniues, some staues in fire warmd.

[13]

This non-uniform series of miniature men gives rise to just such a conflict of forces within Alma as that which was implied by the Affections:

> Fly fast, and saue your selues from neare decay,

> Here may ye not haue entrance, though we would:
> We would and would againe, if that we could;
> But thousand enemies about vs raue.
>
> [12]

The conflict between wanting and preventing the entrance of the knights constitutes a rare example of Alma's weakness. Here at the beginning of the canto we see the multiple forces contained within a human being viewed as a single entity. Spenser is again contrasting the unity and harmony of the natural forces inside man's frame with the tensions and complexities of actual human life as it fragments the body.[56]

The same holds for the three mental faculties, which have been discussed in terms of their philosophical implications by Harry Berger in *The Allegorical Temper*.[57] Here the characterization is generated quite directly out of the anatomical or psychological function. The "mad or foolish" Phantastes, the reasonable and wise man "of ripe and perfect age" who contemplates the present, and the absentminded Eumnestes who objectifies the activity of memory, are, I think, less important for representing three kinds of thought in the world than for demonstrating that these separate faculties within man's body are each heavily tinged with a multitude of moral implications. By diversifying and depicting these faculties, Spenser breaks down the overall abstraction of the temperate man into personified particles which cast doubt upon the perfect harmony and unity of man's condition.

The resolution of the *discordia concors* derives from the place of the Alma episode in the whole of Spenser's second book, and the essential factor in the ninth canto is the experience of Guyon and Arthur within Alma. The Affections and the mental faculties are characterized to some extent, but Guyon and Arthur are fully realized—and life-size—characters who lose none of their liveliness when they are miniaturized for entrance into the human body. It is their experience which typifies the tension between harmony and discord in the conduct of mortal life. Ariosto, as has been mentioned, moralizes the gems of Logistilla's castle as mirrors in which the observer can see his own virtues and vices. Spenser, elaborating this idea, turns Alma into a mirror of the two knights. Shamefastness and desire for praise are elements in Alma's

---

56. The description also suggests Spenser's memory of the rebellious Irish peasantry.
57. *The Allegorical Temper* (New Haven: Yale University Press, 1967), pp. 77–85.

microcosm and are present as part of Alma's being. The damsel whom
Arthur meets not only recognizes the wellspring of Arthur's activity
which he has hidden from himself but she also stands for that very
impulse herself. The same recognition occurs, I think, to Shamefast-
ness, although she is abashed by it and does not speak. Spenser's "el-
ementated body" thus acts as a mirror for Guyon and Arthur because
in the diversity of Alma they find their own essences expressed. This
has the effect of universalizing the picture we see in Alma because it
seems to impinge directly upon the heroes.

The heroes' reaction to this self-recognition is even more interesting
than the mirroring itself. Arthur's body reacts immediately:

> Yet with faire semblaunt sought to hide the breach,
> Which chaunge of colour did perforce vnfold,
> Now seeming flaming whot, now stony cold.
>
> [39]

He cannot hide his feelings, for his body gives him away. Further, it
gives him away by dissolving into a multiple mass, at once hot and
cold, hiding and revealing. In this recognition of his essential quality,
Arthur finds his body becoming just that sort of multiple container
which the House of Alma has demonstrated the body to be. The same
motif is continued in the confrontation of Guyon and Shamefastness.
She herself is a mass of contending forces which show in her body,
"the whiles her louely face / The flashing bloud with blushing did
inflame" (43). Within her we can readily see the effects of a citadel of
separate forces which are less than totally cooperative. When Guyon is
made to recognize her quality, his reaction is an exact mirror of those
physical effects in her which provoked it: "The Elfe did blush in
priuitee, / And turnd his face away." Guyon's own forces multiply
and separate. Spenser's castle of the body is a mirror of man in general
and also of particular men.

The position of the Alma episode in the Book of Temperance
reflects a number of ways in which Spenser sums up the esthetic tradi-
tion of interpreting and allegorizing the body. Like his predecessors,
Spenser affirms the perfection and harmony of the body as a work of
God and of nature. But Alma's situation is weak. The dangers to her
form and balance are found within her own anatomy and in the war
against her senses waged by Maleger. The reason for this weakness as

well as for her triumph over it are in the affirmation of life forces. As has so often been pointed out, the world of Book Two is the world of mortality; it contains little grace, little love, and much death. Throughout Spenser's survey of intemperance, imbalance among the senses is closely associated with death. Nature is a double force, at once the earthly fallen matter out of which are made such forces as Mortdant's original sin, Mammon's cave, and the source of Maleger's strength, and also the source of life, which, as Guyon tells Mammon, needs no excess to sustain itself. The struggle to find the golden mean which occupies both Guyon and Alma is the struggle to stay alive. Guyon's affirmation of life is in the knightly struggle, which throughout is contrasted with the tortures of self-doubt; while Alma, and Arthur, her champion, must face the antilife forces head-on.

It is for this reason that Maleger is not a personification of intemperance, but rather of death. His body, in contrast to Alma's, is almost without form and self-contradictory: "Full large he was of limbe, and shoulders brode, / But of such subtile substance and vnsound, / That like a ghost he seem'd, whose graue-clothes were vnbound" (11. 20). The interdependence of his own body with his mother earth gives him earth's powers of mortality. He represents a summation of Mortdant, the death doer, of Pyrochles ("dying daily, daily yet reuiue") and of the deathly qualities of Mammon's cave. Each of these situations of death has been primarily self-contradictory: Mortdant is the death giver who dies; Pyrochles dies but revives enough to die again even after Arthur triumphs over him when he shouts "I not ouercome do dye, / But in despight of life, for death do call" (8. 52); and Mammon's riches, which are supposed to give lordship over the world, are in fact instantly death producing.

The underlying self-contradiction which has riddled the lives of these intemperate characters is that between life and death. Maleger is the essential image of this contradiction in physical terms:

> Flesh without bloud, a person without spright,
> Wounds without hurt, a bodie without might,
> That could doe harme, yet could not harmed bee,
> That could not die, yet seem'd a mortall wight.
>
> [11.40]

But, significantly, Alma is also an image of simultaneous life and death: "imperfect, mortall, foeminine . . . immortall, perfect, masculine."

Alma's and Arthur's victory over Maleger is not the victory over death, for in this book of mortality that is impossible, but rather the victory over the torturing strife between life and death. We have seen that Spenser affirms the body for its own sake at the same time as he recognizes that its unity only serves to contain the complexities of mortal life. The affirmation of temperance as an affirmation of life is a rich rereading of the whole esthetic tradition. Whether among the scholastics, the Renaissance estheticians, the architects, or the poets, the body has represented a natural or divine ideal, specifically that of *discordia concors*. Spenser comes to grips with the dangers to that ideal, the dangers of *discors*. He suggests that an acceptance of the body—like the poet's own acceptance—is an acceptance of life, and in that proper acceptance of life resides the temperance needed to retain the ideal harmony of discord, which can, even at its best, seem so precarious.

4

Astrophil and Stella:
The Human Body as Setting for
the Petrarchan Drama

1

When Petrarch walks through "boschi inospiti e selvaggi" and yet sees and hears nothing but forms of Laura, he epitomizes the spirit of metamorphosis at the heart of Petrarchan love poetry. The poet sets his passionate desire over against his drive to experience or to understand the cosmos around him. These latter moral and spiritual drives are forever distorted and subverted by the drives of love, and poetic expression of this distortion is often a metamorphosis of the world into the lady. Petrarch does not experience the savage forest because his more passionate desires annihilate the objective world around him and substitute the image of Laura:

> Ch' i' l'ho ne gli occhi; e veder seco parme
> Donne e donzelle, e sono abeti e faggi
> Parmi d'udirla, udendo i rami e l'òre
> E le frondi e gli augei lagnarsi, e l'acque
> Mormorando fuggir per l'erba verde.[1]

In this metamorphosis and substitution, the human body plays a special role. We have seen that in a multitude of ways the reading of the human body has always been an essential means for grasping man's

1. Francesco Petrarca, *Le Rime*, ed. Giosuè Carducci and Severino Ferrari (Florence: Sansoni, 1957), 176. 7–11.

place in the cosmos. This technique of "reading" objects in order to discover subjective truths is at the heart of the Petrarchan tradition, particularly in the sonnets of Sir Philip Sidney. The simplicity and objectivity of Sidney's Petrarchan poetry derive at least partly from an emphasis upon minute details of the poet's life which are expanded poetically without ever losing their original simplicity. This reading of objective matters is closely akin to the imaginative and metaphoric reading of the human body which is our subject. The allegorizers, too, expand the body imaginatively without losing track of the objective corporeal frame which remains at the heart of their cosmic speculation. Thus buried in the Petrarchan system is a need to grasp and measure the cosmos. The traditional means of doing this is the human body allegory.

Yet the body would not be so important in Petrarchan poetry if it were merely one of many similar objects of meditation, like the grammar rules which Sidney can meditate upon and use to transform Stella's "No, no" into a "yes." The unique significance of the body lies in the fact that it is the consummate expression and locus of the poet's desparate love at the same time as it is an image of the harmony which eludes him. The body, then, may take both parts of the struggle: the body is the cosmos, and the body is the locus of sexual desire. The body is also a bridge between the two, which the poet can never seem to cross. The result of these multiple significations for Sidney is that *Astrophil and Stella* almost seems to be a meditation on the body, forced upon the poet because he sees the body wherever he turns. The experience of his love is like that of the Promethean hero struggling between reason and passion, unable to realize his drives. Yet the stage upon which this drama is enacted is not the vast world linked to the cosmos in the lives of a Tamburlane or an Antony, but rather the little worlds of the poet's body and his lady's, both of which are also linked to the cosmos.

Like all literature which makes use of the body image, *Astrophil and Stella* demonstrates a tension between fragmentation and union. The poetic technique itself expresses this tension. Sidney's sonnets are often studies in *chiaroscuro*: behind the tiny, intricate experience of each sonnet there tends to be a wholeness which can be grasped by the reader, but which is skewed and obscured by the poet's perceptions of it. This wholeness may be an external narrative which is obscured by the poet's psychological point of view, but often it is the human body—

either the poet's or Stella's or an abstract body—which stands as a reminder of unity and harmony, but which the poet only calls up in a couple of telling allusions. These allusions speak of the body's multiplicity, whether in the glories of Stella or the pains of Astrophil. The body is at once the physical stage of the drama and the image of its spiritual implications. All the traditions of the human body image are telescoped into the struggle of one individual, multiple in his drives, to win the heart of another, multiple in her powers. The body can be locus, technique, and meaning.

Before turning to *Astrophil and Stella*, where the force of the human body image is most tellingly felt, it is important to note that this image was essential to the tradition in which Sidney was writing. Only one of Petrarch's *Rime* was translated by both fathers of the English Petrarchan tradition, Wyatt and Surrey. This is "Amor, che nel penser mio vive e regna," (*Rime*, 140), which becomes Surrey's "Love that doth raine and live within my thought" and Wyatt's "The longe love, that in my thought doeth harbar." Here is Surrey's version:

> Love that doth raine and live within my thought,
> And buylt his seat within my captyve brest,
> Clad in the armes wherin with me he fowght
> Oft in my face he doth his banner rest.
> But she that tawght me love and suffre paine,
> My doubtfull hope and eke my hote desire
> With shamfast looke to shadoo and refrayne,
> Her smyling grace convertyth streight to yre.
> And cowarde love than to the hert apace
> Taketh his flight where he doth lorke and playne
> His purpose lost, and dare not show his face.
> For my lordes gylt thus fawtless byde I payne;
>   Yet from my lorde shall not my foote remove.
>   Sweet is the death that taketh end by love.[2]

No poem could be more essentially Petrarchan in its conventions, and none could better epitomize the imaginative use of corporeal metaphors. The objective scene of this poem's action is the lover's own body, separated into parts and transformed into a little world. The plot distinguishes between the face, which is the outward expression of the poet's "hote desire," and the heart, which is love's natural seat, where

2. Henry Howard, Earl of Surrey, *Poems*, ed. Emrys Jones (Oxford: Clarendon Press, 1964), p. 3.

he is protected and safe, but where he cannot reach his beloved.

The poet's body is allegorized in several ways. It is a geographical territory which at some point in the past—corresponding to the moment when the lady was first seen—was conquered by a lord. This lord, love, built his capital at the central point of his newly conquered territory presumably because the safest policy is to stay at the farthest point from possibly hostile boundaries. And in fact when the lord does travel to boundary regions, he encounters considerable difficulty with the neighboring territories.

The most consistent allegorical construction within this sonnet is the political image of the body. The breast, or heart, is the seat of the lord, which should be occupied by the lover's reason. But this lord of reason was defeated by another lord and banished completely. The new lord takes over the seat of government, but is not in fact able to keep all the parts of the commonwealth in smooth operation and cooperation. The external force of the commonwealth tries to cooperate with the new lord but is so repulsed by the neighboring commonwealth that the new lord must return to his stronghold where he has apparently not gained full power over the territory. The Petrarchan lover is quite literally beside himself, split between reason and passion, and the traditional vision of the human body as a commonwealth offers the poet the opportunity to objectify this doubleness.[3] The image of the body comes to realize in concrete terms the multiple forces within a single man. The particularly Petrarchan version of these multiples includes, as we shall see, separation and unity both within the individual and between the lover and the lady.

2

The sonnets in *Astrophil and Stella* are generally narrations, some sequences of real events and some sequences of mental events. The human body can play a number of significant roles in these narrations. Perhaps the most basic function of the body is as literal locus for the action. The body bridges the gap between concrete narrative events

---

3. The body is also a geometric construct (the heart at the center, the face at the outer edge) and an iconographic subject since the arms which Love wears and which then appear in the lover's face are a visualized allegorization of his looks of desire and hot blushes.

and the abstract emotions which the speaker is undergoing. In Sonnet
53, for instance, the body is the setting for action within and between
the lovers:[4]

> In Martiall sports I had my cunning tride,
>> And yet to breake more staves did me addresse:
>> While with the people's shouts I must confesse,
> Youth, lucke, and praise, even fild my veines with pride.
> When *Cupid*, having me his slave descride
>> In *Marse's* liverie, prauncing in the presse;
>> "What now sir foole," said he, "I would no lesse,
> Looke here, I say." I look'd, and *Stella* spide,
>> Who hard by made a window send forth light.
> My heart then quak'd, then dazled were mine eyes,
> One hand forgott to rule, th' other to fight.
> Nor trumpets' sound I heard, nor friendly cries;
>> My Foe came on, and beat the aire for me,
>> Till that her blush taught me my shame to see.

This sonnet has as much plot as any in the whole sequence: Sidney
decides to ride in yet another tournament, but Stella's observation of
him, which he notices as he is entering the lists, paralyzes him on the
sidelines. In consequence, his opponent thrashes about unable to find
him, and the poet is only rendered capable again at the humiliating
sight of Stella's blush.

Placed between the action of the tournament and the emotional
sequence within and between poet and lady is the bodily theater of
action. The speaker is himself seen as a body whose organs have ab-
stract values: "Youth, lucke, and praise, even fild my veines with
pride." "Youth, lucke, and praise" are the stuff of Sidney's life in his
courtly role, particularly as the veins have always been associated with
social commerce and with the maintenance of life. At the beginning of
the sonnet, then, Sidney's body is constructed of forces both positive
and unified. He is quite literally the creature of his courtly role.

The appearance of Stella turns his body to doubt and disunity:

> My heart then quak'd, then dazled were mine eyes,
> One hand forgott to rule, th' other to fight.
> Nor trumpets' sound I heard, nor friendly cries.

[10–12]

4. Citations are to *The Poems of Sir Philip Sidney*, ed. W.A. Ringler (Oxford: Clar-
endon Press, 1962).

The body in these lines is both a literal and metaphoric scene of action, but the two are nearly inextricable. The metaphoric kernel is contained in the eleventh line. The idea of a stable commonwealth which had been evoked by the image of flowing veins is now contradicted by a picture of bodily disintegration. Sidney alludes to two traditional allegorizations of the hands: as the individuals who actually execute the king's will, and as the fighting men.[5] This doubleness of purpose ("rule," "fight") immediately suggests the multiple forces within the poet, and when both these actions are forgotten an already multiple body is thrown into complete disunity.

Surrounding this line and elaborating its metaphoric overtones are two lines in which the body is treated more literally. The relations among them demonstrate quite revealingly how Sidney joins literal and metaphoric bodies. The original sight of Stella at the tournament, so confusing and embarrassing to the poet, produces a literal over-working of bodily functions which represents a perversion of their true purpose. The heart, in traditional allegorical terms, should be the secure seat of the king (or of reason) and ought not to quake; the eyes are usually allegorized as some kind of fact-finding organ, and they defeat themselves by being overimpressed with what they see. This self-defeat becomes more pronounced in the twelfth line, when the sight of Stella, far from leading to an excess of sense experiences as was implied earlier, produces anaesthesia.

But the sonnet as a whole is not nearly so negative as a reading of these three lines suggests, and the positive forces which Stella launches are also objectified in corporeal terms. Stella herself possesses a multiple body, though less is said of it since she appears only on the sidelines of the poem, and only in terms of her effect upon the poet. Stella, we are told, "hard by made a window send forth light." Here Sidney touches on rather a different allegorical tradition in which the body is a building whose eyes are beacons. Far from being a perversion of the natural function (like the poet's eyes which are "dazled"), this beacon of light from the castle of Stella's body is intended as a guide to her wandering knight. From Stella's point of view, then, the glance is an attempt to bring their bodies together—in both literal and metaphoric terms. Literally she stares into his eyes. Metaphorically she sends forth the beacon of light which should enable him to see. Yet as so often

---

5. John of Salisbury used both in *Policraticus*. See chapter 2.

happens in these sonnets, the union of lovers' bodies, whether literal or metaphoric, leads to a complete disunity within the mind or body of the poet. In this case the poet's senses explode and are not guided by the beacon of light.

The final line, however, produces a kind of happy ending. Stella's blush proves that her own bodily unity is crumbling in response to her admirer's humiliation, for blushes were a traditional bodily objectification of warring feelings within the spirit.[6] The effect of Stella's bodily disunity is to return Sidney to something like unified control over himself. The beacon of light which her strong "castle" sent forth achieved just the opposite of its intent. But the bodily sight of her confusion actually does succeed: "her blush taught me my shame to see." They are joined again by a successful look at each other's faces, and Sidney's forces are themselves unified into action. The negative aspect of this happy ending is in the sight which the poet's newly restored eyes behold, as his shame is a constant reminder of the self-perpetuating movement between a split self, union with his beloved, and back to a split self.

The body as scene of the action has special relevance to the sonnets about poetic creation, whose source is in the poet's body and whose inspiration is in the beloved's. The famous opening sonnet illustrates the connection between poetic creation and the human body:

> Loving in truth, and faine in verse my love to show,
> That the deare She might take some pleasure of my paine:
> Pleasure might cause her reade, reading might make her know,
> Knowledge might pitie winne, and pitie grace obtaine,
>   I sought fit words to paint the blackest face of woe,
> Studying inventions fine, her wits to entertaine;
> Oft turning others' leaves, to see if thence would flow
> Some fresh and fruitfull showers upon my sunne-burn'd braine.
>   But words came halting forth, wanting Invention's stay,
> Invention, Nature's child, fled step-dame Studie's blowes,
> And others' feete still seem'd but strangers in my way.
> Thus great with child to speake, and helpless in my Throwes,
> Biting my trewand pen, beating my selfe for spite,
> "Foole," said my Muse to me, "looke in thy heart and write."

The pattern resembles that of Sonnet 53: the poem constructs a triangle consisting of the poet, the lady, and an activity which both unites and

6. Compare Guyon and Shamefastness in Spenser's House of Alma.

divides them, in this case the attempt at poetic inspiration. Again, the main business of the sonnet is the poet's own internal process, but a parallel is drawn to a presumed process within the lady. Her internal action, the straightforward progression described in the first quatrain, is not seen in corporeal terms. But the poet's own body does act as a scene for his progression. He searches through the inspiration of others "to see if thence would flow / Some fresh and fruitfull showers upon my sunne-burn'd braine." The brain here is less the seat of reason than of wit. "Sunne-burn'd" immediately turns the body into a geographical metaphor: the brain is a stretch of land which has been parched by the sun, i.e., the lady, and since passionate real life in the person of Stella has dried up this part of him, only the peaceful contemplation of literature can refresh it, he thinks.[7] He assumes that his entire body and self are sunburned and proceeds to look outside of himself. But as external inspiration fails him, he finds his own body all that much fuller, "great with child to speake, and helpless in my Throwes."

The much interpreted final sentence suggests two readings, each of which uses a traditional allegorization of the heart. One reading suggests that when Sidney looks in his heart he will see Stella, and she will give him all the inspiration which others' feet cannot.[8] The heart is the seat of government which has been occupied by Stella. She has displaced all others, including the poet's own reason, and instead of his reason he has her image as a guide. Had Stella not occupied this garrison, Sidney's reason would probably have led him altogether away from the composition of poetry, but when Stella's image is monarch of this little world, its major industry becomes poetic. The other reading suggests

7. Neil Rudenstine, in *Sidney's Poetic Development* (Cambridge, Mass.: Harvard University Press, 1967), pp. 197–201, suggests that Astrophil's brain is sunburned not by the lady but by the surfeit of literary models he has been consulting. This is an ingenious and suggestive reading, though I think it is secondary to the more accepted one (offered by Ringler) that Stella is the sun that has parched the poet's mind.

8. The lady's dwelling in the poet's heart is a classic Petrarchan *topos*. See Lisle C. John, *The Elizabethan Sonnet Sequences* (New York: Columbia University Press, 1938), especially p. 59 and p. 196. A particularly straightforward example—unlike most of Sidney's—is Shakespeare, Sonnet 24: "Mine eye hath play'd the painter and hath steel'd / Thy beauty's form in table of my heart; / My body is the frame wherein 'tis held, . . ." (*Shakespeare's Sonnets*, ed. W. G. Ingram and Theodore Redpath [London: University of London Press, 1964]). For this *topos* in Sidney, see David Kalstone, *Sidney's Poetry* (Cambridge, Mass.: Harvard University Press, 1965), pp. 126–28.

that in his heart the poet will find himself, instead of finding the warmed-over poetic inspirations of others. The muse is urging him to write his own self, and this self is identified with the body. The idea is quite appropriate to the imagery which develops in the whole sonnet sequence, for the human body is seen as nature's real work of art. The structure of the body metaphor in this first sonnet gives the poem an unclouded happy ending. When the poet discovers that he is one with his lady, that she is present in his body, he also becomes one with himself, for his uncertainties about how to fit his words to his woe disappear. So, too, presumably does the sunburn with the cooling shower of inspiration from the lady.

Sonnet 50 repeats the corporeal terms for poetic inspiration of the first sonnet, but judges them more harshly. Here there is no more mystery about the "child" which the poet is so painfully carrying:

> *Stella,* the fullness of my thoughts of thee
> Cannot be staid within my panting breast,
> But they do swell and struggle forth of me,
> Till that in words thy figure be exprest.

[1–4]

He knows now that Stella is present in his body, but his thoughts of her have become too great to be held within his body any longer. The union of bodies here is unsatisfactory since the "infant" is vaster than the "mother." The excess is let off as poetic words, and these are equated with Stella's body, "thy figure." The words nonetheless fail to equal her body: "With sad eyes I their weake proportion see, / To portrait that which in this world is best," but this failure does not restrain the poet because his own body is too full of Stella for him to keep silent. When he tells us, "I cannot chuse but write my mind," he is in a sense uniting himself with his lady via poetry, since his mind is her body, just as his heart was her body in the first sonnet. But unlike the situation in the first sonnet, Stella's body in Astrophil's mind is not altogether satisfying: the criticism of his own poetry here suggests that her body and his mind do not do each other justice. In fact the conclusion, as in so many of the sonnets, is an endlessly repeating action, the birth and death of "those poore babes" which attempt to imitate Stella and to which the poet must again give birth because of the fullness of his thoughts. The circular pattern of the sonnet as a whole reinforces this repetition: Sidney keeps these poor babes alive (undeservedly) because on their faces is written Stella's name. The imitation of her body is thus unsatisfying.[9]

3

In our treatment so far, Sidney's use of the human body as locus for his narratives, however fanciful, has been largely literal and concrete, resulting more from the natural turn of his poetic mind than from the desire to build an allegory. But in objectifying the complexity of his own feelings and experiences, Sidney often uses the body as the vehicle for multiple metaphors. The most straightforward of his metaphoric techniques with respect to the body is that familiar functional differentiation which we have seen in all the traditions of human body allegory. Each anatomical feature is linked in some way with an external object that shares its powers. Thus in Sonnet 90, "*Stella* thinke not That I by verse seeke fame," he says of her, "Thine eyes my pride, thy lips my history." Her eyes are his pride because in them he finds rare expressions of good will to him. And her lips are his history because her few words to him form the verbal basis of his life. There is a further sense in which the body is metaphorical, since "pride" and "history" become the components of his verse in this sonnet. Consequently, Stella's eyes and lips are respectively the impulse and the articulateness of Sidney's poetry.

Another of Sidney's metaphoric techniques is the transformation of various features of the body into a composite machine. This we find in Sonnet 11, "In truth, o Love, with what a boyish kind":

9. The poetry that is compared to the lover's body is not always Sidney's own, and the process is somewhat different when he refers to other poetic representations. In Sonnet 45, "Stella oft sees the verie face of wo," Sidney compares her indifference to his pain with her tearful involvement in a fictional tragedy, and he urges her to view him as such a tragedy. Here Sidney allegorizes the face as the cover of a book which describes what is inside the man. This is an ancient trope widely used in Petrarchan poetry, again envisioning the body as a bridge between internal action and personal communication. "E 'l core ne gli occhi e ne la fronte ho scritto," says Petrarch in *Rime* 76. But Sidney goes further by suggesting a meteorological body metaphor: "my beclowded stormie face." This suggestion is continued when Stella's reaction to the fictional tragedy is seen in terms of her own bodily processes and described in meteorological terms as well: "Pitie thereof gate in her breast such place / That, from that sea deriv'd, teares' spring did flow." Her reaction, then, is appropriate and in the same metaphoric kind, but it is misplaced, since she is not in fact reacting to her lover's storms.

So when thou saw'st in Nature's cabinet
Stella, thou straight lookst babies in her eyes,
In her cheeke's pit thou didst thy pitfould set,
And in her breast bopeepe or couching lyes,
    Playing and shining in each outward part:
    But, foole, seekst not to get into her hart.

                                    [9–14]

The eyes are not the gateway for the barbs of love proceeding from lady to poet. Rather, they enable Cupid, as a boyish spirit, to enter into Stella's body and take it as his own. This identification of Stella and Cupid via the eyes is possible because the eyes are mirrors. This is true scientifically because of the anatomical mechanism of sight, physically since one can theoretically see one's reflection in another person's eyeballs, and linguistically since the eyes are *pupulae* and Cupid is a *pupulus.* But the mirror is only the beginning of the machine. By manipulation of the cheek and the breast Cupid is able to set a trap for the lover, thus differentiating the parts of Stella's body as varied parts of a machine. But as the final line indicates, the machine has more parts than Cupid is willing to tamper with, for the trap to catch the poet would not be as effective if Cupid had entered Stella's heart.

    Another metaphoric approach to the body in Sidney's sonnets makes use of a multiple onrush of metaphors for a single, otherwise simple, objective reality. This type of metaphor making, which one sees in such places as *Astrophil and Stella, The Temple,* the works of Sir Thomas Browne, and of Donne, is a fascinating study in itself. The human body is only one basis of many behind this kind of metaphor.[10] The most revealing example in Sidney with a corporeal feature as reference is Sonnet 102:

Where be those Roses gone, which sweetned so our eyes?
    Where those red cheeks, which oft with faire encrease did frame
    The height of honor in the kindly badge of shame?
Who hath the crimson weeds stolne from my morning skies?
How doth the colour vade of these vermillion dies,
    Which Nature's selfe did make, and selfe engraind the same?
    I would know by what right this palenesse overcame
That hue, whose force my hart still unto thraldome ties?
    Gallein's adoptive sonnes, who by a beaten way
    Their judgements hackney on, the fault on sicknesse lay,

10. See, for example, *Astrophil and Stella,* 79, in which the kiss is subjected to a multitude of metaphoric treatments.

> But feeling proofe makes me say they mistake it furre:
> It is but love, which makes his paper perfit white
> To write therein more fresh the story of delight,
> While beautie's reddest inke *Venus* for him doth sturre.

Instead of the multiple body whose every feature has an individual metaphoric significance, we have here a single corporeal feature allegorized with multiple significances. The complete miniature world is constructed not from the multiplicity and totality of Stella's body, but rather from the variety of reactions which a single feature calls up in Astrophil's mind.

Each of the questions which form the octave of this sonnet enables the poet to read this feature of Stella's body in terms of a different traditional allegorization. The first question, in which the cheeks "sweetned so our eyes," refers merely to visual beauty. The second treats the body as a moral exemplum: a blush in the cheeks was a sign of the indecency of the lover's proposals. The third places the cheeks in a cosmic framework, in "my morning skies," like those zodiacal or mystical diagrams in which man's body was inscribed in the cosmos. The fourth question treats the body as a work of art, a careful process of dyeing to reach the proper color. The final question sees the body as a political force, placing the lover in "thraldome." These microcosmic allegorizations continue even into the sestet, where the reference to Galenic medicine at last treats the body as the thing itself, the locus of health and sickness.

The final image, which the poem presents as the correct one, turns the tables on those that precede. Since it presents the cheeks as *tabulae rasae*, it controverts all these earlier interpretations. At the same time it fulfills the analogies of the first eight lines, since these comparisons were in fact "the story of delight" which Love, with the help of the poet, wrote in Stella's cheeks. Sidney, then, calls attention to his human body metaphor as a catchall of interpretations by presenting this onrush of possibilities.

The sonnets which combine all these metaphoric treatments of the body are often based on a narrative fable. One of the most suggestive of these fables is the account of how Love gained control of all the parts of Stella which inspire her lover, but not of her heart, which if controlled by Love would respond to the poet's pleas. This fable of course lends itself to expression by means of a multiple body metaphor, as has been suggested above in our discussion of Sonnet 11, which only makes use of the body metaphor in the last five lines. Sonnet 12 begins by seeing Stella's body as a series of machines which serve Cupid's purposes:

> *Cupid,* because thou shin'st in *Stella's* eyes,
>   That from her lockes, thy day-nets, none scapes free,
>   That those lips swell, so full of thee they bee,
>   That her sweete breath makes oft thy flames to rise,
>   That in her breast thy pap well sugred lies,
>   That her Grace gracious makes thy wrongs, that she
>   What words so ere she speakes perswades for thee,
>   That her cleare voyce lifts thy fame to the skies.

[1–8]

These lines are an interesting combination of all the techniques discussed above: functional differentiation, the machine based on cooperative working of different features of the body, and the multiple interpretation of a single image in parallel series. The machine described in the first two lines suggests a complicated and compressed metaphor. The eyes are again mirrors, as in Sonnet 11, but of a very specific kind, the sort made very brilliant in order to attract larks, who alight on the mirrors only to be trapped by the birdcatchers in nets, the technical name of which was "day-nets."[11] This image has something of that functional differentiation we saw in Sonnet 90, for the hair is not only so beautiful that it traps the lover's regard, but it is also made of netlike material and therefore resembles a literal trap.

The images which follow in the octave continue to be largely literal and functional in their metaphoric treatment of the human body. At the same time, they are not unlike the onrush of images of Sonnet 102 because they come in such a steady rhythm, and because they lead in the sestet to the same sort of ambivalence that we saw in the later sonnet. The swelling lips, the breath as bellows of Love's flames, the breasts as larder of his sweet food, and the voice as his advocate are merely separate imaginative essays rather than part of a single machine. The result, at least in the octave, is that the body is not well enough unified to be successfully differentiated. Just as the multiple object in Sonnet 102 was not so much Stella's cheeks as her lover's mind and wit perceiving them, so here the different forces that can be read into Stella's body do not stand as representation of the multiplicity of Stella so much as of the abstract and mythological powers of Cupid.

The sestet, however, alters the force of the images in the first lines:

11. Ringler, ed., *Poems,* p. 465.

> Thou countest *Stella* thine, like those whose powers
> Having got up a breach by fighting well,
> Crie, 'Victorie, this faire day all is ours.'
> O no, her heart is such a Cittadell,
>   So fortified with wit, stor'd with disdaine,
>   That to win it, is all the skill and paine.

[9–14]

Sidney here invokes the familiar tradition of the body–castle, and because this image of the body is in itself such a catchall, it partially succeeds in bringing all those powers mentioned in the octave together as part of a single machine or castle. But this citadel is made of abstract rather than bodily components ("Wit," "disdaine"), so that it does not so much join with the functional machine of the octave as stand beside it in the guise of yet another metaphoric approach to the power of love seen through Stella's multiple body.[12]

4

In order for the image of the human body to work dynamically, the poet must be at least as interested in the possibilities for multiplicity as in its ultimate unity. Indeed, the image characteristically creates a tension between fragmentation and unity. Thus in Sonnet 5, "It is most true, that eyes are form'd to serve," he postulates on the one hand an absolutely single-minded reading of the body, suggesting themes of platonic love, and on the other hand, the baser, more physical and more diverse approach to bodily beauty, "Which elements with mortall mixture breed." In the final line he acknowledges the purity and truth of single-minded Platonism but himself opts for the "Mortall mixture." Thus from here on, the analysis of *Astrophil and Stella* will be largely an inquiry into the ways in which Sidney uses the body metaphor to multiply and diversify his characters, and to establish the three basic forces which animate the sequence: the attraction of Stella, the strength of Love, and the transforming power of Astrophil's spirit.

12. Also see Sonnet 29, "Like some weake Lords, neighbored by mighty kings," another territorial metaphor of the body. Sidney creates a complete citadel which is at once the traditional Petrarchan lady and the castle of the body: "her eyes / Serve him [Love] with shot, her lips his heralds arre: / Her breasts his tents, legs his triumphall carre: / Her flesh his food, her skin his armour brave." The image of the body–castle and the discreteness of its parts emphasize the strength inherent in the union of diverse elements within Stella's spirit as imaged forth by her body.

The simplest of the traditional ways in which the body is separated into parts is the praise of the lady's beauty: the poet describes each feature in idealized terms and compares it by metaphor or simile to some wondrous thing in the cosmos outside the human body. This poetic *topos* long predates even Petrarch and continues after Sidney in English letters at least until Lord Herbert's time. Most of these are not truly microcosmic metaphors because the comparisons are not part of a consistent overall image. Petrarch, who was a master of this *topos*, unifies these descriptions of the body by including his own reactions to its various features. All the features seem to conspire together to overpower the poet in a particular way. Thus in 198, "L'aura soave al sole spiega e vibra," Laura's beauties together overthrow the poet, and in 157, "Quel sempre acerbo et onorato giorno," the force of Laura's image engraves itself in his heart and memory. These unities are not really corporeal.

Sidney makes use of a physical image which unifies the descriptive praise and gives it true microcosmic force in Sonnet 9:

> Queene *Vertue's* court, which some call *Stella's* face,
>   Prepar'd by Nature's chiefest furniture,
>   Hath his front built of Alabaster pure;
> Gold is the covering of that stately place.
> The doore by which sometimes comes forth her Grace,
>   Red Porphir is, which locke of pearle makes sure:
>   Whose porches rich (which name of cheekes endure)
> Marble mixt red and white do enterlace.
>   The windowes now through which this heav'nly guest
> Looks over the world, and can find nothing such,
> Which dare claime from those lights the name of best,
> Of touch they are that without touch doth touch,
>   Which *Cupid's* selfe from Beautie's myne did draw:
>   Of touch they are, and poore I am their straw.

This sonnet demonstrates the relations between medieval allegorical traditions and the Petrarchism of the English Renaissance. The description is strongly indebted to the tradition of the body–castle; in fact, it is a veritable précis of the House of Alma. The same three consistent levels of metaphor which we saw in Alma are present here: the "building" is sound architecturally, anatomically, and morally. In order to give the body–castle a distinct moral identity he identifies it as "Queene *Vertue's* court." This identity specifies the terms of the praise, both their objective form and their moral force. Not only is the praise unified physically by the castle image and morally by the reference to Queen Virtue, but all the descriptions are tied to precious stones, alabaster, gold, porphyry, marble, etc., which can apply to all three levels of the metaphor: they traditionally resemble the features of the face, they can literally—and in medieval times allegorically—be the materials of construction of a great palace, and they have the perfect attributes of purity, beauty, and truth for the moral description which the poem attempts to evoke. Because of all these unities Sidney's sonnet of praise succeeds rather more in unifying than in diversifying Stella's physical or spiritual image.[13]

The idealized description which is invariably the business of these sonnets of praise is not conducive to differentiation because multiplicity would limit the impression of absolute perfection always associated with oneness. For that reason the circle is the real physical counterpart for the image of these poems, not the unwieldy irregularity and diversity of the human body.[14] The body is used in its multiple guise more to suggest sheer quantity of wonders than variety. But as was suggested before, uniformity is not the most typical of Sidney's poetic intents. Almost all of the fables which Sidney reverts to in these poems, whether they are narrative, mythological, or abstract, turn around some kind of split within or between the lovers, or at least a tension between centrifugal and centripetal forces. These tensions are as close as one can come to the subject of *Astrophil and Stella*, and again and again Sidney uses the human body as their image.

The traditional Petrarchan division of the body's organs is between the heart and the eyes. Characteristically, this can be either a separation or a union. Love's beams enter through the eyes and pierce the heart so that the two can work cooperatively. On the other hand, since the heart often stands for reason even at the same time as it is the emblem of irrational love, the heart can be the stern voice of rationality or virtue opposing the pure physical attractions represented by the action of the eye. Sidney does not make nearly so much overt use of the traditional heart

13. See Shakespeare, Sonnet 53, in which the poet tells the young man "that millions of strange shadows on you tend." The paragon calls up a multitude of references in the outside world, but within himself he remains one and indivisible: "you like none, none you, for constant heart."

14. A specific case in the "First song." Each stanza is devoted to praise of Stella's features but the unifying element is the refrain, "Only in you my song begins and endeth," suggesting that the body is the circle of perfection, the ever-renewing inspiration of Sidney's verse at the same time as it is a collection of individual features upon which he can meditate.

and eye partnership as either Petrarch or Shakespeare.[15] Yet the two are
frequently coupled as if accidentally, and I think the traditional rela-
tions between these organs of a multiple body are clearly being called
up by Sidney in those sonnets where he makes reference to them.
Sidney splits the body between heart and eye for a variety of purposes
ranging from complete unanimity between them to utter fragmenta-
tion. Further, unlike Petrarch and Shakespeare, he manipulates the rela-
tions among the hearts and eyes of both lovers so that both union and
fragmentation can apply to the lovers' individual psyches, to the attrac-
tions they hold for each other, and to the progress of the affair.

The simplest use of heart and eye is as two parts of a multiple but
unified machine. They are assigned slightly different functions, but
their efforts tend in exactly the same direction. Thus in Sonnet 65,
Sidney uses the fable of Cupid as wandering beggar:

> For when, nak'd boy, thou couldst no harbour find
> In this old world, growne now so too too wise:
> I lodg'd thee in my heart, and being blind
> By Nature borne, I gave to thee mine eyes.
>   Mine eyes, my light, my heart, my life, alas.
>
> [5–9]

Here the traditional process seems to be reversed or at least altered.
Cupid's dart does not enter through the eyes, for love here is not the
result of the lady's dazzling beauty. Instead Cupid enters directly into
the heart, which stands here more as the potential seat of reason than as
the traditional emblem of love. The hearts of the inhabitants of "this
old world" are "too too wise," their forts of reason too secure to harbor
the boy.

But the poet is in a different position. Just as his heart has a double
significance—citadel of reason and emblem of love—so too do his eyes.
Their blindness works on the plane of reason: the eyes, which are tradi-
tionally the most important counselors of the king reason, have been
rendered blind, and therefore the king himself is given over to irra-
tional powers. But the eyes also function as the gate of love, for in giv-

15. Outside of *Astrophil and Stella*, the combat between heart and eye is probably the
prime Petrarchan *topos* and certainly the most common instance of human body imag-
ery. See John, *Elizabethan Sonnet*, pp. 93–95. Of the *Rime* the most interesting in this
connection are 3 ("Era il giorno ch'al sol si scoloraro," which Spenser adapted as *Amoret-
ti* 16); 39 ("Io temo sí de' begli occhi l'assalto"), and 84 ("Occhi piangete," a dialogue
of heart and eyes). For Shakespeare, see Sonnets 24, 46, and 47.

ing them over to Cupid, as the poet does in line 8, he gives up hope of their gaining the power of counselors to reason and turns them instead into slaves of love. In this guise they may learn to see, but they will only be able to see the dazzling beauty of the beloved.[16] Thus in these lines the heart and the eye are seen in two different but simultaneous relations, as the Petrarchan love machine and as the allegorical representation of man's reason.

The cooperation of heart and eye with this double allegorical significance is one of Sidney's most characteristic images for the simultaneous attraction and repulsion of the love affair. We see it also in Sonnet 5:

> It is most true, what we call *Cupid's* dart,
> An image is, which for our selves we carve;
> And, fooles, adore in temple of our hart,
> Till that good God make Church and Churchman starve.
>
> [5–8]

This sonnet, which is filled with traditional platonic categories, suggests the familiar citadel of reason in the phrase "temple of our hart" only to contrast it violently with the kind of idolatry which has actually gained possession of reason's seat.

Throughout *Astrophil and Stella* Sidney tends to make more of the eye than the heart. Consequently, tensions or separations between the two are often assigned to different allegorical aspects of the eyes with only an occasional reference to an allegorized heart. An interesting example of a delicate tension between the forces of heart and eye is Sonnet 105, which consists of an onrush of various metaphors for seeing and has only one mention—though a very telling one—of the heart:

> Unhappie sight, and hath she vanisht by
>   So neere, in so good time, so free a place?
>   Dead glasse, doost thou thy object so imbrace,
> As what my hart still sees thou canst not spie?
> I sweare by her I love and lacke, that I
>   Was not in fault, who bent thy dazling race
>   Onely unto the heav'n of *Stella's* face,
>   Counting but dust what in the way did lie.

16. Blind love is a great subject of Renaissance iconography. In the Neoplatonic system, this blindness may signify profound vision. See Erwin Panofsky, *Studies in Iconology* (New York: Oxford University Press, 1939; rpt. 1967), pp. 95–129, and Edgar Wind, *Pagan Mysteries in the Renaissance* (New Haven: Yale University Press, 1958; rpt. 1967), pp. 53–81. Also see below, chapter 5.

> But cease mine eyes, your teares do witness well
> That you, guiltlesse thereof, your Nectar mist:
> Curst be the page from whom the bad torch fell,
> Curst be the night which did your strife resist,
>   Curst be the Cochman which did drive so fast,
>   With no worse curse than absence makes me tast.

The tension in this sonnet is not between the forces of love and rationality, but rather between the powers of sense and of memory within an individual already given over to love. Something like the same distinction, though, is preserved, since the heart is the seat of pure love not necessarily bound to the experience of the senses. By concentrating on the eyes and by suggesting a contrast between the body's eye and the mind's, Sidney diversifies the whole body into physical and spiritual forces. The physical side is unsatisfying as the lady has departed from his literal sight. This departure Sidney describes in both narrative and anatomical terms: the coachman has taken her away, but the light which enabled her lover to see her has been put out as well. The abstract side, on the other hand, seems richer because his heart still retains the sight of his beloved.

Yet the emotional impetus for the poem suggests a union of heart and eye in deprivation because the tone implies that the purely abstract retention of the beloved's image is far from satisfying to the poet. He seems in fact to be castigating his body for being split between these opposites and for being unable to make the abstract concrete. The telling lines are those of the second quatrain. In the eighth line the physical process of vision is turned into a metaphor for the distance which separates people. The dust which lay between the lovers represents both Sidney's scientific version of how they saw each other and the true obstacle to their union. Thus the sensuous act of seeing is the only union possible, and at the same time it suggests the complete hopelessness of such a union. Sidney is multiplying the body by means of opposing implications of a single anatomical organ.

The real separation of forces between the heart and the eye almost invariably involves not just the poet's eyes but also communication between the two pairs of eyes, a communication which then leads to a fragmentation among anatomically expressed forces within the poet. This process can be seen in miniature in Sonnet 47:

> What, have I thus betrayed my libertie?

> Can those blacke beames such burning markes engrave
> In my free side? or am I borne a slave,
> Whose necke becomes such yoke of tyranny? . . .
> I may, I must, I can, I will, I do
> Leave following that, which is to gaine to misse.
> Let her go. Soft, but here she comes. Go to,
>   Unkind, I love you not: O me, that eye
>   Doth make my heart give to my tongue the lie.

                                                              [1–4,10–14]

The emotional impetus for this sonnet is the poet's feeling of help-
lessness, his total inability to order events or feelings as he would like
them. The black light which is shed by the lady's eye is the first and
strongest power over which he has no control; it fragments his will,
his words, and his body. The "lie" here is in fact all those traditional
truths which the poet's heart, as the seat of his reason, expresses in the
first eleven lines of the poem. Truth is turned into lies by the lady's
attractiveness, and on the corporeal level the union between the lovers'
eyes leads to a disunifying union among the organs of the poet. Her
eyes make of his heart and tongue a machine which overturns all
traditional truths.[17]

The basic fable behind the diversification and multiplication of the
self in Sidney and other Petrarchan poets is that the power of love
enters one or both of the lovers and turns them from singleness into
multiplicity. The power of love is objectified in the person of Cupid,
and the diversification is realized in terms of a multiple body. When
applied to the lady, this diversification is generally a source of strength,
as in Sidney's Sonnet 43:

> Faire eyes, sweet lips, deare heart, that foolish I
> Could hope by *Cupid's* helpe on you to pray;
> Since to himselfe he doth your gifts apply,
> As his maine force, choise sport, and easefull stay.
>   For when he will see who dare him gainesay,
>   Then with those eyes he lookes, lo by and by

---

17. In Sonnet 76, Stella's eyes are compared with the sun, and she is transformed
into a complete metereological system. As the poet, basking in this "sun," moves from
"rosie morne" to "noone," his own body is thrown into multiple confusion by an organ
of Stella's body. His dazzled eyes, short breath, long looks, etc., are the concrete cor-
poreal signs of spiritual confusion and disintegration, while the power and constancy
of Stella's allegorized body dramatize her complete self-containment. Such is the pattern
in Sidney: the more unified the image of Stella's body, the more diverse the poet's.

Each soule doth at *Love's* feet his weapon lay,
Glad if for her he give them leave to die.
   When he will play, then in her lips he is,
Where blushing red, that *Love's* selfe them doth love,
With either lip he doth the other kisse:
But when he will for quiet's sake remove
   From all the world, her heart is then his rome,
   Where well he knowes, no man to him can come.

The breakdown of love's powers into eyes that wound, lips that play, and heart that conceals and protects is a sign of strength because the diversified organs are so thoroughly united in their purpose. Love's perfect bodily machine attracts victims, leads them on, and then retires in safety. It is akin to the machines in Sonnets 9 and 29. There too the image is of Stella, with the poet a helpless victim who cannot break into the machine's perfection, so effectively does it exclude him. In this case the very syntax of the poem demonstrates the unity of diversities, for it is an example of correlative verse.[18] The trio of organs which opens the sonnet is perfectly picked up and rounded first by "maine force, choise sport, and easefull stay," and then with the symmetrical descriptions which follow.

When the corporeal diversity is applied to the poet, the power of love produces self-contradictions which weaken him. This is perhaps the most essential use of the body image in all Petrarchan poetry. As has been suggested, the poet is literally beside himself, and parts of his body are stretched concretely or abstractly beyond the physical limit possible within the bounds of sanity. Petrarch usually describes this disintegration in ornamental fables. In "Mira quel colle, o stanco cor mio vago" (*Rime*, 242), Petrarch is separated from his own heart, with which he engages in dialogue. He cannot keep his heart because it is irrecoverably given over to Laura. His disintegration is not the result of being tortured by his unrequited love, but rather a sign of the steadfastness of his affection. Indeed in the next sonnet he expresses considerable pleasure at this split between himself and his heart, since he can so readily sympathize with his heart's inexorable attraction to Laura.

For Sidney this disintegration tells more of the hopelessness than of

18. See Ringler, ed., *Poems*, p. 406. Sidney was fond of this form and used it most blatantly in the *Old Arcadia* ("This cave is dark, but it had never light"). See also *Astrophil and Stella*, 100.

the vastness of his love. The split may stand for no more than a momentary discomfort, as in Sonnet 51, when his ears are forced to listen to Stella's small talk, though

> Meane while my heart confers with *Stella's* beames,
>   And is even irkt that so sweet Comedie,
>   By such unsuted speech should hindred be.
>
> [12–14]

This sonnet perfectly juxtaposes two multiple bodies, hers strong in its unified diversity and his disintegrating. Though her tongue and eyes may tell different stories, there seems to be no problem of decorum in her mind. But the poet's ears and heart are thrown into disunity by his ardor. His ears are forced to treat the conversation as a simple social amenity, while his sight of her eyes inflames his love. The "Comedie" whose tone is broken by seriousness is not Stella's behavior, which in its own terms is perfectly consistent, but the poet's tortured interpretation of it.

The more emotional sonnets show the poet's mind and body disintegrating into a mass of contradictions. In Sonnet 19, for example, a physical image leads to a whole sequence of oppositions within Sidney's mind:

> On *Cupid's* bow how are my heart-strings bent,
>   That see my wracke, and yet embrace the same?
>   When most I glorie, then I feel most shame:
> I willing run, yet while I run repent.
> My best wits still their owne disgrace invent.
>
> [1–5]

The problem is a straightforward one: Sidney is helplessly drawn to a love that tortures and disgraces him. The opposing forces within him are matched evenly, so that there is no hope of peace.

In Sonnet 94 the same problem is described in somewhat subtler and, at the same time, more corporeal terms:

> Griefe find the words, for thou hast made my braine
>   So darke with misty vapors, which arise
>   From out thy heavy mould, that inbent eyes
> Can scarce discerne the shape of mine owne paine.
>
> [1–4]

The poet's brain is the concrete territory of reason, and his eyes, whose

job it is to perceive reason, are helpless before the "misty vapors" which
have clouded the territory. At the same time as the poet's self is ex-
tended to something like a meteorological cosmos, the ideal of the
closely unified single individual still remains. Thus when his eyes
cannot see his own misery, he is completely beside himself. The rhetoric
of the quatrain demonstrates this disintegration as forcefully as the
statement itself. Grief is the cause of the vapors, and grief is the pain
which the vapors cover. He begins the quatrain knowing his pain, and
so disintegrated is he that in four lines his own pain has clouded itself
over.

The fragmentation of the poet's self, for which the multiple body
stands as an image, leads to a kind of union with his lady. Here too the
body is an important image. In traditional Petrarchan terms, the
sonneteer may be beside himself, but since his true self is one with his
love and since he feels united with his love, he is united with himself
after all. The traditional expression of this union in corporeal terms is
the picture of the lady which is stamped on the heart of the lover: "Ma
'l bel viso leggiadro, che dipinto / Porto nel petto."[19] For most son-
neteers, this physical union is a joyous experience which compensates
for all the fragmentation of the self which the love provokes. Shake-
speare, after castigating himself for self-love, sets it right by demon-
strating that his self is in fact the Young Man: " 'Tis thee (my self)
that for myself I praise, / Painting my age with beauty of thy days."[20]

In *Astrophil and Stella* this presence of the lady within the poet is
nearly always expressed in terms of an allegorized body, and this image
tends to give the union a tentative and desperate quality. Sonnet 36 is
perhaps the best example:

> *Stella*, whence doth this new assault arise,
> A conquerd, yelden, ransackt heart to winne?
> Whereto long since, through my long battred eyes,
> Whole armies of thy beauties entred in.
>   And there long since, *Love* thy Lieutenant lies,
> My forces razde, thy banners raisd within:
> Of conquest, do not these effects suffice,
> But wilt new warre upon thine owne begin?
>   With so sweete voice, and by sweete Nature so,
> In sweetest strength, so sweetly skild withall,

19. *Rime*, 96. 5–6.
20. Sonnet 62. 13–14.

In sweete stratagems sweete Arte can show,
That not my soule, which at thy foot did fall,
   Long since forc'd by thy beames, but stone nor tree
   By Sence's priviledge, can scape from thee.

The poet's body is a battleground, not under the lively and romantic occupation of Cupid as in the traditional version ("Amor che nel penser mio vive e regna"), but rather a decimated territory with forces vastly outnumbered by the conquering army and hence hopelessly defeated: "conquerd, yelden, ransackt, . . . razde." The heart is again the main force of the poet's body, and defeat is total. Union with the lady does provide, here as in the other sonneteers, a kind of peace and wholeness within. In its defeat the poet's body is unanimous and cooperative: the eyes and heart conspired in perfect harmony. In fact it is the overthrow of reason (in the heart) which has produced this unanimity. The sonnets of personal fragmentation treat the heart as the feeble erstwhile citadel of reason, still struggling impotently against the eyes or other organs which are overcome by passion. Only once the fight is lost, as in Sonnet 36, can reason be silent and an unsatisfactory peace be proclaimed.

The peace is not unsatisfactory simply because Sidney would rather have stopped loving Stella. The pain results from the tendency of this defeat never to bring peace but merely to open the way to more fighting and more defeats. In Sonnet 36 he asks, "do not these effects suffice, / But wilt new warre upon thine own begin?" In Sonnet 40, "Since then thou hast so farre subdued me, / That in my heart I offer still to thee, / O do not let thy Temple be destroyd." In concrete terms, the cause of this recurrent battle and defeat is Stella's unwillingness either to offer a token of love or to deny it completely. This produces a paradoxical torture realized in the imagistic structure of the poems as a presence of Stella in the poet's body bringing nothing but pain. The image proclaims the fact that union in equality between the two lovers is impossible, or at best fleeting. Astrophil's body has been defeated by Cupid leading Stella's forces, i.e., the various elements of her beauty. Until she too is defeated by Cupid, until her body turns from the strong unified citadel to fragmented confusion and thence to unanimity in defeat, the lovers are unequal and hence irreconcilable.

Only when Stella's self-possession falters does this union become momentarily possible. Thus after offending her, he says, "all thy hurts in my hart's wracke I reede; / I cry thy sighs; my deere, thy teares I bleede" (93. 13–14). But even this union of their bodily functions is in the expression of pain. The hopelessness of their love, as the images of the body present it, derives from the fact that the fragmentation and union of their bodies can never quite coincide. This was apparent in Sonnet 53, where Stella's strength made him weak and Stella's weakness made him strong. The best example in terms of images realized dramatically is at the end of Sonnet 66:

> *Stella's* eyes sent to me the beames of blisse,
> Looking on me, while I lookt the other way:
>> But when mine eyes backe to their heav'n did move,
>> They fled with blush, which guiltie seem'd of love.
>
> [11–14]

Perhaps the final essential fragmentation for which the body stands as image is the split between the body itself and the spirit. In poetic terms Sidney realizes this split by juxtaposing the literal body and the fancifully allegorized body. The literal body stands for the poet's passion and the allegorical body represents the wit which is an attempt to master this passion. This is the rhetorical tension in Sonnet 73:

> And yet my Starre, because a sugred kisse
> In sport I suckt, while she asleepe did lie,
> Doth lowre, nay, chide; nay, threat for only this:
> Sweet, it was saucie *Love,* not humble I.
>> But no scuse serves, she makes her wrath appeare
>> In Beautie's throne, see now who dares come neare
> Those scarlet judges, threatning bloudy paine?
>> O heav'nly foole, thy most kisse-worthie face,
>> Anger invests with such a lovely grace,
> That Anger' selfe I needs must kisse againe.
>
> [5–14]

The poet's passion stole the kiss. He tries to separate this force from himself, calling it "Love," who earlier in the sonnet is described as "still a boy, and oft a wanton." "Humble I" is the poet who makes conceits and thus turns his passion into a series of harmless expressions. To prove his point, he goes on to invent one of these conceits. Stella's face becomes a royal court with a queen (beauty) and stern judges (the lips). But the poet trips himself up in the last line. The allegorical body which he depicts is so attractive that he must break out of the image and kiss the real body. Her lips are no longer "scarlet judges," but irresistible, real attractions. He can no longer claim that he is not responsible for the original kiss, since the wit that was supposed to master passion has rekindled it.

The same structure of thought is found in Sonnets 52 and 71, where Stella herself is arrayed on the side of virtue and the poet on the side of desire. In each case virtue and love struggle for possession of Stella's person. In 52 this struggle is overt, and it is realized conceptually rather than in terms of an allegorical body. But in 71, thirteen lines of the sonnet go to make up the image of Stella's body as the book of virtue, but this image is destroyed by the insistently sensual attraction of the body when "Desire still cries, 'give me some food.'" Thus the body comes to stand for both forces in the ultimate tension within Sidney's sonnet sequence. The poet writes in order to overcome his lust. The more wittily he writes and the more completely he transforms the brutal facts into fanciful conceits and allegories, the more he conquers the power of love. The conceits and allegories of the human body represent some of Sidney's highest poetic flights. Yet at the same time the body is the source of his lust, and the more he reads the "book" of Stella's body platonically, the more tempted he is to throw away the book and cry for food.

The Faerie Queene:
Allegory, Iconography, and the Human Body

The goal in considering the metaphor of the human body has been to
study one small chapter in the history of the imagination and its uses,
to consider one particularly fertile subject which could inform and be
informed by the habits of mind peculiar to poets of the Renaissance.
The Faerie Queene is a culminating instance of the habits of mind we
have associated with the metaphor of the body in its widest sense,
perhaps in wider senses than have been considered so far. Spenser's epic
is not basically contructed on the principles of the human body, nor
does the body—apart from a few episodes—have as much structural
relevance to the poem as to many of the works considered earlier, but
The Faerie Queene can stand at the end of this study because it demon-
strates how the traditions surrounding the metaphor of the body
penetrated consciously and unconsciously into the texture, the methods,
and the meanings of a vast poetic creation. A discussion of certain of
the poem's basic qualities will illustrate the relevance of those tradition-
al styles of thought associated with the corporeal metaphor. I shall then
proceed to a reading of three books of the poem, not proposing that the
human body is the key to all its mysteries but rather reconsidering the
narrative and the poetic texture in the light of the notion that the world
is a body and the body is a world.

1

Thus, all these fower (the which the ground-work bee
Of all the world, and of all liuing wights)

To thousand sorts of *Change* we subiect see:
Yet are they chang'd (by other wondrous slights)
Into themselves, and lose their natiue mights;
The Fire to Aire, and th'Ayre to Water sheere,
And Water into Earth: yet Water fights
With Fire, and Aire with Earth approaching neere:
Yet all are in one body, and as one appeare.

[7.7.25]

I well consider all that ye haue sayd,
And find that all things stedfastnes doe hate
And changed be: yet being rightly wayd
They are not changed from their first estate;
But by their change their being doe dilate:
And turning to themselues at length againe,
Doe worke their own perfection so by fate:
Then ouer them Change doth not rule and raigne;
But they raigne ouer change, and doe their states
maintaine.

[7.7.58]

In these stanzas from the Mutability Cantos I believe we can read many of the conscious and unconscious preoccupations of the poem. They stand first of all as a challenge and a reply: Mutability's cosmology, in which the elements are subject to constant change and discord though they are contained within one body, as opposed to Nature's cosmology, in which the very endlessness of the change is an assurance that essences are unchanging. Yet as significant as the opposition between the two points of view is the similarity of their underlying presuppositions. Both Nature and Mutability are enunciating versions of *discordia concors*. Mutability sees all the elements of creation in constant strife and yet all contained within what appears to be one body, while Nature grants the presence of change as continual discord harmonized by a god-given creative principle evident in nature's own vitality.

Each of these points of view has a long heritage, some of which has been covered in these pages. The harmonized strife of the elements as an essential cosmological principle goes back to Empedoclean influences and permeates medieval descriptions of the creation.[1] The birth of the

1. See "A Medieval Commonplace in Spenser's Cosmology," in Rosemund Tuve, *Essays*, ed. Thomas P. Roche, Jr. (Princeton: Princeton University Press, 1970), pp. 49–64.

four elements out of primordial matter was the first recognition in a platonic creation story of the inherent multiplicity of the cosmos. From that birth the elements became essential types of multiplicity, rather like the human body but with a much more abstract harmonization to balance the multiplicity. Bartholomaeus Anglicus, for instance, sees between the elements "contrariousnes and strife, by reason whereof they work togethers, and suffer, and ingender, and corrupt. . . . And elements be neuer idle: but be continually in doing & suffering: & so they neuer rest, nor cease off generation & moving."[2] Theories about the harmonization of the elements' discord vary tellingly. They tend to be abstract: based upon love, as in the Empedoclean tradition, upon mysterious "inclinations of things among theselues"[3]; or upon Neo-platonic and mystic conceptions of the One, which is God, "who forasmuch as he is one, and innumerable things of himselfe, and con-taineth them within himselfe."[4] Mutability's version of the harmoniza-tion is based less upon these systems than upon the structure and whole-ness of the body. This will be of great significance in understanding Spenser's use of the body as an image of cosmic wholeness.[5]

Nature's version of the *discordia concors* is of somewhat less concern to us because it is purely abstract. Dame Nature sees change in non-physical terms and harmonizes the change with a Neoplatonic worship of the One, in this case rather abstract, though Spenser can make the same principle palpably physical in the Garden of Adonis.[6] Nonetheless, it is important to realize that the very paradoxical quality of Dame Nature's argument itself represents a harmony of discord, an attempt to reconcile the multiplicity of creation with the unity of an essential principle. Kathleen Williams has argued this point very eloquently:

> The opposites of life and death, the elements on whose balanced conflict the universe is sustained, the circling seasons, all moving before Nature for her judgment on their meaning, gather together the implications of the pastoral cycle, the hieros

2. *Batman vppon Bartholome* (London, 1582), sig. 154r.

3. Bartholomaeus Anglicus, cited in Tuve, *Essays*, p. 53.

4. An addition to Batman's commentary credited to Henry Cornelius Agrippa, cited in Tuve, *Essays*, p. 53.

5. Marjorie Nicolson in *The Breaking of the Circle* (New York: Columbia University Press, 1962), p. 12, cites other instances in English Renaissance poetry of elemental strife at the time of the creation, e.g.: "For Hot, Cold, Moist, and Dry, four champions fierce, / Strive here for mastery, and to battle bring / Their embryon atoms" (*Paradise Lost*, 2. 897–99).

6. See below, pp. 241–44.

gamos of Venus and Adonis, and much else with which the poem has been concerned. The marriage of opposites, about which so much of Spenser's imitation has been organized, is identified with the highest of ordering powers below God himself, Nature whose authority not even Mutability dreams of questioning.[7]

The essential similarities between these versions of *discordia concors* suggest that the tensions contained within them—as well as between them—represent crucial polarities upon which the whole fabric of *The Faerie Queene* can be stretched. All of these voices belong to the poet. The poet himself is faced with unavoidable strife among all the elements of creation. He depicts this multiplicity with great artistic multiplicity, and then at the end of his life and work he is begging to be reminded that there is a harmony to the discord.

The synthesis of *discordia concors* which Spenser derives from the last cantos is itself highly mutable, for it offers little promise of stasis. Dame Nature's abstract cosmology offers a never ending process of change from essences to shadows to more shadows ultimately working their way back to essences which are no more permanent than the shadows. When we apply this process to the concrete cosmology offered by Mutability, we see a world of tense multiplicity unified by a corporeality that ultimately breaks down in the face of elemental strife and is reunited only to break down again.

In this combination of abstract and concrete unifications of diversity lies an essential fact of Spenser's poetic cosmos. In surface, structure, and meaning, *The Faerie Queene* is continuously in flux from the One to the Many and back. The poem's vision of the world is not unlike that of the single stanza in the House of Alma: an endlessly precarious, almost Sisyphean attempt to seek unity and essence in the face of multiplicity. Because of this overriding preoccupation, the poet concentrates upon methods which by their nature express unity and multiplicity at the same time. Spenser's goal is to create structures which are a bit like those mannerist paintings that depict a landscape and a face at once,[8] or like

7. *Spenser's Faerie Queene: the World of Glass* (London: Routledge, Kegan Paul, 1966), p. 231. E. Donald Elliott, Jr. has suggested to me that Spenser wrote the Mutability Cantos partly as a comment upon the unfinished state of his own work, meaning to place them at the end of the poem wherever he was forced to leave off writing it. Its unfinished condition, then, proves beyond a doubt the ravages of Mutability; and, in case he did complete twelve—or possibly twenty-four—books, he could throw away the Mutability Cantos knowing that he had defeated her.

8. I think particularly of certain works attributed to Giuseppe Arcimboldi, especially Plates 19–22a in Benno Geiger, *I Dipinti Ghiribizzosi di Giuseppe Arcimboldi*. These are

Rorschach inkblots: we look at a structure and see it as hopelessly tortured and diffuse; we blink and look again only to see it as a familiar, homely wholeness.

Two poetic methods in particular receive this Spenserian treatment: allegory and iconography. Allegory suggests at once the multiplicity of intricate analogical narratives and the unity of a hierarchic world view in which it is possible to build a poetic structure parallel to a divine or abstract structure. Iconography suggests at once the multiplicity of interpretations and the unity of the object which is being interpreted. In both cases, it seems to me, the human body offers one concrete basis for the method. For, as the whole present study has documented, the body is that quintessential construct which is at once single and multiple. Since Spenser is very much concerned with the concreteness and objectivity of his allegory and iconography, the human body stands at the nexus of his method and vision.

2

Since it is beyond the present purpose to summarize the nature of Spenserian allegory, I shall merely isolate a few features of allegory which are intended to clarify *The Faerie Queene* rather than to capture its essence. I think the point has not been made sufficiently clear by theorists that allegory almost inevitably presupposes the creation of a cosmic wholeness which is at the same time a cosmic reduction. That is, the allegorical poet gives up circumstantial *mimesis*—an imitation of the details of daily life—for a broad mimetic act much more nearly parallel to God's creation. This parallel of the artist and God is implicit in the esthetic tradition discussed above in chapter three. It forms one of the bases of Sidney's *Defence of Poesie*: "Onely the Poet . . . lifted up with the vigor of his own invention, doth grow in effect into an other nature; in making things either better than nature bringeth foorth, or quite a new, formes such as never were in nature."[9]

M. H. Abrams has called this created wholeness the "heterocosm,"

---

fantastic landscapes which become profile portraits if turned ninety degrees; or, in the case of "Homo Omnis Creatura," a landscape which in the same vertical direction is also a face.

9. *The Prose Works of Sir Philip Sidney*, ed. Albert Feuillerat (Cambridge, Eng.: Cambridge University Press, 1963), 3:8. See also my afterword.

and in regard to the Romantic Period has used it to prove that "a poem is an object-in-itself, a self-contained universe of discourse, of which we cannot demand that it be true to nature, but only, that it be true to itself."[10] In the sixteenth century, however, the heterocosm is the province of the allegorical poet, and the meanings or implications of the created world are very different. In traditional allegorical poetry, this heterocosm is created parallel to much the same image of the cosmos which has animated speculation on man or man's body as microcosm. This is implicit in many of the generalizations about allegory offered by Angus Fletcher. According to Fletcher, the allegorical cosmos is a composite system organized in a rigidly heirarchical fashion. Each individual force within the system has its own *daimon*, and this subdivision produces a cosmos which is "fractionated," but at the same time unified by its reliance upon strict hierarchy: "If nature is a composite system all parts and aspects of which are daemonically controlled, and if man acts only within such a system, the allegorical agent—whose paradigm is daemonic man—is always a division of some larger power."[11]

At the same time as the allegorical heterocosm copies the fragmentation of the macrocosm, it harmonizes the cosmos is a number of ways, both copied from the macrocosm and original to the poet. The imitative harmonization is derived from the idea of cosmic hierarchy. Fletcher points out that the Greek term *Kosmos* refers not only to "world" but also to the kind of ornamental language which represents the transformation of the real cosmos into fictive allegory. Thus *Kosmos* "signifies (1) a universe, and (2) a symbol that implies a rank in a hierarchy. As the latter it will be attached to, or associated with, or even substituted for, any object which the writer wants to place in hierarchical position."[12]

The non-hierarchical unification of cosmic fragmentation, at least as important for our consideration of Spenser, derives from the poet's own creation of wholenesses, instead of mere references to traditional cosmic wholeness. The major expression of this wholeness in allegorical poetry is the distillation of a total experience or world view into a complex poetic machine—not the humanoid machine which Fletcher

10. *The Mirror and the Lamp* (New York: Oxford University Press, 1953), p. 272.
11. Fletcher, *Allegory*, p. 60.
12. Ibid., p. 109.

describes and for which he cites Spenser's Talus and Čapek's robots—
but rather a concrete, visual machine, composite of many parts, rep-
resenting a complete experience through which the allegorical hero
must pass.[13] These two reductions of the cosmos, the hierarchical
miniature and the allegorical machine, are central to Spenser's poetic
method and closely tied to his use of the human body.

The early adventures of Artegall in Book V offer perhaps the clearest
instances of Spenser's praise for the wholeness of the cosmos, a praise
that recognizes but accepts the discord contained within the wholeness.
We can see this theme presented both by mimesis and by the use of an
allegorical machine. The allegorical core is contained in Artegall's
meeting with the Communist Giant. Like the argument between Mu-
tability and Nature this confrontation takes place between two recog-
nitions of the cosmos as *discordia concors*. The Giant plans to make peace
among the elements:

> For why, he sayd they all vnequall were,
> And had encroched vppon others share,
> Like as the sea (which plaine he shewed there)
> Had worne the earth, so did the fire the aire,
> So all the rest did others parts empaire.
>
> [5.2.32]

The speaker errs by engaging in a slavish pursuit of equalization which
repudiates the wholeness of the cosmos, since the unity of the cosmos is
inseparable from its internal discords. Weighing is not in itself wrong—
Artegall had, in fact, been taught by Astraea "to weigh both right and
wrong / In equall ballance with due recompence" (5.1.7)—but any
weighing must take into account the world as it is, full of multiplicity
and individuality.

The elements must not be harmonized and equalized,

> For at the first they all created were
> In goodly measure, by their Makers might,
> And weighed out in ballaunces so nere,
> That not a dram was missing of their right,
> The earth was in the middle centre pight,
> In which it doth immoueable abide,

13. On the connection between allegory and "machine," compare Gregory the
Great's definition: "Allegoria enim animae longe a deo positae quasi quandam machinam
facit, ut per illam levetur ad deum" (*Super Canticum Canticorum Expositio* in *Patrologia
Latina*, ed. Migne [Paris: Garnier, 1855], 97: 467).

Hemd in with waters like a wall in sight;
And they with aire, that not a drop can slide:
Al which the heauens containe, and in their courses guide.

[5.2.35]

What is most interesting for us is that in defending the *discordia concors*, Spenser tells the creation story and conceives of strife among the elements as a traditional map with four layers comprised of the four elements. By reminding us of the creation, Spenser presents the Giant as a false creator and rederives the act of creation in his own poetic terms. In resolving an abstract argument with a concrete map, he demonstrates his propensity to understand the world by reading it physically. This cosmological map depicting the harmonized strife of the elements represents one version of Spenser's mimetic heterocosm.

But Spenser's heterocosm is more than a map of the macrocosm with layers of earth, water, air, and fire. Despite Rosemary Freeman's feeling that in this episode "the literal–physical and the spiritual–conceptual do not conform satisfactorily with each other,"[14] it seems to me that the praise of wholeness here is imaged forth with a remarkably rich poetic machinery. The balance is itself a Spenserian allegorical machine, compact and unified but at the same time suggesting the world's multiplicity. It epitomizes the whole esthetic tradition in which the world can be grasped by proportional reduction. The Giant's misuse of the scale casts doubt upon systematic microcosmic reduction,[15] but the image of equality which the scale conveys, while incorrect as applied by the Giant, is a perfect expression of God's impartiality to His creatures:

All creatures must obey the voice of the most hie.
They liue, they die, like as he doth ordaine,
Ne euer any asketh reason why.
The hils doe not the lowly dales disdaine;
The dales doe not the lofty hils enuy.
He maketh Kings to sit in souerainty;
He maketh subiects to their powre obay
He pulleth downe, he setteth vp on hy;
He giues to this, from that he takes away.
For all we haue is his: what he list doe, he may.

[5.2.40–41]

14. *The Faerie Queene: a Companion for Readers* (Berkeley: University of California Press, 1970), p. 270.

15. Compare the criticism of measurement which Spenser echoes from Isaiah 40:12, "Who hath measured the waters in the hollow of his hand and meted out heaven with the span. . . ."

The scale is a machine which typifies the concepts of unity offered by the platonic or Neoplatonic image of the One,[16] and also those offered by the organic view of the State. At the same time, the differences among these terms which God loves so equally are imaged forth in the scale's potential for inequality and, at least in the stanza above, they have much in common with that physical *discordia concors* in the fable of the belly.

If Spenserian allegory is based partly upon the creation of microcosms and cosmic machines, two adventures which frame that of the Giant will illustrate the technique more cosmologically and more corporeally. The dispute between Amidas and Bracidas objectifies and dramatizes the differing views of *discordia concors* which separated Artegall and the Giant. Only a circumstantial, man-made equality could assign identical islands and seemingly identical brides to the two brothers. The sea, like the balance scale, destroys this trivial equality by eroding Bracidas's island in favor of Amidas's at the same time as it switches the brides and bestows Philtera's treasure upon Lucy. This apparent destruction of equality cannot be undone—the inexorability of the erosion is a concrete response to the social theory offered by the Communist Giant—but this natural action creates a new and deeper equality. As Kathleen Williams expresses it, "Amidas has the land and the avaricious Philtera, Bracidas the treasure and Lucy: each of the four is more suitably matched and more justly served, than in the days when the islands were equal."[17] The tale is another Spenserian heterocosm, a miniature myth of the creation. For the whole world is just such a mass of multiple inequalities as characterize the final fate of the two brothers: geographically the world is made of large islands and small, and economically, the world is made of those with treasure and those without. When Spenser demonstrates the deeper natural equality among this apparent multiplicity, he is reviewing, and affirming, the creation with all its harmonized discords.

The dispute between Sanglier and the squire turns on the same issue of false equality opposed to the true, though Spenser is here defying the social hierarchy which he seems to support so single-mindedly in Book V. Sanglier stands with the Giant and Amidas as an exponent of illusory

16. This is reminiscent of the "scientific" or second degree of contemplation discussed in chapter 3, which saw the world in tension between the variety of created nature and the unity of the divine creating spirit. See above, pp. 119–21.

17. Williams, *Spenser's Faerie Queene*, p. 187.

equality. Sanglier's knightly station leads him to assume that he is worthy of the fairer maid, who happens to be in the possession of the squire. When Artegall calls him to account for this and for the murder of his own lady, he gives Sanglier the choice which Solomon offered the two mothers, an opportunity designed by the hero to give Sanglier's notions of equality full play:

> Sith then (sayd he) ye both the dead deny,
>   And both the liuing Lady claime your right,
>   Let both the dead and liuing equally
>   Deuided be betwixt you here in sight,
>   And each of either take his share aright.

[5.1.26]

Artegall is suggesting—ironically, of course—that since the abstract issue seems so equal and unresolvable, the booty must itself be divided equally. Further, since the exponent of equality has already divided one lady in two parts, why not continue the process and divide the second lady?

The reader and the squire recognize that this argument is absurd. Erosion cannot be undone, mountains cannot be weighed in a balance and equalized with valleys: these are natural, physical wholenesses which must be accepted as they are. By the same token, the human body is a natural, physical wholeness—traditionally parallel with the cosmos and with society—and it cannot be "equalized" by being sliced in half. The disputants get what they deserve: the squire, who accepts life even with the potential pain of losing his lady, gets her, and Sanglier, who demands "equality," must carry half of a lady with him. The episode is important because it illustrates that Spenser's allegorical concern with microcosmic wholenesses can center on the traditional microcosm, the human body. As we shall see, the image of the body is often realized much more fully than in these scant references. Yet the striking parallels among these three episodes in Book V demonstrate that Spenser's allegorical method is consistently microcosmic and that cosmology, society, and personality—all of which are being "weighed" in these cantos—can be contained and unified in such poetic machines as that offered by the body.

The Book of Justice being what it is, the poet is never very specific about the elements of his *discordia concors* (significantly he relies upon the traditional and unrevealing earth, air, fire, and water), and the allegorical vehicles, e.g., balance scale, islands, human body, are not endowed with the fullest range of concreteness and complexity. But we have already seen in the House of Alma that Spenser allegorizes an abstraction like temperance by creating a multiple heterocosm—in this case the corporeal microcosm—which defines the abstraction through a multiplicity of independent yet interrelated actions. These multiple actions resemble the parts of a machine rendering the original abstraction precarious but at the same time vivid and dynamic. The richness of Spenserian allegory inheres in this recognition that abstractions are multiple and can be subdivided. His poetic means of conveying this richness consists of creating multiple allegorical vehicles which are diverse in their parts but unified by their external shape and place in the narrative. In this, they resemble the picture of man presented by the House of Alma. The body, with its internal diversity and external unity, is a natural image for such an expression.

The House of Alma is exceptionally explicit in its treatment of the body, but a few other examples of corporeal allegorization will illustrate the deeper penetration of corporeal metaphors into Spenser's work. Guyon's adventures take him from outward examples back to sources—such is the movement of the whole book from Amavia to Acrasia—and if temperance has its obvious corporeal source in Alma, so too does the book contain corporeal sources of intemperance. The Cave of Mammon exemplifies Spenser's imaginative propensity for wholeness in the image of a machine which at least borrows the form of the human body. The description of the sources of cupidity illustrates the definition of an abstraction by means of cosmos and microcosm:

> Then gan a cursed hand the quiet wombe
>   Of his great Grandmother with steele to wound,
>   And the hid treasures in her sacred tombe,
>   With Sacriledge to dig. Therein he found
>   Fountaines of gold and siluer to abound,
>   Of which the matter of his huge desire
>   And pompous pride eftsoones he did compound;
>   Then auarice gan through his veines inspire
> His greedy flames, and kindled life-deuouring fire.

[2.7.17]

The stanza defines avarice historically. The poet begins with an anthropomorphic Grandmother Earth, one of whose non-human attributes is the containment of gold and silver. The first greedy man destroys the earth's natural wholeness by digging for the gold and silver. In imagistic terms the destruction penetrates further when the gold and silver are added to his own anatomy. Spenser uses the alchemical term "compound" so as to bridge the gap not only between earth and human body but also between concrete and abstract. In this new, postlapsarian human anatomy, gold is contained in the body and becomes the "matter" of desire and pride. Avarice is finally the product of all these forces, concrete, abstract, terrestrial, and corporeal. Once gold and silver are metaphorically flowing in the circulatory system, then avarice can literally flow and produce flames and fire. The image moves from an anthropomorphic cosmos to a cosmomorphic human body.

From this human body of avarice, whose veins flow with fire, it is a short step to seeing Mammon's Cave as the literal picture of an avaricious man's internal anatomy and psychology. The refinement of the gold is one of Spenser's great allegorical machines:

> One with great bellowes gathered filling aire,
>   And with forst wind the fewell did inflame;
>   Another did the dying bronds repaire
>   With yron toungs, and sprinckled oft the same
>   With liquid waues, fiers *Vulcans* rage to tame,
>   Who maistring them, renewd his former heat;
>   Some scumd the drosse, that from the metall came;
>   Some stird the molten owre with ladles great;
> And euery one did swincke, and euery one did sweat.
>
> [2.7.36]

The current which runs this machine is clearly the "greedy flames" and "life-deuouring fire" that the first greedy man assumed into his anatomy, and the process of refinement involves the same transformation. While this machine is not specifically anthropomorphic, the description is parallel to that of Alma, and its complexity and tension mirror the internal state of the intemperate man.[18] Like the inkblot, the image is at once of a unified wholeness acting in an evil enterprise and of a multitude of component parts each behaving differently. This is

18. Compare the allegorical body machine describing Acrasia's effect upon Verdant in the Bower of Bliss: "And all that while, right ouer him she hong, / With her false eyes fast fixed in his sight, / As seeking medicine, whence she was stong, / Or greedily depasturing delight: / And oft inclining downe with kisses light, / For feare of waking him, his lips bedewd, / And through his humid eyes did sucke his spright, / Quite molten into lust and pleasure lewd; / Wherewith she sighed oft, as if his case she rewd" (2.12.73).

true of the earth that contains the gold, of Mammon's machine, and of the human body.

Spenser's definition of courtesy offers exceptionally interesting examples of his use of the body as an allegorical wholeness. The drive of the Many toward the One becomes increasingly insistent in the last half of *The Faerie Queene*. Of all the virtues depicted in the books, courtesy is the most internalized, for the characters of Book VI are continually reminded that they must look in themselves for strength and virtue. In keeping with this emphasis, Spenser abandons overt cosmology—there is no equivalent of the *discordia concors* in the Temple of Venus or the sense of Justice as cosmic organizing principle—and concentrates more upon what might be called micro-cosmology.

The book's central moral lesson, the Hermit's speech to Timias and Serena, goes no further than the human body in its vision of total harmony:

> For in your selfe your onely helpe doth lie,
>   To heale your selues, and must proceed alone
>   From your owne will, to cure your maladie.
>   Who can him cure, that will be cur'd of none?
>   If therefore health ye seeke, obserue this one.
>   First learne your outward sences to refraine
>   From things, that stirre vp fraile affection;
>   Your eies, your eares, your tongue, your talk restraine
> From that they most affect, and in due termes containe.
>
> For from those outward sences ill affected,
>   The seede of all this euill first doth spring,
>   Which at the first before it had infected,
>   Mote easie be supprest with little thing:
>   But being growen strong, it forth doth bring
>   Sorrow, and anguish, and impatient paine
>   In th' inner parts, and lastly scattering
>   Contagious poyson close through euery vaine,
> It neuer rests, till it haue wrought his finall bane.
>
> [6.6.7–8]

The hermit is telling the story of man's fall *sub specie corporis humani*. The anatomical process beginning with the outward senses and proceeding thence to the more serious realm of the inner parts exemplifies Spenser's propensity for wholeness and for concrete, visualizable allegorization. The anatomy here is equivalent to a map of the cosmos created perfect and yet ready to fall. As we saw in *Astrophil and Stella*, the body is at once the metaphoric image of God's cosmic wholeness and also a specific and unique part of creation, one which is literally very susceptible to immoral disorder. By locating the cosmology in the body, Spenser here reminds us of the actual link between micro- cosm and macrocosm: the misuse of the outward senses is the germ of that disease which, in the Fall, poisoned both the body of a man and the body of the world.

Courtesy is the highest of virtues within this personal microcosm, and Spenser recurrently describes it as an animating, life-giving force within the bodily machine:

> For his exceeding courtesie, that pearst
> Her stubborne hart with inward deepe effect.
>
> [6.1.45]

> That well in courteous *Calidore* appeares,
>   Whose euery deed and word, that he did say,
>   Was like enchantment, that through both the eyes,
>   And both the eares did steale the hart away.
>
> [6.2.3]

The body, which can be fragmented and poisoned by the Fall, becomes a unified allegorical machine when the outward senses are confronted with courtesy. In the personal world of Book VI, courtesy restores the wholeness to the cosmology and to Spenser's allegorical images.

3

If a major component of Spenserian allegory is the image of whole- ness, an equally strong vector is a fragmentation of the wholeness into a multitude of component parts and possible interpretations. We are speaking here of two complementary kinds of multiplicity: the in- herent complexity of the image and the variety of objects or abstrac- tions which it depicts. Both belong very properly to the domain of Renaissance iconographical imagination. Allegory and iconography are complementary uses of the imagination. In each case a partly hidden abstraction generates objective images or stories. In allegory the imaginative movement tends toward the perception of the abstract core, while in iconography it tends toward the variety and objectivity offered by the concrete images. In *The Faerie Queene*, the flow from intricate idea simply allegorized to simple idea rendered with intricate iconography is endless and circular.[19]

According to C. S. Lewis,[20] the essential feature of the iconographic imagination is a transformation of the One into the Many. The ideal is *multum in parvo*, a phrase which can refer at once to multiple images (e.g., the four ladies attending Queen Perfection in the masque contained in *Cynthia's Revels*) and to simpler images which are loaded with varieties of traditional wisdom (e.g., the paintings of Botticelli). In much the same way Spenser takes simple ideas and enriches them through the use of multiple images which become the vehicles for multiple interpretations.[21] In this technique Spenser is an orthodox Neoplatonist. As we saw in the first chapter, Pico identifies human nature with multiplicity in *De Hominis Dignitate*. Since man has no such fixed position as do angels or beasts, he can share all their qualities. Through the experience of this multiplicity the individual can discover the One, and only by believing in the ultimate One can the experience of the Many be meaningful. Man is the chameleon, while God, according to Ficino in his commentary on Plotinus, "has knowledge of things not by a multiplicity of thoughts about an object, but by a simple and firm grasp of its essence."[22] Spenser's iconographic imagination is constantly attempting to reach the One via the esthetic experience of the Many.

The human body, as an essential image of *multum in parvo*, is central to the iconography of *The Faerie Queene*. In its simplest use the body is a subject for Spenser's descriptive iconography. This approach makes use of a relatively straightforward image of the body interpreted in a

19. Compare Edgar Wind's discussion of allegory (*Pagan Mysteries*, pp. 26–27): "If allegory were only what it is reputed to be—an artifice by which a set of ideas are attached, one by one, to a set of images—it would be difficult to account for its nefarious use. Since there is little demand for repeating the simple, and no advantage in doubling the complicated, an image designed to duplicate a thought should be either superfluous or distracting. But persuasive allegory does not duplicate. If a thought is intricate and difficult to follow, it needs to be fastened to a transparent image from which it may derive a borrowed simplicity. On the other hand, if an idea is plain there is an advantage in tracing it through a rich design which may help to disguise its bareness."

20. *Spenser's Images of Life*, ed. Alastair Fowler (Cambridge, Eng.: Cambridge University Press, 1967), pp. 6–11.

21. Compare Angus Fletcher's discussion of how the allegorical hero generates sub-characters, in *Allegory*, pp. 35–41.

22. Cited in Wind, *Pagan Mysteries*, p. 207.

multitude of ways. This is rather like the sonnet of descriptive praise which we met in *Astrophil and Stella*. Belphoebe, for instance, appears in Book II having little connection with the narrative, standing almost purely as an iconographic emblem. In contrast to Alma's earthly body, Belphoebe's is viewed and iconographically interpreted on a cosmic plan. Because she is chaste and beautiful, her body is a microcosm of heaven. Her face is of the angels "Cleare as the skie, withouten blame or blot" (2. 3. 22). Her eyes are God's light, too brilliant to be subjected to wanton love, "For with dredd Maiestie, and awfull ire, / She broke his wanton darts" (2. 3. 23). But her forehead is the seat of triumphant love, whose "good and honour might therein be red: / For there their dwelling was" (2. 3. 24). Her voice is heavenly music, and her eyelids are the abode of graces and of grace. She is herself a temple of the gods, for her legs are "Like two faire marble pillours . . . / Which doe the temple of the Gods support" (2. 3. 28). She is also an epitome of nature: her breasts are like "young fruit in May" and "whether art it were, or heedless hap, / As through the flouring forrest rash she fled, / In her rude haires sweet flowres themselues did lap, / And flourishing fresh leaues and blossoms did enwrap" (2. 3. 30).

This description of a character who has no further role to play in Book II serves to inscribe the perfect human body in a figurative circle of the cosmos. The multiplicity of the description equates Belphoebe with the cosmos in much the same way that Pico equates *homo chamaeleon* with the cosmos: since man, and in this case man's body, can imitate the variety of the cosmos, he must be its epitome and center.

But richer in implication and more characteristic of Spenser's poetic iconography than the descriptive praise is the creation of multiple, partly independent bodies which are tied to each other and yet whose differences cover worlds of diversity. Spenser draws upon the fact that the human body has the power to reproduce itself. He can thus depict multiplicity in the literal regeneration of the human body at the same time as he derives unity from the oneness implied in the reproductive act. Alternatively, he can create a poetic self-regeneration of the human body.

The myriad groups of similar characters with similar names which so often subdivide and enrich a simple abstract concept, are related not only by their parentage but also by a kind of symbiosis among their physical forms. The human body is essential to this poetic technique because of another of its essential paradoxes: it is identical from man to man, as the generality of Alma demonstrates, and at the same time it is the basic image of each man's individuality. Groups of characters like Malecasta's six courtly knights are at once separate individuals typifying different aspects of the overall abstraction and also different aspects of a single individual. This individual is undergoing that metamorphosis which, in the Neoplatonic scheme, is necessary for the ultimate discovery of one's identity in the most literal sense of that word. The god Proteus, whose metamorphoses are purely corporeal, is the image of human multiplicity in the Neoplatonic system because identity is inextricable from physical form. Thus Proteus is at once the changeable, individual man of Spenser's Book III and also—to the mythographers—an image of nature in all her multiplicity.[23] The metamorphoses of Proteus, which render his body microcosmic, are parallel in style and content to the poet's transformation of such concepts as courtly love, Venus, or slander, into groups of characters who are shadows of each other.

Spenser's treatment of the three Graces offers perhaps the richest demonstration of his participation in the iconographic tradition. The dance of the Graces on Acidale seems in many ways the most essential of all the allegorical centers in the poem. One cannot help draw the conclusion that Spenser knew as he wrote it that he was reaching the climactic end of his poem, just as the speeches of Prospero force us to think of Shakespeare as viewing the close of his creative life. In Neoplatonic mythography, the three Graces represent a quintessential image of the flow from the One to the Many and back. The simplest expression of this flow is the moral interpretation of the Graces, for in a variety of ways they were made to represent the offerings of bounty which we make and those which we get in return.[24]

23. Thomas P. Roche, Jr., in *The Kindly Flame* (Princeton: Princeton University Press, 1964), p. 160, cites Proclus on Proteus: "In se complectentem omnes rerum formas in mundo genitarum." See also A. Bartlett Giamatti, "Proteus Unbound: Some Versions of the Sea God in the Renaissance," in *The Disciplines of Criticism*, ed. Peter Demetz, Thomas Greene, and Lowry Nelson, Jr. (New Haven: Yale University Press, 1968), pp. 437–77.

24. The standard positions of the Graces—two standing face front and the center one back to us but face in profile—were variously interpreted. Seneca, in *De Beneficiis*, 1.3, interprets the picture as meaning that men ought to be generous in giving, thankful, and generous in return, while Servius (*In Vergilii Aeneidem*, 1.720) sees it as a two part motion, "because for one benefit issuing from us two are supposed to return." (Wind, *Pagan Mysteries*, pp. 28–35.)

A more interesting, and a complementary, derivation of the universal flow is to be found in the cosmic interpretation of the Graces. The Graces were, in Panofsky's words, "thought of as qualifications of the entity that was Venus."[25] This relationship is important both for the cosmic meanings of a three-in-one Venus and for the philosophic and poetic presuppositions of the trinitarian concept itself. The cosmic meaning of Venus and the Graces begins to be clear when we realize that the flow of bounty which they symbolized was a kind of universal organizing principle, as Edgar Wind has explained:

> All we must remember is that the bounty bestowed by the gods upon lower beings was conceived by the Neoplatonists as a kind of overflowing (*emanatio*), which produced a vivifying rapture or conversion (called by Ficino *conversio*, *raptio*, or *vivificatio*) whereby the lower beings were drawn back to heaven and rejoined the gods (*remeatio*). The munificence of the gods having thus been unfolded in the triple rhythm of *emanatio*, *raptio*, *remeatio*, it was possible to recognize in this sequence the divine model of what Seneca had defined as the circle of grace: giving, accepting, and returning.[26]

Further, since love was the essential medium of this flow from the gods, to men, back to the gods, the subdividing and reuniting of Venus becomes the kernel of the whole system. Ficino in his *Commentary on Plato's Symposium* sees Venus as a cosmic model, the *machinae membra*, whose parts "are bound to each other by a certain mutual affection so that it may justly be said that love is a perpetual knot and binder of the world."[27] It has already been suggested how Spenser's imagination fixed upon cosmic models in the image of the *machinae membra*; and I think this iconographic cosmology is central to the scene on Acidale.

But the method of the Graces' union with Venus is as important as its meanings. Neoplatonic mythography was animated by the desire to discover cryptic and hidden branches of knowledge, particularly those which demonstrated that apparent opposites were united and apparent unities were separable into opposites. Thus the mythographers derived pleasure from such non-classical hybridizations as Venus–Diana or Hermathena and thus they could subdivide a unity like Venus into *emanatio*, *raptio*, and *remeatio* or *amor*, *pulchritudo*, and *voluptas*. Their interest in hidden knowledge led them to understand these subcategories as infolded in the unity of Venus.

25. *Studies in Iconology*, p. 168.
26. Wind, *Pagan Mysteries*, pp. 37–38.
27. Ficino, *Commentary on Plato's Symposium*, trans. Sears Jayne (Columbia: University of Missouri, 1944), p. 152.

The invention or the allegorization of the three Graces then unfolds the richness and multiplicity embedded in the One. Wind explains this process in terms that apply with startling accuracy to Spenser's technique:

When the Venus–Virgo becomes "unfolded" in the three Graces, as we have seen, each Grace represents a less "complicated" state of mind than the "infolded" Venus from whom they descend. Theoretically, the process of explication could be continued indefinitely: and the farther it proceeds, the plainer are the elements obtained. But so long as the elements remain interdependent, they all partake of each other's nature, and pure externality is never reached.[28]

The subdivision of a large abstraction into elements which are partly independent and partly interdependent is a keystone of Spenser's poetics. His treatment of the Graces demonstrates these abstract relationships and begins to suggest how the human body could realize this curious combination of separation and union.

In many respects the scene on Acidale merely summarizes the tradition as described above. Like Ficino's *machinae membra*, the Graces are the model of a cosmos whose currency is bounty and love, and hence they together infold the mysteries of the unified Venus: "Those three to men all gifts of grace do graunt, / And all, that *Venus* in her selfe doth vaunt, / Is borrowed of them" (6. 10. 15). Colin Clout's gloss of the Graces is classic iconography whose content is Neoplatonic and whose method is Panofskian:

> Therefore they alwaies smoothly seeme to smile,
>   That we likewise should mylde and gentle be,
>   And also naked are, that without guile
>   Or false dissemblaunce all them plaine may see
>   Simple and true from couert malice free:
>   And eeke them selues so in their daunce they bore,
>   That two of them still froward seem'd to bee,
>   But one still towards shew'd her selfe afore;
> That good should from vs goe, then come in greater store.
>
> [6.10.24]

The human body is used in its simplest visual sense here, as an iconographic emblem to be read morally.

Spenser's more individualistic and imaginative treatment of the iconographic tradition shows itself largely in the realm of the relationship among the Graces and between their diversity and the unities which they encompass. Spenser suggests visually that the Graces are

28. Wind, *Pagan Mysteries*, p. 205.

independent yet totally and harmoniously linked with each other by means of their own forms and the shapes which their movement creates. The whole passage seems to be creating and annihilating forms, suggesting independent elements of perfection ("Diuine resemblance, beauty soueraine rare, / Firme Chastity, that spight ne blemish dare" [6.10.27]), and destroying independence in a whirl of dance, circularity, and repetition.[29]

The circle and the dance are, of course, traditional parts of the iconographic subject, but Spenser emphasizes the unity and perfection of the form and the interdependence of the figures within it so as to reestablish the imagistic contact of the Graces with the whole cosmic dance. Once the image of the whole cosmic dance is suggested, the combination of independence and interdependence of the figures within it comes to express the tension between the inexorability of cosmic harmony and the fragility of human order. The familiar imagery and theme we saw in the House of Alma are repeated in the relation between the perfect circles of the dance and the linear intrusion of Calidore which breaks it. The human forms within the dance are significant not so much because of specific anthropomorphism as because they are capable either of fitting together to produce a perfect circle, or of diversifying and disappearing.

Spenser's treatment of the Neoplatonic concept of infolding and unfolding demonstrates his use of iconography especially clearly. The allegorical poet, as Angus Fletcher points out, breaks up large abstractions by causing his characters to generate individualistic subtypes of themselves. This description characterizes the whole tradition of the trinitarian Venus, both in Spenser and before. When Spenser creates the figure of Colin Clout's lady in the middle of the Graces, he alters and elaborates the whole process by returning from the Many to the One and returning to rather a different One from that with which he began. The rhetorical process begins with Venus, who is perfection,

29. Compare Harry Berger's description in "A Secret Discipline: *The Faerie Queene* Book VI" in *Form and Convention in the Poetry of Edmund Spenser*, ed. William Nelson (New York: Columbia University Press, 1967), p. 67: "In this great passage there is not only the circling of thoughts which unites the parts of time, but the circling of words in rhythmic repetition, echoing and reechoing, as they imitate the movement of the figures around a center beyond the reach of language; and at the same time the rising and cresting of vision as it moves from the dale to Ariadne's crown, then returns to Colin, Rosalind, and Calidore only to ascend once more, in Colin's explication, to the Sun of the world."

continues through the multiplicity of the Graces and maidens "Whose sundry parts were here too long to tell," and ends with a reunification in the person of the shepherdess standing at the midpoint of all the circles. The links among these similar forms are less corporeal than linguistic, revolving around multiple use of the word "grace." The shepherdess is a fourth Grace, but she is also a summation of all possible graces and hence a summation or reunion of the three Graces: "Another Grace she well deserues to be, / In whom so many Graces gathered are" (6.10.27). Thus as a return to the One, Colin's shepherdess is Venus. But Spenser elaborates on the Neoplatonic One-Many-One process by effecting a metamorphosis in the One. In transforming Venus into Colin's lady, he is giving new life and new familiarity to an abstraction and bringing it closer to the locus of Book VI, the interior of the mind.

Spenser's version of the tripartite process personalizes the Neoplatonic system. He begins with a Venus who is a perfection of beauty and love, diversifies her into the three Graces who represent that cosmic love defined by the triple *emanatio, raptio,* and *remeatio,* and reunites her in the figure of poetic inspiration as personified in Colin's shepherdess. In this process, Spenser redefines love as poetry. All the multiplicity of figures in Spenser's own narrative seems now to be only the middle term in a Neoplatonic movement from cosmic love back to a version of cosmic love which is completely internalized and definable only as poetry. This is the quintessential Spenserian method, and though the human body is only very obliquely the means of movement from the One to the Many and back, still the style of movement is so epitomized here it can be applied to the more corporeal instances of Spenser's imagination.

Before passing on to more detailed consideration of that multiplicity of narrative, it is worth mentioning that at one point in Book VI the Blatant Beast experiences an infolding and unfolding which, despite the unconventionality of the icon, are in the mythographic tradition and rather closer than the three Graces to the style of the whole poem. The beast has as many different significations as there are individuals menaced by him, but in the case of Timias at least, the beast is very clearly an infolding of three qualities:

> Three mightie enemies did him most dispight,
> Three mightie ones, and cruell minded eeke,

> That him not onely sought by open might
> To ouerthrow, but to supplant by slight.
> The first of them by name was cald *Despetto*,
> Exceeding all the rest in powre and hight;
> The second not so strong but wise, *Decetto*;
> The third nor strong nor wise, but spightfullest *Defetto*.

[6.5.13]

When we are told that "The *Blatant Beast* the fittest meanes they found
/ To work his vtter shame, and throughly him confound" (6. 5. 14), it
becomes clear that the beast is a trinity infecting the world with despite,
deceit, and defeat. Like the Graces, they are an iconographic subject
which can be read visually:

> But most of all *Defetto* him annoyde,
> Creeping behinde him still to haue destroyde:
> So did *Decetto* eke him circumuent,
> But stout *Despetto* in his greater pryde,
> Did front him face to face against him bent.

[6.5.20]

Spenser goes further here than with the Graces in specifying the ways
in which the trinity is a physical machine of separate parts still depen-
dent upon each other and upon the unity which they unfold:

> Oftimes their sundry powres they did employ,
> And seuerall deceipts, but all in vaine:
> For neither they by force could him destroy,
> Ne yet entrap in treasons subtill traine.
> Therefore conspiring all together plaine,
> They did their counsels now in one compound.

[6.5.14]

The three-part movement from the One to the Many to the One
progresses in this case from the Blatant Beast through the Despetto
group back to Timias himself, for his wound acts as a summation of
his whole earlier experiencing of gaining, losing, and regaining the love
of Belphoebe. In building this triple machine, Spenser suggests that the
Blatant Beast is itself a composite body made up of three interdepen-
dent human bodies.[30] Just as the Despetto group is physically inter-

---

30. The Beast is characteristically seen as multiple, particularly in respect to tongues,
which are its major weapon. In Canto One, it "did seeme a thousand tongues to haue, /
That all in spight and malice did agree" (6.1.9), and in Canto Twelve, "therein were a
thousand tongs empight, / Of sundry kindes, and sundry quality" (6.12.27).

nalized within the Blatant Beast in its inception, it seems internalized within Timias spiritually in its effect, once the beast has bitten the squire. In this little icon, then, we can see a remarkable number of Spenser's preoccupations: the wholeness or machine which creates an allegorical heterocosm; the iconographic subject which infolds a multiplicity of qualities and then unfolds them; the creation of bodies which are part independent and part interdependent; above all, the simultaneous vision of the Many and the One.

4

The present chapter will concentrate upon a reading of Books I, III, and IV of the poem, the books which offer the greatest range and interest for the subject of the human body as cosmic model and iconographic subject. In the Book of Holiness, the quest is largely internal, so that multiplicity and unity are to be found within the bodies of the hero, his friends, and his adversaries. In the Book of Chastity the multiplicity of the body is that provided by love, either in terms of the womb's fruition or the mind's fancies. In the Book of Friendship, the pattern is reversed: a multiple, or more specifically, double, world is struggling to be united in one body in the act of love.

The Book of Holiness is at once the most physical and most psychological of the quests. Red Cross journeys through the multiplicity of the fallen world in order to find a Oneness that represents at the same time his own knightly force, his native virtue, and his mission of salvation. The multiplicity of evil is produced by the evil powers' ability to multiply and diversify the human body, and this in turn produces within Red Cross a psychological multiplicity that disables him from discovering his Oneness. But through the very completeness with which he experiences the multiple evil, as in the Neoplatonic scheme, and through the unified multiplicity of the good powers, Red Cross is capable of discovering the One in all its fullness, and at the very end he learns to diversify and multiply that One within himself. The hero's psychological action consists of seeing in the corporeal diversification produced by Archimago and Duessa the unfolding of evil's fullness and range. So long as he believes in the truth and independence of each illusory corporeal form, he is blind to the unfolding process, and so long as he adapts to these various forms, his own self diversifies to match them in multiplicity and in error. This unfolding of evil can only be infolded into a unified good by means of multiple images of good which unfold holiness for the spiritual instruction of the hero.

The essential power of evil in the first several cantos of Book I is the power of error, for Error herself stands as both an introduction to and a summation of the hero's experience in combating all the uncertainties of the "wandring wood." This battle with Error, which opens the poem, demonstrates how the multiple body of evil captures Red Cross into its own fragmentation. Error is a beast made of several diversified parts and often described in multiple terms: "Halfe like a serpent horribly displaide, / But th'other halfe did womans shape retaine / Most lothsom, filthie, foule, and full of vile disdaine" (1. 1. 14). Error's body multiplies in two separate ways. She has "a thousand yong ones, which she dayly fed, / Sucking vpon her poisonous dugs, eachone / Of sundry shapes, yet all ill fauored" (1. 1. 15); and in the course of the fight "she spewd out of her filthy maw / A floud of poyson. . .   . Her vomit full of bookes and papers was, / With loathly frogs and toades, which eyes did lacke" (1. 1. 20). By multiplying the monster's body, Spenser differentiates the abstract forces of Error, represented by her thousand children, from concrete errors of man, represented by her vomit full of books and papers. The monster's body, then, is a cosmic model depicting the wholeness of error, but it also contains diversified parts (e.g., abstract forces, books and papers, mother, children) whose discords can destroy each other from the inside in the battle with the hero.

The confrontation of Red Cross and Error epitomizes in emblematic terms his relations with the multiple evils of his quest. At first he and his adversary are complete opposites. He is purity, singleness, and light; she is corruption, multiplicity, and darkness. "His glistering armor made / A litle glooming light" in her cave, and "light she hated as the deadly bale." Then the Many overcomes the One to the extent that he is no longer separate from her:

> Tho wrapping vp her wrethed sterne arownd,
> Lept fierce vpon his shield, and her huge traine
> All suddenly about his body wound,
> That hand or foot to stirre he stroue in vaine:
> God helpe the man so wrapt in *Errours* endlesse traine.

[1.1.18]

This is the first of many interweavings of psychological and physical states. When the "double forces," i.e., the multiplicity, of Error entrap the hero, he is momentarily wrapped in her endless train. He comes face to face with his own capacity for error, thus discovering another facet of his own multiple self.

As so often happens, Una drives him on to find his real self just as he is wavering among uncertain alternatives. "Shew what ye bee," she cries out to him, and this admonition prompts him to reject error within himself, to find a unity which does not include the monster. Yet Error's multiplicity remains, especially at this point in his quest, a powerful weapon against him. Her disgusting vomit, which surrounds the hero with innumerable "deformed monsters," at first makes him less than himself, for despite Una's inspiration "His forces faile, ne can no longer fight." Even when the thought of shame finally leads him to self-possession, he is only "Halfe furious vnto his foe." Nevertheless, he masters himself, "resolv'd in mind all suddenly to win, / Or soone to lose," and destroys the monster. But her own multiple spawn has a life of its own, deriving completely from their mother's life. This mutuality between the little monsters and the wellhead of error is so great that they destroy themselves. Multiplicity and self-regenerating mutuality are the greatest powers of the evil force, but this internal discord is also its undoing.

The moment when Red Cross is trapped in the multiple embrace of the monster Error, when he loses his single, unified force, which is incarnate in the aptly named Una, epitomizes the relation between the hero and the multiple bodies of evil. The next body diversified by the powers of evil is that of Una herself. Archimago

> Had made a Lady of that other Spright,
> And fram'd of liquid ayre her tender partes
> So liuely, and so like in all mens sight,
> That weaker sence it could haue rauisht quight:
> The maker selfe for all his wondrous witt,
> Was nigh beguiled with so goodly sight:
> Her all in white he clad, and ouer it
> Cast a blacke stole, most like to seeme for *Vna* fit.

> [1.1.45]

This is Archimago's corrupt use of the elements in an antitype of God's corporeal creation, a spirit whose equality to the real Una is as false as the equality advocated by the Communist Giant. "Liquid ayre" is an evil parody of true creation via the four elements.

Spirit Una helps to define both the real Una and the mental state of Red Cross. Just as this Una's body is identical to the real and yet ultimately distinguishable, so is her "love" for the hero. Spirit Una is a multiple creature not only in physically being Una's double but also in being filled with the fashionable doubts and fears of passionate love. She speaks in oxymorons: "For hoped loue to winne me certaine hate"; and her body itself is engaged in an internal struggle: "There she stopt with teares; / Her swollen hart her speach seemd to bereaue." This multiplicity and passion in Spirit Una act to purge the real Una of those qualities traditionally associated with romantic love. Spirit Una reveals as much about Red Cross as about Una. Error triumphs over Red Cross at first only enough to ravish his senses and convince him that the real Una might speak to him as this one does, but the creation of the Spirit Squire who makes love to Spirit Una transforms Red Cross into a self-torturing body, similar in fact to Spirit Una: "He could not rest, but did his stout heart eat, / And wast his inward gall with deepe despight, / Yrkesome of life, and too long lingering night" (1.2.6). The description recalls the speech of Spirit Una in the previous canto. Archimago and the spirits which he has created by corporeal analogy have turned Red Cross momentarily into a fit mate for this passionate false Una. Thus the hero's separation from Una in the second canto is both an external sundering and an internal straying from the path leading toward the One.

Una's own gullibility when faced with Archimago's impersonation of Red Cross demonstrates that she too is susceptible, both internally and externally, to the powers of evil. But Una, though equally gullible, is much less culpable than her knight. Archimago's impersonation is more authentic than Spirit Una. The false Red Cross is not the opposite of the true but only an exaggeration of certain knightly qualities. Una's weakness in accepting false Red Cross is the weakness inherent in true love, and this would have expressed itself in the same fashion had the real Red Cross returned at this point giving the actual excuse for his absence. (In fact when they are reunited much later Una forgives him much as she forgave the false Red Cross.) Thus Spenser's comment at this ostensible reunion is as apt for the real Red Cross as for the false: "She has forgot, how many a wofull stowre / For him she late en-

dur'd; she speakes no more / Of past: true is, that true loue hath no
powre / To looken backe" (1.3.30).

Red Cross's double demonstrates some of the weakness inherent in
Una's love, bringing her a bit closer to Spirit Una, whose love was all
weakness. But Archimago's impersonation also brings to light some of
Una's strength, for unlike the earlier impersonation it produces some
real interplay between impersonator and role. The advent of Sansloy
forces Archimago to play his role much more seriously than he had
intended to do. In this moment of danger Una urges him on; and
though Archimago "did faint through feare," "yet his Lady did so
well him cheare, / That hope of new good hap he gan to feele" (1.3.34).
For the moment Archimago forgets that he is only playing a part and
is almost turned into the real thing by Una's encouragement, a force
which will be important later to Red Cross himself. The corporeal
wholeness which Archimago produces in the image of the image of
God has an inherent power of attraction to God's purposes despite its
own creator's attempts to control it. In addition, Una's power is set
in diametric opposition to this multiplying body of evil. Archimago
has the magical protean power to transform himself and his sprites into
any human body at all; Una very nearly has the human power of truth
and faith to undo that magic and turn the false into the real.

Una's most important double is, of course, Duessa. Una is single,
faithful, true, and unchanging, while Duessa is saturated in multiplicity,
both within her own body and spirit and in those of the individuals
who are linked with her. Duessa's multiplicity takes the particular form
of containing diametric opposites, giving her the opportunity not of
being all things to all men like the protean Archimago, but of playing
one or the other of two opposing roles. She is oxymoron incarnate:
she can be simultaneously Fidessa or Duessa, and both "fowle" and
"welfauored." She has monstrous nether parts, but she can seem to
Red Cross "the fairest wight, that liued yit" (1.2.30).

"I that do seeme not I, Duessa am," she tells Night, and the opposi-
tions in her false message to Una's father capture her essential double-
ness: "Therefore since mine he is, or free or bond, / Or false or trew,
or liuing or else dead. . . . Thy neither friend, nor foe" (1.12.28). At
this point, when Una has Red Cross and Duessa wants him (or seems
to), the doubleness of this message helps define the real difference be-
tween the two women and thus the nature of Una. Duessa's ability to

vacillate between extremes and to imitate them represents an unwill-
ingness to accept the universe as it is and an attempt to create a false one
in its place. Una, by contrast, is strong, active, and committed. She
does not choose to deal with opposites of herself, but her steadfastness
succeeds because she deals with the world as it is, without the ability or
desire to retreat into a pose which mirrors the world's multiple vagaries.
Thus while Duessa frequently complains of her father's undeserved
wrongs, she simply uses that misfortune as a pose. But Una truly
achieves her father's redemption, accepting the help of Red Cross yet
chiding him when he is in error.

   The implications of Duessa's multiplicity are elaborated by a large
number of characters, beings, and settings with which she is linked.
Some of these multiple bodies merely add a decorative, emblematic
force to the multiplicity of Duessa's own body. At Orgoglio's den she
rides "her manyheaded beast, / And euery head with fyrie tongue did
flame, / And euery head was crowned on his creast, / And bloudie
mouthed with late cruell feast" (1.8.6). More relevant to Duessa's
particular kind of multiplicity is the description of Night's chariot in
which she rides:

> Her twyfold teme, of which two blacke as pitch,
> And two were browne, yet each to each vnlich,
> Did softly swim away, ne euer, stampe,
> Vnlesse she chaunst their stubborne mouths to twitch;
> Then foming tarre, their bridles they would champe,
> And trampling the fine element, would fiercely rampe.
>
> [1.5.28]

The implied reference to Plato's discordant steeds of reason and passion
in the *Phaedrus* offers yet another composite cosmic vision embodied in
an iconographic image. This image is part of Duessa and of her body,
itself made of opposing parts "each to each vnlich," for she too can
choose to move softly or violently at will.

   The physical and spiritual state of the House of Pride extends and
elaborates Duessa's corporeal multiplicity. The kernel of this analogy is
an implied anthropomorphism. Though the House of Pride seems
magnificent and beautiful, it is ultimately weak and, like Duessa's, "all
the hinder parts, that few could spie, / Were ruinous and old, but paint-
ed cunningly" (1.4.5). The House of Pride is a multiple, composite
container of evil, subdividing it and rendering it incarnate. Like the

machine in Mammon's cave, this procession of Lucifera and her six fellow deadly sins is a micro-universe containing the *discordia concors* of evil within the body of the House of Pride.[31] The emphasis upon discord within the wholeness demonstrates the weakness of the multiple body, arising from the struggle of the various evil forces within. Each of the deadly sins is consumed and ultimately either destroyed or rendered impotent by its own sin. Idleness leads the procession but is a bad leader since he "knew not, whether right he went, or else astray" (1.4. 19). Gluttony vomits up his own surfeit, which is then loathsome to him. Lechery, despite his success with women, was an "unseemely man to please faire Ladies eye" (1.4.24). Avarice has no heir. Envy consumes itself most literally, for "inwardly he chawed his owne maw"(1.4.30). And Wrath, despite his desire for destruction, "of his hands . . . had no gouernement" (1.4.34).

Like any multiple heterocosm in *The Faerie Queene*, the House of Pride represents an unfolding of characteristics that are infolded into several of the individuals connected with it. It stands as an objectification of their complex or tense internal states. This is already evident in the case of Duessa: once she is linked to the House by its anthropomorphic and similar form, the complex of qualities inside magnifies her and glosses her mysteries for Red Cross's benefit.

But if the House of Pride is an unfolding of Duessa, it is in turn re-infolded by Lucifera. Lucifera stands to the House of Pride as Alma to the House of Temperance: its principal inhabitant but at the same time its overall composite identity. If we consider Lucifera as the product of a three-part process like the one in which Colin's shepherdess was generated out of Venus via the Graces, it becomes apparent that the hero is beholding personal faithlessness (a lack, in Rosemund Tuve's terms, of both *veritas* and *fides*)[32] transformed into the seven deadly sins and yielding in Lucifera a cosmic sin which denies the whole moral fabric of the universe. Duessa is a usurper of Red Cross's love, but Lucifera is a universal usurper. Like many of Spenser's grandest images of evil she represents a corrupt great chain of being spanning the highest and lowest in a hellish parody of the true universe. It is for this reason

31. Alastair Fowler (*Spenser and the Numbers of Time*, p. 73) suggests that the procession "is also a deliberate travesty of the conventional representation of Sol with his retinue of lesser planets." If this is true, the passage depicts yet another physical microcosm.

32. See *Allegorical Imagery* (Princeton: Princeton University Press, 1966), pp. 120–25.

that she is pridefully "looking to heauen" and in the same stanza, "in her hand she held a mirrhour bright, / Wherein her face she often vewed fayne" (1.4.10). This juxtaposition represents a perverted relation between macrocosm and microcosm, as we see again in the universe-spanning link between Phoebus, whom she resembles, and Pluto and Proserpina, who are her real parents. Pride is a denial of mortal life, which operates between Lucifera's extremes, and thus it is a cosmic version of Duessa's doubleness, as well as an unwillingness to accept life as it is.

Finally, just as Spenser had Red Cross physically "become" the monster Error as a means of expressing the psychological interdependence of the two figures, so too the hero represents a larger unit in which Duessa, the House of Pride, and Lucifera can be contained. His own passivity, which has been interpreted as uncompromising indifference to the sin,[33] can also suggest that pride's pageant represents the hero's mental state at that moment. Consequently, any active response from him would confuse or clutter that assertion. Certainly his subjugation to Duessa implicates him in the process that unites Duessa, Lucifera, and the seven deadly sins.

If the House of Pride demonstrates the self-defeating tensions of multiple evil, Fradubio's story demonstrates its potential strength. This is a story of repeated bodily metamorphoses. First, the lightness of Fradubio's love, his willingness to take on Duessa when he already has Fraelissa, turns the two women into seemingly identical forms in his eyes: "So doubly lou'd of Ladies vnlike faire, / Th' one seeming such, the other such indeede" (1.2.37). Fradubio is blind to moral differences, and this blindness enables Duessa to get Fraelissa completely in her power. When Duessa produces the fog which turns Fraelissa into a "foule ugly forme," Duessa in fact changes her own body for Fraelissa's, for it is Duessa who really bears an ugly form under a beautiful exterior. Fraelissa, who was of one beautiful form, is metamorphosed into a being like Duessa who contains diametric opposites. Fradubio is completely deceived by this exchange and thus treats Fraelissa as he ought to have treated Duessa.

Fraelissa's metamorphosis into a tree grows naturally out of Fradubio's lack of faith and insight into the earlier metamorphosis. When he sees the double image of Duessa as a witch he attempts to escape her,

33. C. S. Lewis, *Spenser's Images*, pp. 29–30.

failing to recognize how he is implicated. But this escape is impossible. By consorting with the powers of evil and having faith in them, he has transformed himself psychologically into one of them just as his lack of insight transformed Fraelissa physically. Fradubio's metamorphosis into a tree places him in a kind of limbo, a helpless victim of Duessa's powers to transform her own body and those of others. Until he is bathed in a living well, he is, like Duessa, both human and less than human, "Wretched man, wretched tree."

The significance of these transformations is to be found in the parallel between Fradubio and Red Cross. Red Cross is temporarily a victim of the same blindness that was so fatal to Fradubio. In fact it is in picking off a branch as a love token for Duessa that Red Cross causes Fradubio to speak. Red Cross has also rejected his own pure love and turned to the two-faced Duessa, and he too believes that not Duessa but his original love is the double-dealer Yet the hero cannot at this point realize that he is looking in the mirror. He tries to escape completely from any involvement in Fradubio's fate when he "The bleeding bough did thrust into the ground, / That from the bloud he might be innocent" (1.2.44), just as Fradubio tried to wash his hands of Duessa once he had seen her to be a witch. In the final stanza Red Cross's Duessa undergoes one of her pretended metamorphoses, supposedly in horror at this narration, and the hero is so completely convinced that in comforting her he quite forgets Fradubio's pains. Duessa's power over Red Cross throughout her alliance with him is very similar to her power over Fradubio. Unlike the poem's later heroes, Red Cross recognizes little about the implications of his predicaments. He does not recognize his own doubles, a blindness which suggests his inability to grasp the meanings of multiplicity, and he has difficulty in coping with simultaneous opposites. He is a naive version of Una, for he believes whatever he sees to be single and truthful. Thus he accepts Duessa as Fidessa and allows her multiple powers to trap him, but he does not recognize their multiplicity clearly enough to see her hypocrisy and to purge the psychological multiplicity in himself.

The remaining multiple evil which besets Red Cross in the earlier part of his quest is the trio of Paynim brothers, Sansfoy, Sansloy, and Sansjoy. This trio is the *discordia concors* of opposition to Christian values, subdividing this opposition as did the three forces which unfolded the power of the Blatant Beast against Timias. They render the multiplicity of paganism all the stronger by their capacity to be in three places at once. Yet despite these fragmenting qualities of the trio, the spiritual concord among them is so strong and the personality differences so minimal that Spenser, having separated the three qualities to anatomize paganism, is in fact suggesting that they are inseparable in the absence of real Christianity.

These interrelations are partly corporeal and partly based on the revenge principle which underlines their opposition to Christianity.[34] Born of and closely identified with the earth, the brothers are linked by a code of revenge for each other's defeats that turns them into a single composite person. Sansloy cries out to Archimago, whom he takes to be Red Cross, "Life from *Sansfoy* thou tookst, *Sansloy* shall from thee take" (1.3.36), and later as Sansjoy fights with Red Cross over his brother's armor,

> At last the Paynim chaunst to cast his eye,
>   His suddein eye, flaming with wrathfull fyre,
>   Vpon his brothers shield, which hong thereby;
>   Therewith redoubled was his raging yre.
>
> [1.5.10]

In that "redoubled" I think we can read the same kind of corporeal union which will more explicitly link Priamond and his brothers in Book IV. The code of vengeance that spiritually joins the brothers has momentarily given Sansjoy in his own body the strength of his defeated brother in addition to his own.

Like the other multiple evils of Book I, this trio of brothers helps to define virtue and unity. The closeness of these brothers is a false unity, a lack of self-reliance that turns each of them into less than a whole person. They contrast with and point up the true unity of Una, who is more than capable of seeking aid in her adversity but remarkably self-reliant when alone. The antichristian code of revenge diminishes man's humanity, for rather than standing as an individual under God, Who alone can judge and dispose, the revenger denies God as king and judge and loses his self in the person whom he is avenging.[35]

---

34. See Williams, *Spenser's Faerie Queene*, p. 15.

35. In addition, by being woven into so much of the narrative, the pagan brothers can act as poetic mirrors of the good characters. The imagery of Red Cross's fights with Sansfoy and Sansjoy recurrently stresses the mutuality of the struggle. In the case of Sansfoy, the two combatants stand symmetrically, "sencelesse as a blocke" until Red

By the midpoint of Book I, the threats to Red Cross from the multiple body of evil are by and large past, even though in some respects Orgoglio and the dragon are multiple monsters like Error, and Duessa lingers on until the very end. Nevertheless, from the sixth canto on it is largely the hero himself and the forces of good that are seen in multiple terms. It has already been suggested that the multiple evils in the first half of the book refract Red Cross himself into a multiple body having various forces in disharmony with each other. At the very entrance into the dark wood, Red Cross and Una "wander too and fro in wayes vnknown, / Furthest from end then, when they neerest weene, / That makes them doubt, their wits be not their owne" (1.1.10). In each of his succeeding adventures, he is temporarily lost in the multiplicity of evil, wrapped in Error's train or eating his inward heart out, and then, endowed with either the grace of his special mission or a brief spark of native virtue or self-possession, he triumphs over his adversaries. But this process leading from knightly prowess to an understanding of his mission to discovery of himself is only previewed in the first half of the book, since the enemies, though they mirror the hero's state, are fundamentally separate from him. In the second half the forces of good, Una, Satyrane, and Arthur, are themselves seen in multiple terms, and the hero engages in struggles with new evils which turn him into a multiple world.

Red Cross's essential state is an uncertainty about both himself and his misfortunes, and the multiplicity of the evils and of his own psyche realizes these uncertainties poetically. Una and Arthur, however, are completely certain of themselves and are weakened only by their misfortunes. Their multiplications, then, are either signs of personal strength and completeness or else tensions between their internal fortitude and their wavering fortunes. The imagery with which Una's multiple body and spirit are evoked tends to convey strength and wholeness. Her body is a "stubborne fort" which will not yield to Sansloy (1.6.3), and it is also a strong meaningful force that civilizes the Salvage Nation and enables the savages to "read her sorrow in her count'nance sad" (1.6.11). She also represents both Venus and Diana in

---

Cross transcends the parallel condition when his "sleeping spark / Of natiue vertue gan eftsoones reuiue." In the case of Sansjoy, the two fighters are clearly opposed, but they are described in parallel terms and they are subjected to encouragement from Duessa that each takes to be intended for him alone.

the sight of old Sylvanus, and these, as we know from Books III and IV, are the Alpha and Omega of womanhood. Similarly, Arthur in himself is strong and whole, as we can see from the perfection of his armor, made all of diamond so that "From top to toe no place appeared bare / That deadly dint of steele endanger may" (1.7.29).

In both cases their strength rests to a considerable extent on the power of their love, but the misfortunes of this love split them apart. Arthur asks Una "to disclose the breach, / Which loue and fortune in her heart had wrought" (1.7.42), and each of them dissolves internally when misfortune threatens to triumph over love. At Archimago's mention of Red Cross's supposed death, "That cruell word her tender hart so thrild, / That suddein cold did runne through euery vaine, / And stony horrour all her sences fild / With dying fit" (1.6.37), and at later bad news from the Dwarf her body again betrays her weakness, for the Dwarf has "To rub her temples, and to chaufe her chin, / And euery tender part does tosse and turne: / So hardly he the flitted life does win, / Vnto her natiue prison to retourne" (1.7.21).[36]

In Arthur's case the misfortunes of not finding his love or knowing his fate turns wholeness into fragmentation. His unrealizable love he describes as a "fresh bleeding wound, which day and night / Whilome doth rancle in my riuen brest" (1.9.7), and we can see for ourselves how his breast is riven, for "as he spake, his visage wexed pale, / And chaunge of hew great passion did bewray" (1.9.16). All these images of the body treat it as a cosmic wholeness, a natural tower of strength. These descriptions suggest an innate wholeness in Una and Arthur that is fragmented because the fallen world has subverted the natural perfection of the body. Each of the good characters, however in control of himself, lacks the ability to turn fortune in his favor. Una is destined to overcome but has not the power to effect this victory on her own, while Arthur has knightly power but a destiny which, though beautiful, he seems powerless to fulfill. The wholeness of the good powers is fragmented by misfortune or by the multiple strength of the evil powers. It remains for Red Cross to discover his own wholeness, for once he has seen that, he alone will be able to combine personal power and a destiny touched with grace.

36. See also the moment when Red Cross seems to succumb to Despair, "Which, when as *Vna* saw, through euery vaine / The crudled cold ran to her well of life" (1.9. 52).

Una and Arthur are towers of strength, and even in their misfortunes they are involved in grandiose internal struggles. Red Cross, on the other hand, suffers bodily dissolution before he can suffer fragmentation. In continuing to dally with Duessa, in drinking of the soporific stream, and in being captive to Orgoglio, he suffers a loss of body, which in the context of the multiple body image suggests a loss of all the elements of the self:

> His sad dull eyes deepe sunck in hollow pits,
>   Could not endure th' vnwonted sunne to view;
> His bare thin cheekes for want of better bits,
> And empty sides deceiued of their dew,
> Could make a stony hart his hap to rew;
> His rawbone armes . . .
>   Were cleane consum'd, and all his vitall powres
> Decayd, and all his flesh shronk vp like withered flowres.
>
> [1.8.41]

The hero's loss of self is remedied by Arthur's power and Una's steadfastness, but almost immediately Red Cross is transformed into a debilitating fragmentation by the force of Despair. More than any other of the evils Red Cross meets, Despair is an objectification of the hero's internal voice, a figure who is both united with and separate from the hero's self. Despair himself suggests this doubleness by disclaiming any responsibility for Trevisan's misery: "None else to death this man despayring driue, / But his own guiltie mind deseruing death" (1.9.38). He is a physical mirror of the hero's state of mind, for he even resembles the Red Cross of Orgoglio's dungeon: "his hollow eyne / Lookt deadly dull, and stared as astound; / His raw-bone cheekes through penurie and pine, / Were shronke into his iawes" (1.9.35).

This internal voice constantly makes use of multiples and opposites in order to win the upper hand in a struggle within the hero's self: "Sleepe after toyle, port after stormie seas, / Ease after warre, death after life does greatly please" (1.9.40), or "Feare, sicknesse, age, losse, labour, sorrow, strife, / Paine, hunger, cold, that makes the hart to quake" (1.9.44). Despair's multiplicity, expressed both in himself and in the tug-of-war he inspires within Red Cross, represents the ultimate version of evil's multiple power because it depends upon all the earliest mistakes of Red Cross and because its power of fragmentation is most internal. The voice of Despair succeeds in moving the action from the healthy sphere of knightly battles to a world of strife within, as Una recognizes when she chides Red Cross: "What meanest thou by this reprochfull strife? / Is this the battell, which thou vauntst to fight / With that fire-mouthed Dragon, horrible and bright?" (1.9.52).

Red Cross, riddled with internal dissension, is not yet ready for that greater battle, and all that the single good force of Una can do is to shame him into departing from Despair's cave. His peculiarly fragmented internal state can only be treated by a multiple version of the good, and this he experiences in the House of Holiness. If Una is the image of individual holiness, then Coelia is the image of multiple holiness unified. The various forces of Coelia work on each of the multiple strands that make up Red Cross's self. Under Fidelia's guidance he is "greeu'd with remembrance of his wicked wayes, / And prickt with anguish of his sinnes so sore, . . . / But wise *Speranza* gaue him comfort sweet, / And . . . / Made him forget all that Fidelia told" (1.10. 21–22). The House of Holiness is another of Spenser's multiple machines, and it unfolds the essence of Una much as the House of Pride unfolded Duessa.

The regimen is so exhausting and the hero's desire for internal peace so great that through penance and repentance he tries again to destroy his self in order to conquer its multiplicity. This he is saved from by the multiple image of Charissa, surrounded with loving children and served by seven beadsmen. It is she, finally, who prepares him to accept his life and his self, even though the vision of the New Jerusalem reawakens his desire to avoid external battle since he is so fatigued of strife within.

In conversation with the hermit Contemplation, Red Cross discovers his past, his future, and hence his self. By naming him as Saint George, the hermit shows the knight how the grace, of which he has all along been the instrument, is inextricable from his own identity, "the way that does to heauen bound" (1.10.67). This grace and this destiny release Red Cross from strife within and send him forward to God's strife in the world. From this point on, he is one with himself and is therefore able to multiply in his own strength as so many of his enemies had earlier. Now that he has realized himself, Una is able to urge him on in the next canto, "The sparke of noble courage now awake, / And striue your excellent selfe to excell" (1.11.2). This is the only internal striving left for him: having finally discovered an excellent self, he can now try to surpass it.

This new self-multiplication is perfectly demonstrated by the fight with the dragon. The dragon is itself a multiple creature, having elements of hill, mountain, eagle, boat, etc. Consequently the fight requires constant new reserves of power from the hero, forcing him each day to find new strengths in himself. He reaches the point where "three mens strength vnto the stroke he layd" on the first day and his hands grow greater from baptism on the second, until, on the third day, quickly and without special outside help he slays the beast. Red Cross has excelled himself by multiplying his own powers with the help of truth, grace, and his personal destiny, but in the final triumph these multiple powers, unlike the weak interdependence of the evil characters, are fully subsumed in his self. Concord triumphs even over the *discordia concors*, at least for a time.

5

In Spenser's Book of chastity and love, the human body plays a major role in both method and meaning. The book is in large part concerned with the purging of fantastic, imaginary types of love and the glorification of love that leads to wholesome generation and to the fulfillment of destiny. The human body in itself and in its transformations is integral to the image of both good and bad love. False love consists of a fantasy world peopled by multiple physical forms that objectify the changeable illusions within the bad characters' imaginations. True love is defined by its close link with generation, a bodily fulfillment leading to the reproduction of the body. The tension between fantasy love and generative love stands as the essential issue of the book. Britomart, while not perhaps changing psychologically as in a *Bildungsroman*, moves through a world which gradually rids her of the mere image of her lover in the mirror and readies her to meet in the flesh the man with whom she will fulfill the destiny of her womb.

Spenser's method in Book III centers upon corporeal reproduction, both literal and poetic. If one carries, as Joyce did in *Ulysses*, the idea of the human body so far as to assign to each book a part of the anatomy, Book III would undoubtedly be the book of the womb, not only for the meaning of reproduction but also for the poetic method. Groups of characters born literally or figuratively in the same womb are frequent here. Their origins are a corporeal expression of *discordia concors*:

union in the womb is contrasted with their own independence as psychological and allegorical figures. They represent the unfolded qualities of the essence contained within the womb of their origin. The literal act of reproduction diversifies and spreads that essence through the world of the poem, and the poetic reproduction unfolds the moral meanings for the reader.

The clearest examples are Amoret and Belphoebe, and Argante and Ollyphant. The birth of Chrysogone's twin daughters is so steeped in mother nature that they become an incarnate definition of nature. Chrysogone herself is a child of nature, who, on the day of the twins' conception, "bath'd with roses red, and violets blew, / And all the sweetest flowres, that in the forrest grew" (3.6.6). She is chastity itself, while the sun's beams, which impregnate her, are the essence of fertility. Both principles are basically natural. Spenser joins them literally by bodily union and thematically by the fruit of that union. The sisters' glorious and simultaneous conception suggests the unity of nature. At the same time they are separate and complementary beings who can refract the single force of nature into two parts, the chaste and the loving. Each part, as we shall see, has its pitfalls and its glories, but their bodily union proves that in a perfect state their meanings are joined: "These two were twinnes, and twixt them two did share / The heritage of all celestiall grace" (3.6.4).

While Argante and Ollyphant are morally the opposite of Chrysogone's twins, the poetic method of their generation is similar. Their conception is the result of powerfully anti-natural forces. Their father was Typhoeus, one of the Titans, "which did make / Warre against heauen." In addition, he was opposed to the natural order by being cannibalistic and by begetting the twins on his own mother, Earth. So while Amoret and Belphoebe are children of two natural forces, Argante and Ollyphant are born of two earthly forces, i.e., the Titans, so earthbound that they could not reach heaven, and Mother Earth herself. Perhaps the most important difference between the two groups of twins is the relationships within the pair. Argante and Ollyphant are surrounded by images of bodily union: Typhoeus "drunk with bloud of men" and incestuous with his mother, and the twins themselves, who "Whiles in their mother's wombe enclosed they were, / . . . In fleshy lust were mingled both yfere, / And in that monstrous wise did to the world appere" (3.7.48). Amoret and Belphoebe, apart from the union

involved in their being twins, are conceived in purity and are inde-
pendent from each other. Their conception was not sensual and their
birth not painful; they are independent as they were parted at birth.

Each pair of twins has its own figurative progeny: Amoret and
Belphoebe give rise to the duality of fertility and chastity, while Ol-
lyphant torments knights and Argante "ouer all the countrey . . . did
raunge, / To seeke young men, to quench her flaming thrust" (3.7.50).[37]
This difference sets the pattern for the moral and allegorical force of all
the characters who are paired in body, birth, or meaning. In Book
III—and this distinguishes it from the Book of Friendship—inde-
pendence from one's double is by and large a sign of virtue, while union
in body or spirit generally suggests enslavement to the fantasy world
inhabited by the false forms of love.

If all love in Book III moves between the extremes of multiple
fantasies and the affirmation of life and reproduction, then perhaps the
exact midpoint, and therefore the tensest struggle, is to be seen in the
relationship of Timias and Belphoebe. The explicit agonies of the squire
and the more covert tensions within his love constitute a pageant seen
in decidedly corporeal terms. Timias's original wound is sustained in
the fight against lechery, whose allegorical representation in the three
fosters exemplifies the image of multiple progeny from a single womb.
When there is one foster, Timias is a reasonable match for him, but the
fosters are "three / Vngracious children of one gracelesse sire." They
complement each other in gracelessness, and though they are not differ-
entiated allegorically, they do function as distinctly separate parts of a
composite machine attacking Timias. The first throws a dart that
pierces the squire's armor but does not wound him, the second gets him
in the thigh, the third tries to kill him with a club and is defeated.
Timias's wound is the collective work of all three brothers, and it
demonstrates in allegorical terms that the young man is not entirely
invulnerable to the sin of lechery.

The sight of Belphoebe transforms this bodily taint of lechery into
the equally corporeal passion of love. At first Belphoebe believes that
the traces of blood she sees are from the wild beasts she has been shoot-
ing, and this mistake becomes the truth as the wounds from her

37. Argante's body is, in fact, a festering place of unnatural acts: "Did wallow in all
other fleshly myre, / And suffred beasts her body to deflowre: / So whot she burned in
that lustfull fyre, / Yet all that might not slake her sensuall desyre" (3.7.49).

attractiveness overshadow the fosters' wound. The dangers of lechery
to Timias's body, which he might easily have shaken, pale beside the
fragmentation produced in his body by love:

> O foolish Physick, and vnfruitfull paine,
>   That heales vp one and makes another wound:
>   She his hurt thigh to him recur'd againe,
>   But hurt his hart, the which before was sound,
>   Through an vnwary dart, which did rebound
>   From her faire eyes and gracious countenaunce.
>
> [3.5.42]

As in the Petrarchan tradition, Timias's heart is occupied by the
enemy, and the forces of reason within are not powerful enough "the
passion to subdew, / And loue for to dislodge out of his nest" (3.5.44).

The squire's mental state perfectly mirrors the fragmentation within
his body. Tormenting himself in a three-stanza sequence of sophistries,
Timias pictures love first as a blot to the woman's honor, then as service
due her in return for her nursing him, then as a meek and humble
offering from his lowly self to her divinity. The squire's immaturity
can be read in these conceptions of love and in his association of love
with death. These multiple fantasies, associated throughout the book
with false love, express in spiritual terms the physical fragmentation
Belphoebe produces within his body, and the association of love with
death very nearly proves itself true in Timias's body when, with his
third vow, his health takes a serious turn for the worse:

> he was forst at last,
>   To yield himselfe vnto the mighty ill:
>   Which as a victour proud, gan ransack fast
>   His inward parts, and all his entrayles wast,
>   That neither bloud in face, nor life in hart
>   It left, but both did quite drye vp, and blast.
>
> [3.5.48]

False love, here and elsewhere, begets multiple fantasies and death, but
true love produces life and regeneration of the body. Timias's ills are
not hopeless, but he needs the guidance of Belphoebe to lead him from
a morbid love to a regenerating love.

Belphoebe comes closer to understanding love, as is apparent from
her relation to the corporeal image. Her body is also love's playground.
Her sympathy for the youth, which is the beginning of their love,

arises from a curious joining of their bodies. She sees him wounded on the ground, "woxen pale and wan," and her own body mirrors this reaction: "all suddeinly abasht she chaunged hew, / . . . But when she better him beheld, she grew / Full of soft passion and vnwonted smart: / The point of pitty perced through her tender hart" (3.5.30). She, too, is wounded, but her wound leads toward life rather than death, as her pity leads her to nurse Timias back to life. Her body, rather than being a place of taint, confusion, and fragmentation, is the soil in which grows the flower of chastity, which God "did in stocke of earthly flesh enrace / That mortall men her glory should admire: / In gentle Ladies brest" (3.5.52).

Belphoebe fails because in the extremity of her devotion to chastity, she is unable to perceive Timias's love, and therefore ultimately incapable of bringing him back to life. She bestows nature's cordials upon him but not her own. Thus her pity is nearly as far from life-giving as is Timias's false love. True love is to be found in regeneration, a fact which neither of them has perceived, and only at the end of the canto do we begin to see Belphoebe moving toward this realization. Spenser refers to her "fresh flowring Maidenhead," an oxymoron that implies a childbearing destiny, and finally she is described as combining chastity with love:

> she was so curteous and kind,
> Tempred with grace, and goodly modesty,
> That seemed those two vertues stroue to find
> The higher place in her Heroick mind:
> So striuing each did other more augment,
> And both encrease the prayse of woman kind,
> And both encrease her beautie excellent;
> So all did make in her a perfect complement.
>
> [3.5.55]

This "perfect complement" is another instance of personal wholeness in the image of a microcosmic machine. The struggle between giving in to Timias for his life's sake and remaining pure initiates a recognition of love's meaning.

The Garden of Adonis, which directly follows the unresolved Timias and Belphoebe episode, acts as an answer to the lovers' problems, for the Garden is the essential home of generation. Here Spenser's association of love with multiple forms of progeny is asserted with particularly universal force. In contrast to pageants of multiple false love like the tapestries in Castle Joyous, the decorations of Busyrane's house, and the Masque of Cupid, the infinite forms of the creatures in the Garden of Adonis are natural. The art, even of the gardener, is banished, for, as the painless birth of Amoret and Belphoebe demonstrated, true natural regeneration needs none of the art that characterizes courtly love or lust. The creatures of the garden affirm life in the way that Timias so sorely needed. In the place of false multiple forms, these creatures are endowed with real life, i.e., with eternal matter: "The substance is eterne, and bideth so, / Ne when the life decays, and forme does fade, / Doth it consume, and into nothing go, / But chaunged is, and often altred to and fro" (3.6.37).

True form, like the spirit of love which is its source, is the mortal principle's only bridge between the temporal and the eternal. Consequently, it represents temporal man's only means of attaining the eternal. Like man himself, form is mortal and subject to time, for each individual form passes under time's scythe. Yet because these forms are endowed with eternal substance, they return to the garden after their death,

> And grow afresh, as they had neuer seene
> Fleshly corruption, nor mortall paine.
> Some thousand yeares so doen they there remaine;
> And then of him are clad with other hew,
> Or sent into the chaungefull world againe,
> Till thither they returne, where first they grew:
> So like a wheele around they runne from old to new.
>
> [3.6.33]

The very mutability of the forms makes them eternal because mutability enables them to return to earth through endless metamorphoses. The endless fruit of the human womb represents the innumerable metamorphoses of man's form, and in the diversity of these corporeal forms lies eternity and the conquest of multiplicity.

It is important that this place of true forms is also the place of true love. All the torturing falseness of fantasy love is excluded from the relationships in the garden:

> For here all plentie, and all pleasure flowes,
> And sweet loue gentle fits emongst them throwes,
> Without fell rancor, or fond gealosie;

> Franckly each paramour his leman knowes,
> Each bird his mate, ne any does enuie
> Their goodly meriment, and gay felicitie.
>
> [3.6.41]

This remarkable peacefulness is both a natural and a supernatural phenomenon. It is natural in the sense that "Franckly each paramour his leman knowes," that discord and falsehoods are banished. It is supernatural in that the eternity of the forms makes death of love impossible, even though the forms may change. This is apparent in the relationship of Venus and Adonis:

> . . . she her selfe, when euer that she will,
> Possesseth him, and of his sweetnesse takes her fill.
> And sooth it seems they say: for he may not
>   For euer die, and euer buried bee
>   In baleful night, where all things are forgot;
>   All be he subject to mortalitie,
>   Yet is eterne in mutabilitie,
>   And by succession made perpetuall,
>   Transformed oft, and chaunged diuerslie:
>   For him the Father of all formes they call;
> Therefore needs mote he liue, that liuing giues to all.
>
> [3.6.46–47]

I think we are meant to see that this is the fate of all who truly love, whether living in the Garden of Adonis or not. Since all bodies are the children of Adonis, they all bear something of his immortality. True love between a man and a woman begets bodies, and in those forms the lovers are "eterne in mutabilitie." One's progeny is the succession of forms in which love can be reenacted, even though within the progeny the original forms of the loving parents are frozen in timelessness like Venus and Adonis in the garden. For this reason, the fact that "There is continuall spring, and haruest there / Continuall, both meeting at one time" (3.6.42) is not simply an image of supernatural paradise but an indication that the act of love and love's reproduction of forms are inextricable from each other.

As a bridge between the eternal and the timeless, the Garden of Adonis also spans all the orders of the cosmos, illustrating the link so crucial to Spenser's thought between the individual human body and the body of the world. Thus the garden not only bears a message for the individual man but is also itself anthropomorphic. "Right in the middest of that Paradise, / There stood a stately Mount, on whose round top / A gloomy groue of mirtle trees did rise, / Whose shadie boughes sharpe steele did never lop, / . . . And from their fruitfull sides sweet gum did drop, / . . . Threw forth most dainty odours, and most sweet delight" (3.6.43)—this is surely a picture not only of the principle of regeneration but also of its concrete form in the human body. The implied pun on Venus's mount joins together the eternal process of creation with the individual act of love. The Garden of Adonis, for all its wonders, is not an imaginary place, but rather just that place sought by all the good and bad lovers of Book III. All the lovers may find something, but only the good ones will find that place which is at once the garden of earthly delights and the key to eternal life.

Most of the book's texture consists of departures from the canons of true love as expressed in the Garden of Adonis. The first, Castle Joyous, demonstrates in relatively emblematic terms how false love leads to a variety of fanciful forms and imaginings. Malecasta lives in a world of courtly love, and Spenser anatomizes and criticizes that tradition in the description of her castle and in the events that take place there. Our introduction to the milieu immediately casts it in the light of multiple forms as we see a single knight fending off with great difficulty six other knights. Even before we learn the identities of any of the seven knights, it is clear that the multiplicity of the six suggests wanton love, while the uniqueness of the one indicates faithfulness. As the single knight says, "These sixe would me enforce by oddes of might, / To chaunge my liefe, and loue another Dame, / That death me liefer were, than such despight, / . . . For I loue one, the truest one on ground" (3.1.24).

The six are another example of groups of characters born together: "all sixe brethren, borne of one parent, / Which had them traynd in all ciuilitee, / And goodly taught to tilt and turnament" (3.1.44). This collective heritage is morally ambiguous. Such knightly training would stand them in good stead if they were servants of true love, but their names, which we learn in the next stanza, prove that they are six subdivisions of courtly love. The single knight, on the other hand, is Red Cross, who by his link with Una has become associated with indivisibility. The six knights are an unfolding of the multiple motives and forms within courtly love. But, as in the case of the twin giants or the three Paynim brothers, their forms and qualities are conceptually inextricable from each other.

It is, in fact, Britomart who defines the six knights by contrast. She is the antithesis of the six knights, not because she is indivisible like Red Cross, but because her multiple qualities have individual independence and collective real force. Their collective machine made up of Gardante, Parlante, Iocante, Basciante, Bacchante, and Noctante is wanton, decorative, and interdependent. But a seemingly superfluous description of Britomart juxtaposed with that of the knights compares and contrasts her in terms of the composite corporeal image:

> For she was full of amiable grace,
>   And manly terrour mixed therewithall,
>   That as the one stird vp affections bace,
>   So th' other did mens rash desires apall,
>   And hold them backe, that would in errour fall.
>
> [3.1.46]

Thus Britomart is herself a two-handed engine, but each of her parts is strong and sincere, and together they have genuine force. For this reason her fight with the six knights at the beginning of the episode takes a different form from Red Cross's. In his struggle, "Mainly they all attonce vpon him laid, / And sore beset on euery side around, / That nigh he breathlesse grew" (3.1.21), but Britomart is miraculously able to combat them one at a time: "She mightily auentred towards one, / And downe him smot, ere well aware he weare, / Then to the next she rode, and downe the next did beare. / Ne did she stay till three on ground she layd . . ." (3.1.28–29). Britomart's double forces have the special power to divide and conquer those groups which, in the service of false love, are each other's shadows.

The six knights are not the only multiple fanciful forms in Castle Joyous. The Venus and Adonis tapestry treats love in a series of wanton pictures, at once vagaries of the imagination and overdecorated physical representations. Venus's first image of love is "the bitter balefull stowre, / . . . with many a feruent fit" (3.1.34). Next her love is transformed into "sleights and sweet allurements," then into a deception, then into the peephole pleasures of watching Adonis bathe, then into a dead body, and then into a flower. These multiple forms of Adonis betoken neither the lustful amours of the House of Busyrane, nor the generative bodies in the Garden of Adonis, but rather a wantonness which is ultimately sterile. Adonis's metamorphosis into a flower is certainly not evil. In fact, he is very pretty, but without sexuality or the powers of generation. Courtly love opposes the true fruition of the Garden of Adonis, not so much by lust as by sterility.

Malecasta herself carries this link between multiple forms and sterility further. Spenser describes her falling in love as a gradual series of transformations within her body. It begins with the traditional glance that produces body-wasting passion:

> She greatly gan enamoured to wex,
> And with vaine thoughts her falsed fancy vex:
> Her fickle hart conceiued hasty fire,
> Like sparkes of fire, which fall in sclender flex,
> That shortly brent into extreme desire,
> And ransackt all her veines with passion entire.

[3.1.47]

Spenser offers here a personal version of the Petrarchan bodily process, for the cause of the heart's desire is not a true vision of beauty (especially since Britomart is not even a man), but rather "vaine thoughts" and "falsed fancy." Once she is in the grip of the passion, she tries to hint of her love to Britomart, but such intimations are meaningless to the warrior maid. Malecasta next experiences multiple externalizations of her fragmented internal state. She "discouered her desire / With sighes, and sobs, and plaints, and piteous griefe, / The outward sparkes of her in burning fire" (3.1.53). This does not bring Malecasta internal peace, for the bodily torment of trying to win her love gives way to the bodily torment of sensuality itself when she thinks consummation is near.

Malecasta's mistake about Britomart's sex is the most telling indication that her love is based on fantasy forms and therefore leads to sterility. Like a courtly sonneteer, Malecasta has created grandiose fantasy images of love out of nothing, since the armor necessary to conceal Britomart's sex must presumably have concealed any genuine attractiveness. She has ignored the human body, whose real form is truth itself, mocking her misguided aspirations. Malecasta's blindness parodies the error behind courtly love: without a real relation between lovers, without a destiny that binds them together, love is nothing but a constructed image, and no affirmation of the body's form and its capacity for regeneration.

Sterility and false love images of another kind are the subject of the episode involving Malbecco, Hellenore, and Paridell. The courtship of Paridell and Hellenore is in part reminiscent of love in Castle Joyous. Their bodies become the stage for "speaking lookes" on the outside and "the wicked engine" of lust on the inside. They invent false forms and shows which deceive the ignorant and innocent while communicating love to each other. But the most interesting aspect of the Paridell–Hellenore story for our purposes is that the two are themselves mutated forms of great ancient ancestors, born not out of the same womb as Paris and Helen but certainly in the same mold. By placing his two characters in the shadow of their ancestors, Spenser both mocks and condemns them.

The doubling is largely comic because the two individuals and the struggle they provoke are so paltry when compared with Paris, Helen, and the Trojan War. In this sense Paridell's narration of his ancestry is itself one of the fantasy forms of false love, spiced up to aggrandize himself and intended to be a sort of *roman à clef* which only he and Hellenore understand. In this respect it is very effective:

> But all the while, that he these speaches spent,
>   Vpon his lips hong faire Dame *Hellenore*,
>   With vigilant regard, and dew attent,
>   Fashioning worlds of fancies euermore
>   In her fraile wit, that now her quite forlore:
>   The whiles vnwares away her wondring eye,
>   And greedy eares her weake hart from her bore.
>
> [3.9.52]

Paridell, when compared to a figure from the Trojan War, is a figment of false love, one of the "worlds of fancies" which lusty young men and women imagine.

At the same time, Spenser takes the parallel seriously so as to condemn Paridell first because his claims to military heroism are complete lies, and second, because the personality traits of Paris as Paridell recapitulates them hardly deserve admiration. In addition, the presence of Britomart sets the Trojan archetype in serious light next to which Paridell's relation to the past is indeed paltry and imaginary. Britomart is herself a true descendant of Troy in body and spirit, a historical metamorphosis of the Trojan ideal like the metamorphoses in the Garden of Adonis. She does not ape Troy's foibles but rather fulfills its destiny, as she herself points out: "a third kingdome yet is to arise, / Out of the Troians scattered of-spring, / That in all glory and great enterprise, / Both first and second *Troy* shall dare to equalise" (3.9.44). This aspect of Troy's greatness, which Paridell "had forgot," is for Spenser the most important, though it is irrelevant to Paridell since it does not help with his seduction. Britomart's relation to Troy is through the womb of regeneration, while Paridell's is merely an image of love's fancy. Again these two sorts of bodies are contrasted.

Malbecco's passion also demonstrates the fanciful forms of false love. The flames that he sees destroying both his money and his love correspond precisely to the false flames which have all along been burning within him. The fires which "Consume his hart, and scorch his Idoles face" (3.10.14), represent at once the loss of the coins, the loss of the woman, and the battle raging within him. Deprived of his love objects, he finally breaks down into just that sort of fragmentation which characterizes the flirtation that robs him of Hellenore: "He rau'd, he wept, he stampt, he lowd did cry, / And all the passions, that in man may light, / Did him attonce oppresse" (3.10.17). Thus Malbecco, who cannot perceive the sham of his own love or of the love that cuckolds him, begins to change literally into those multiple forms that characteristically represent the pretenses of lust.

The transformation continues when Malbecco is among the satyrs: "And like a Gote emongst the Gotes did rush, / That through the helpe of his faire hornes on hight, / . . . He did the better counterfeite aright" (3.10.47). He is turned into one of the images of false love without having any of the pleasures of lust. The goatish satyrs' horns are phallic; Malbecco's are just the opposite. They look the same because they are equally false. His final transformation signals a complete alignment of his body with his mind. Deprived of Hellenore, he has no more reason to be jealous, but again he is the victim of lust's imaginary forms without reaping their pleasure. The world of passion's false forms and imaginings is internalized into a new corrupted human anatomy:

> Ne euer is he wont on ought to feed,
>   But toads and frogs, his pasture poysonous,
>   Which in his cold complexion do breed
>   A filthy bloud, or humor rancorous,
>   Matter of doubt and dread suspitious,
>   That doth with curelesse care consume the hart,

> Corrupts the stomacke with gall vitious,
> Croscuts the liuer with internall smart,
> And doth transfixe the soule with deathes eternall dart.

                                                                    [3.10.59]

Since jealousy is an inevitable part of lustful love, these lines describe the physical state of any who do not love truly. When one is finally alone all the battles and fantasy forms of false love are internalized.

The pattern of false love producing multiple forms and bodies is both inverted and repeated in the pursuit of Florimell, which runs so persistently through Book III. Florimell is herself a morally equivocal figure endangered by a wide variety of love's bodies and fancies, all of whom lust after her. At the same time, she is herself a multiple form since she seems to represent all things to all men, and since she is herself doubled with the creation of False Florimell. Florimell's susceptibility to lusty men is both an internal and external quality, for the chase of which she is the victim suggests an inability to perceive true forms. This ambivalence is particularly apparent during the high speed parts of the chase, when Florimell is so terrified by the danger she is in that she loses her own constancy. Her body itself is disordered at our very first sight of her: "her faire yellow locks behind her flew, / Loosely disperst with puffe of euery blast" (3.1.16). She is hypersensitive to danger, "of each noyse affeard, / And of each shade, that did it selfe present" (3.7.19), so that she cannot tell the difference between friend and foe, between body and "shade." Thus she is unable to realize that Arthur means her well. She sees only the external facts: a foster was pursuing her and he has given way to a knight, but beyond that there appears to her no difference. Since Arthur bears an "vncouth shield and straunge armes" (3.4.51), she assumes he must be evil. Florimell's terror and her lack of perception as to external danger are so great (and this includes two occasions—the witch's hut and the fisherman's boat—when she believes she is safe and is not) because the wavering fear resides ultimately within her: "So fled faire *Florimell* from her vaine feare" (3.7.1).

Union between multiple forms inside and out is the keynote to Florimell's place in the allegory. Externally, she is subjected to a legion of admirers, each of whom undergoes the bodily torment and fragmentation engendered by false love. When the witch's son conceives a lust for her, "Closely the wicked flame his bowels brent, / And shortly grew into outrageous fire" (3.7.16). And at each misfortune to his "love," his body explodes even further. When she departs, the son "knockt his brest with desperate intent, / And scratcht his face, and with his teeth did teare / His rugged flesh, and rent his ragged heare" (3.7.20), and news of her presumed death "would haue algates riued / The hart out of his brest" (3.8.3). The hyena, which does not pursue her out of explicit lust, is nonetheless a corporeal reflection of those who do: "An hideous beast, of horrible aspect, / . . . Monstrous mishapt . . . / That feeds on womens flesh, as others feed on gras" (3.7.22). Even the old fisherman undergoes bodily transmutations when lusting after her: "The sight whereof in his congealed flesh, / Infixt such secret sting of greedy lust, / That the drie withered stocke it gan refresh, / And kindled heat, that soone in flame forth brust" (3.8.25).

The figure of Proteus, her most persistent love, is the highpoint in this sequence of bodily transmutations. He brings the process closer to the mutations of Florimell herself because each of his forms is an attempt to awaken some response in her. In contrast, she is as changeable as he, but always with the opposite desire: "Sometimes he boasted, that a God he hight: / But she a mortall creature loved best: / Then he would make himselfe a mortall wight; / But then she said she lou'd none, but a Faerie knight" (3.8.39). In contrast to those of Proteus, Florimell's waverings are never lies, yet she is forced into a constantly shifting set of poses by the waverers around her.

Florimell's response to Proteus indicates that she contains an internal multiplicity of forms which corresponds to the corporeal metamorphoses of those who pursue her. She can be the object of Arthur's and Guyon's quest as well as of Proteus's, for the heroic knights see her as "the fairest Dame aliue." She makes Arthur think of Gloriana: "Oft did he wish, that Lady faire mote bee / His Faery Queene, for whom he did complaine: / Or that his Faery Queene were such, as shee" (3.4.54). When she is forced to stay with the witch and be adored by the son, she makes a passable pastoral queen. She reflects her lovers' changeability because that is her own essence. As she is passing from the fisherman to Proteus, Spenser tells us that "Her selfe not saued yet from daunger dred / She thought, but chaung'd from one to other feare" (3.8.33). This internal change is perfectly mirrored by her uncertain fate.

The creation of False Florimell represents the clearest indication that she has protean potentialities. False Florimell is from her inception the image of Florimell as seen through the eyes of lust. She is at once Florimell's double and opposite. False Florimell is outside the order of nature ("That euen Nature selfe enuide the same, / And grudg'd to see the counterfet should shame / The thing it selfe" [3.8.5]) because lust would see the pinnacle of beauty as a work of art rather than of nature. She is as beautiful as the real—in the eyes of the majority, who are lustful, even more so—but the elements of her beauty are created by the witch's art. Significantly, a number of these constituents are of the same material as traditional Petrarchan similes for beauty. Her flesh is snow, the red in her cheeks is "perfect vermily," her eyes are "two burning lampes," and her hair is "golden wyre." Thus False Florimell is in the flesh that creature into which the sonneteers have poetically transmuted their ladies. We hardly even need to know that "A wicked Spright with fawning guile" animates the figment. This spirit completes her body and arms her to deal with all those situations that made real Florimell so distraught. The two Florimells are opposites for the obvious reason that their creation, their constituent parts, and their moral meanings are utterly different. But they are double because their bodies appear identical even though one is a real form from the Garden of Adonis and the other is a corporeal illusion fostered by lust and therefore a mirror of lust.

Britomart's love story spans and epitomizes all the concerns of Book III, for her career begins in an immaturity which resembles flaws in the other characters, and it proceeds toward a purgation of these flaws. While the origin of Britomart's love is morally unimpeachable, its very fancifulness suggests the inevitable immaturity of an untried longing. The vision of Artegall in Merlin's mirror is not unlike those multiple visions of false love we saw in the minds of such characters as Timias and Proteus. Though her motives are pure, and the mirror itself is a virtuous protean force, the very sketchy nature of the vision suggests a fragmentation in Britomart's mental state. Her complaint to Glauce is principally concerned with the intangibility of her love: "th'only shade and semblant of a knight, / Whose shape or person yet I neuer saw, / Hath me subjected to loues cruell law" (3.2.38). This is a Malecasta with self-knowledge but without the mature woman's powers either to transform an imaginary love into a real one or to exchange it for another. She is quite rightly afraid she will "feed on

shadows, while I die for food, / And like a shadow wexe" (3.2.44), a
description appropriate to the career of many of the lesser characters in
Book III.

In addition, Britomart's imagined need to disguise her own body on
the visit to Merlin demonstrates a lack of preparedness for meeting her
own destiny, and this Merlin recognizes immediately: "Ne ye faire
Britomartis, thus arayd, / More hidden are, then Sunne in cloudy vele; /
Whom thy good fortune, hauing fate obayd, / Hath hither brought"
(3.3.19). The image of Britomart as the sun, closely connected with her
royal destiny, permeates the book, and at this early stage Merlin sees
that the disguise is an attempt to cloud that sun and deny her good
fortune.[38] The fact that Britomart disguises Artegall in her conversation
with Red Cross may be even a stronger indication that without real
action to win Artegall, she is in danger of a fanciful, wanton love. She
invents these slanders merely in order to allow the real Artegall to
shine and to be able to ask "What shape, what shield, what armes,
what steed, what sted, / And what so else his person most may vaunt?"
(3.2.16). She answers these questions for herself in a way which frag-
ments her own spirit and her image of Artegall:

> But *Britomart* kept on her former course,
>   Ne euer dofte her armes, but all the way
>   Grew pensiue through that amorous discourse,
>   By which the Redcrosse knight did earst display
>   Her louers shape, and cheualrous aray;
>   A thousand thoughts she fashioned in her mind,
>   And in her feigning fancie did pourtray
>   Him such, as fittest she for loue could find,
> Wise, warlike, personable, curteous, and kind.
>
>   [3.4.5]

Her mental state, which gives rise to such a multiple series of imaginary
Artegalls, is the result of inexperience rather than wantonness, but
until the inexperience is remedied it takes a form similar to that of
wantonness.

The fragmentation within Britomart's body at these early stages
mirrors the fancies of her mind. As she herself predicted, the vision of a
shadow Artegall very nearly turns her into a shadow mate for him. At

---

38. See Paul Alpers, *The Poetry of the Faerie Queene* (Princeton: Princeton University
Press, 1967), pp. 393–94.

first she loses all sense of clarity and definition of form: "Sad, solemne, sowre, and full of fancies fraile / She woxe; yet wist she neither how, nor why, / She wist not, silly Mayd, what she did aile, / Yet wist, she was not well at ease perdy" (3.2.27). Once this ailment passes from her mind to her body, she starts to become as shadowy as her love: "through long languour, and hart-burning brame / She shortly like a pyned ghost became, / Which long hath waited by the Stygian strond" (3.2.52). This lack of fulfillment leading to death constitutes the natural process within the shadow world that Britomart must overcome. But even at the time of meeting with Red Cross, her body is still a raging chaos of fragmentation. No lover in Book III, however wanton, undergoes quite such a frenzy of the body as the heroine upon hearing Red Cross praise Artegall:

> But with hart-thrilling throbs and bitter stowre,
> As if she had a feuer fit, did quake,
> And euery daintie limbe with horrour shake;
> And euer and anone the rosy red,
> Flasht through her face, as it had been a flake
> Of lightning, through bright heauen fulmined.
>
> [3.2.5]

Britomart's internal frenzy here is produced by her lack of fulfillment at this stage, her complete lack of knowledge, and the seeming hopelessness of actually reaching Artegall. Only a knowledge of her own progeny and a sequence of knightly action, which are both a matter of her royal destiny, can bring about Britomart's peace.

Merlin's prophecies transform the disordered fragmentation of Britomart's mind and body into an orderly multiplicity. Her body is no longer a battleground of forces and a self-consuming shadow. Rather it is a "Tree, / Whose big embodied braunches shall not lin, / Till they to heauens hight forth stretched bee" (3.3.22). The destiny, which Merlin describes at some length, resembles the histories contained within Alma's mind in Book II. Just as Alma's body contained history because man's mind is a record of the past, so Britomart's body contains history because woman's womb is a record of the future. In this case the future proves that Britomart's vision in the glass was not like the act of a Gardante, who succeeded in wounding her slightly, but rather the beginning of a fulfillment.

The first step in realizing this future is the union with Artegall. Consequently in bodily terms the real form of Artegall becomes the first fruit of her womb: "The louing mother, that nine monethes did beare, / In the deare closet of her painefull side, / Her tender babe, it seeing safe appeare, / Doth not so much reioyce, as she reioyced" (3. 2.11), i.e., at Red Cross's description of the real Artegall. Thus when Britomart is on the true path, the multiplicity in her body and mind is joined. Understanding the fruit of her body corresponds exactly to knowing the form of her love, for both are described as her progeny. It is at this point that she can further multiply her own forms and become a warrior knight and the summit of all warrior knights: Angela, whose armor she wears, Penthesilea, Debora, Camilla, "Yet these, and all that else has puissaunce, / Cannot with noble *Britomart* compare" (3.4.3).

Apart from a few indications that her heart is in the right place during the episodes in Castle Joyous and Malbecco's house, Britomart's only opportunity to prove herself in Book III is the rescue of Amoret from Busyrane's house. The House of Busyrane and the Masque of Cupid, which takes place there, are the distillation in iconographic terms of all wanton love's multiplicity. The tapestry decorations represent the body of wanton love: "A thousand monstrous formes therein were made, / Such as false loue doth oft vpon him weare, / For loue in thousand monstrous formes doth oft appeare" (3.11.51). And the Masque of Cupid represents the mind: "There were full many moe like maladies, / . . . So many moe, as there be phantasies / In wauering wemens wit" (3.12.26).

The metamorphoses of Jupiter for the sake of love are the longest of all the series of transformations in Book III. They have little in common with Adonis's multiple forms, nor are they, like those of Proteus, even meant to deceive. Rather, they give more spice to an endlessly repeated sexual act that does not have the natural beauty of fruition. This dependence of form and pure decorativeness directly contrasts with the distinctiveness and genuineness of the forms we see either in the Garden of Adonis or in the historical fruit of Britomart's womb.

The Masque of Cupid is the exact equivalent of the tapestry in mental terms because it presents a wide range of mutually contradicting inter-

nal states that walk peacefully hand in hand together.[39] Most of the
pairs in the Masque are just those evil complements that have tortured
the minds and bodies of wanton or immature lovers throughout the
book. They tend to represent the link between a wantonness that one
projects to others and a wantonness that one is subject to oneself, e.g.,
Doubt and Danger, Grief and Fury. The multiples of false love coop-
erate in the internal destruction of the individuals who attempt to
practice it, while the multiples of true love are strong and independent.

In entering and destroying the House of Busyrane, Britomart moves,
both concretely and symbolically, from Scudamour to Amoret. When
she is on the outside, she is at first as ignorant of the false forms as is
Scudamour. Together they storm the castle gate only to find that there
is no castle gate, for the house is less a place than it is the picture of a
mind and body. The fires that protect it as walls protect a castle are
internal to both mind and body. Britomart can pass because she is com-
pletely pure—though inexperienced—and because she is "resolu'd to
proue her vtmost might" (3.11.25). Scudamour, who still feels "the
burning torment" within his body, partially belongs to the fires and
therefore cannot pass through them. Once inside, Britomart is initiated
into the mind and body of lust without being tainted by it. Multiplicity,
as we have seen, is its main feature.

But Britomart is constancy itself, proceeding single-mindedly ahead
and prepared to wait for days, if necessary, in order to reach the heart
of the matter. The heart of the matter is not so much Busyrane as
Amoret, for when Britomart bursts through, the forms "streight were
vanisht all and some, / Ne liuing wight she saw in all that roome, / Saue
that same woefull Ladie" (3.12.30). The House was Amoret's mind and
body, and the performance of the masque was a kind of personal com-
munication between Amoret and Britomart. Britomart's vision of
lust's internal state in Amoret and in the House of Busyrane arms her to
proceed with her powers against it and thus prepares her to meet Arte-
gall. Like Red Cross, she has had multiple powers throughout but only
in the final episode is she given the strength and knowledge to combat
the multiplicity of her adversaries. Perhaps this is encapsulated in the
difference between "Be Bold" and "Be Not Too Bold." Once the

39. It is, then, a kind of antitype to the *discordia concors* that Spenser will celebrate in
the Temple of Venus in Book IV.

vision of Artegall in the mirror ended her childhood and the prophesies of Merlin sent her on her knightly quest, she was prepared to "Be Bold." But now that she is shown the exact form (or forms) of her adversary, she realizes that knowledge is as important as strength, that boldness is important, but that she must "Be Not Too Bold." The turning away from boldness suggests a loss of multiplicity in the self and readiness for union. These are the processes of the next book.

6

The movement from the Book of Chastity to the Book of Friendship resembles the step to a higher level on the ladder of Neoplatonic love, though it is not a transition from human love to divine. On the contrary, Book IV is the book of sexual unions, but Spenser exalts these by describing them in terms of Neoplatonic divinity. The matter of Book IV is at once sexual consummation and the transformation of the Many into One. The human body offers an obvious link between these themes since in physical consummation two are made one by their bodies. In the first half of the poem, to be sure, the body was an image of the Many, while the One had implied a transcendence of the body. At this turning point of the poem, Spenser suggests that only through the experience of the body's multiplicity (i.e., within his own and between his and his beloved's) can the lover find the transcendence of the body in union.

This movement from the Many to the One through love can be illuminated by the Neoplatonic interpretation of Blind Cupid. In that scheme, love which can see is concerned with the earthbound matter of carnal passions, i.e., the lady's beauty, but this is, in Plotinus's words, "a wooing of shadows that pass and change."[40] Blind love, on the other hand, can see the One which is beyond the multiple vagaries of the world. The drive toward this vision is strongly implied in Spenser's description of Britomart in Book IV:

> Vpon her first aduenture forth did ride,
> To seeke her lou'd, making blind loue her guide,
> Vnluckie Mayd to seeke her enemie,
> Vnluckie Mayd to seeke him farre and wide,
> Whom, when he was vnto her selfe most nie,

40. See Wind, *Pagan Mysteries*, p. 62.

> She through his late disguizement could him not descrie.
>
> [4.5.29]

"Blind loue" here is richly ambiguous. On the one hand it suggests the "wooing of shadows," for Britomart has spent one and a half books hopelessly pursuing an image in a mirror and has recently met and fought against him without identifying him. Britomart is lost in the world's multiplicity, in the tensions between opposites (she loves her enemy) and in the protean quality of Artegall's body, which can be an image in the mirror and a disguised knight; in these negative respects, her love is blind. On the other hand, the miseries of her predicament are at least partly caused by her use of eyesight rather than insight, for both the image in the mirror and the knightly disguise are *trompes l'oeil*, multiple fantasies of love—of the kind we saw in Book III—rather than true communications or concrete consummations.[41]

At this point, when Britomart is on the verge of penetrating the disguise, the image of blind love suggests a capacity within her to leap from the multiple experience of the world to the One beyond and behind it. The Book of Friendship takes us through the full experience of discord in the body and the self in order to find a concord which is at once corporeal and spiritually transcendent. The unorthodoxy, and at the same time the essence, of Spenser's argument is the equation of the Neoplatonic One with bodily union, whether in sexual consummation or in friendship.

The combination of corporeality and transcendence of the body is most apparent in the figure of hermaphrodite Venus, who represents the purest image of *discordia concors* in *The Faerie Queene*. Venus, "they say,"

> hath both kinds in one,
> Both male and female, both vnder one name:
> She syre and mother is her selfe alone,
> Begets and eke conceiues, ne needeth other none.
>
> [4.10.41]

In one sense, this is a graphic image of bodily union whose ultimate significance is corporeal and sexual. Even the doubleness of the human body—its multiplicity of limbs, which has throughout the tradition

---

41. The iconography of blind love is best treated in Edgar Wind, *Pagan Mysteries*, pp. 53–81. Erwin Panofsky's essay on the subject in *Studies in Iconology* (pp. 95–129), while excellent, is concerned only with the negative interpretation of Cupid's blindness.

been a sign of man's mortality—is here united for "both her feete and legs together twyned/Were with a snake, whose head and tail were fast combyned" (4.10.40). The hermaphrodite derives unity within man's life by depicting the sexual act, in which two are one and which both conceives and begets.

It is almost too obvious to point out the similarity to the description of Scudamour and Amoret in the cancelled stanzas concluding the 1590 edition of the poem: "Had ye them seene, ye would haue surely thought, / That they had beene that faire Hermaphrodite, / . . . So seemd those two, as growne together quite" (3.12.46). Revision of Spenser's plans deprived Scudamour and Amoret of their own sexual act, but gave Scudamour the chance to witness this in the Temple of Venus. It is the real sign of *discordia concors*, and the *concors* is ultimately physical, like many of the most crucial images in the book.

Yet though it may seem natural, the hermaphrodite is also a *lusus naturae* whose implications can diverge from and even contradict sexual union. It is a classic Neoplatonic figure because it contains opposites in one and because freaks of nature were felt to signify the most mysterious and profound of God's truths. This hermaphrodite figure signifies truths concerning the ultimate and hidden perfect state of man, a state which he enjoyed even before the creation of Adam and Eve and which after the fall can only be captured in a seemingly unnatural composite figure. This image realizes the abstract One in corporeal terms. Man can only begin to attain this One by love, and hence the hermaphrodite is a physical definition of ultimate love.[42]

Book IV presents love as the struggle of opposites, a paradox which is infolded in the hermaphrodite and unfolded in Scudamour's approach through the outskirts to the Temple of Venus. At the opening of the canto, his mind is a mirror of the dialectic tension between opposites:

> True he it said, what euer man it sayd,
>   That love with gall and hony doth abound,
>   But if the one be with the other wayd,
>   For euery dram of hony therein found,
>   A pound of gall doth ouer it redound.

[4.10.1]

42. Lewis, *Spenser's Images*, p. 41, quotes Leone Ebreo: "In God the lover, the beloved and their love are all one and the same, and although we count them to be three and say that the lover is informed by the beloved and that love derives from them both (as from the father and mother), yet the whole is one simple unity and essence."

The bit of self-pity is a key to Scudamour's mental state: in the face of seemingly irreconcilable opposites he is a weak man, and this weakness makes him a particularly appropriate figure for the misfortunes of Book IV. The temple, as he approaches it, continues to be essentially double. Twenty knights guard it, and when Scudamour defeats one, "Eftsoones out sprung two more of equall mould" (4.10.10). The porter is Doubt, who is physically double, having "a double face, / Th' one forward looking, th' other backeward bent" (4.10.12), and he is himself paired with Delay, who is spiritually double, since he tries to make wayfarers waver between the alternatives of staying and going ahead. Together, of course, the two are doubles of doubles. Danger is also double: "dreadfull to behold" in front and "deformed fearefull vgly" in the back.

Once past these discordant bodies, Scudamour enters the temple, where the doubleness is at first better resolved. Nature and art exist separately but in harmony, with nature in first place and art in second. Scudamour comes upon the heterosexual lovers, also separate but harmonious, and then the pairs of friends, who are joined even closer for being nearly identical. Near the center of the temple is the triad of Love, Hate, and Concord, which most nearly embodies the simultaneous range and union of the opposites. Again, they are not identical, for Love, the younger brother, was "stronger in his state / Then th' elder, and him maystred still in all debate" (4.10.32). But concord between love and hate leaves them still separate and still potentially struggling with each other. This union remains earthly and is therefore imperfect.[43]

The story of Cambell and Triamond, with its conceptual origins in the family history of Agape's children, illustrates how corporeal union can lead to a transcendence of the body. In bargaining with the fates to allow the life and soul of each son to pass into the next one after death, Agape creates a physical union among them which is closely akin to all the more properly sexual unions in the book. This physical union both assures and proves their essential oneness. The terms have changed since Book I. When the poet unfolds Coelia into Speranza, Fidelia, and Charissa, he enumerates and separates the forces of holiness so that each can have an individual effect on us and on Red Cross. The three brothers in Book IV, as physical offspring of Agape, are the spiritual

43. See Williams, *Spenser's Faerie Queene*, p. 127, on the doubleness of Venus.

offspring of non-sexual love. But they do not subdivide the concept. Rather, each is possessed of the full range of love, and the fact that they are completely complementary without being individualized acts as a definition of love. It is for this reason that they are described in terms of endlessly circular mutuality:

> Stout *Priamond*, but not so strong to strike,
>> Strong *Diamond*, but not so stout a knight,
>> But *Triamond* was stout and strong alike:
>> On horsebacke vsed *Triamond* to fight,
>> And *Priamond* on foote had more delight,
>> But horse and foote knew *Diamond* to wield:
>> With curtaxe vsed *Diamond* to smite,
>> And *Triamond* to handle speare and shield,
> But speare and curtaxe both vsed *Priamond* in field.

[4.2.42]

This stanza demonstrates why in a book so concerned with pairs there is a trio of brothers, for the union of two opposites is essentially tripartite: each member of the pair and the form they take when united. Spenser sets up three knightly dialectics and both separates and unifies the three brothers on the basis of them.

The dialectical idea has its physical counterpart in the plan Agape works out with the fates, for Triamond, endowed with his brothers' lives, becomes the third principle in any union of two, akin to the hermaphrodite, which, as a third sex, is a union of the two sexes. The events of the tournament against Cambell demonstrate the nature of this physical bond among the brothers. When Priamond is killed, his spirit "Did not as others wont, directly fly / Vnto her rest in Plutoes griesly land" but instead travelled "Into his other brethren, that suruiued, / In whom he liu'd a new, of former life depriued" (4.3.13). Physical union, equivalent to an act òf love though born of Agape rather than of Eros, is a means of assuring immortality. In an analogous way, the individuality of two lovers dies with their union and gives rise to a third being, their hermaphroditic being, which is eternal through procreation. The sexual act produces both immortality and extinction. In this case, the being which is created by the act of love among the brothers is a better knight each time the disembodied spirit of a dead brother enters the body of the living.

The assumption of the two dead brothers into Triamond makes him the equal of Cambell in the tournament and thus by giving him a triple dose of Agape prepares him to join his enemy spiritually in a way that parallels the physical union with his brothers. The source of Cambell's special power, by which he can combat the three-in-one strength of his adversaries, is his sister's magic ring, whose force resembles the physical union among his three adversaries. By being able "to staunch all wounds, that mortally did bleed" (4.2.39), the ring reunites flesh with flesh so as to turn death into life. This reunion of separated flesh is the same power which Agape secured for her sons. Even before Cambina comes *ex machina*, the fight between Triamond and Cambell starts to unite them by the very similarity of their responses. They are absolutely equal in fighting, and equal in dying when "both at once fell dead vpon the field, / And each to other seemd the victorie to yield" (4.3.34), then equal in rising up and beginning again.

If the fight is a spiritual union, it is also described as a cosmic and physical one:

> Like as the tide that comes fro th'Ocean mayne,
>   Flowes vp the Shenan with contrarie forse,
>   And ouerruling him in his owne rayne,
>   Driues backe the current of his kindly course,
>   And makes it seeme to haue some other sourse:
>   But when the floud is spent, then backe againe
>   His borrowed waters forst to redisbourse,
>   He sends thc sea his owne with double gaine,
> And tribute eke withall, as to his Soueraine.

[4.3.27]

The figures of Triamond and Cambell are linked with the natural *discordia concors* of the Thames and the Medway, with such unions as that of Florimell and Marinell, and even with political harmony. Cambina merely acts as the external power which helps these tendencies to be realized. In contrast to the similar figures in the Temple of Venus, Cambina is only a peacemaker. Her emblem is not the single eternal serpent, but two serpents "entrayled mutually." The miraculous union that develops between the enemies is in its essence spiritual rather than physical, and as we perceive it at the tournament for Florimell's girdle, it betokens an almost ludicrous degree of mutuality, as when each passes the trophy ceaselessly to the other. The physical union is not irrelevant to this tournament, however, because the success of the friends is partly due to their loyalty to each other and partly due to the fact that each can wear the other's armor.

The tale of Amyas and Placidas provides an almost Shakespearean mirror to the lives of Book IV's titular heroes. The tale begins in just the sort of discord that gave rise to the love of Cambell and Triamond, not between the two young men but in the unnatural attraction between a highborn lady, Aemylia, and the Squire of Low Degree, Amyas. The two are determined to love despite the counsel of friends and relatives. Their inequality leads each of them to painful enthrallment to a monster, and only the friendship of Placidas, in fact his physical similarity to Amyas, and the help of Arthur, can rectify the situation. Placidas's love for his friend is indistinguishable from their physical similarity because only by taking Amyas's place with Poeana can Placidas act upon his love for his friend.

Once the impostor has undertaken his deception, he seems prepared to go all the way with it. It is necessary for the liberty of this composite Amyas–Placidas that he submit to Poeana's wooing. Since this appearance is not a disguise so much as an act of love, Placidas does not lie to Poeana. He "was not bent to former loue," and therefore cheerfully accepts her. In this way he becomes united with his disguise and with his friend. Love of each other and of their ladies has an almost magical power to unite their physical forms. Thus when Aemylia sees Placidas bringing tidings of her love, she does not for a moment consider that she might be seeing Amyas. But when the trio is reunited in rapturous affection, Poeana

> Began to doubt, when she them saw embrace,
> Which was the captiue Squire she lou'd so deare,
> Deceiued through great likenesse of their face,
> For they so like in person did appeare,
> That she vneath discerned, whether whether weare.
>
> [4.9.10]

Arthur's suggestion that nature "by one patterne seene somewhere, / . . . had them made a paragone to be" (4.9.11), sums up their condition in the word "paragone," meaning both a unique pattern of excellence and a match, a mate, or a consort in marriage. It is a key word in the joining of concepts in Book IV, for Spenser creates miraculous prodigies of corporeal union like this pair, brings them together with each other and with their women in order to suggest how unique and beautiful true union is. The sight which inspires Arthur's comment is a corporeal realization of Leone Ebreo's multiples which in true love become "one simple unity and essence."[44]

The meeting of Britomart and Artegall at the midpoint of Book IV, though primarily spiritual, still demonstrates the union of opposites via the body. The story of the lovers who can only be united once they have battled against each other has, particularly in the context of the tournament for Canacee's hand, the force of a bodily union of opposites. The fighting itself prepares for a physical union between them since it is exceptionally intimate, with the two combatants' armor offering remarkably little resistance. Britomart strikes Artegall so hard that "to the tender flesh it went, / And pour'd the purple bloud forth on the gras; / That all his mayle yriv'd, and plates yrent, / Shew'd all his bodie bare vnto the cruell dent" (4.6.15). This stripping away of armor, which results in greater closeness of body to body, is the beginning of their union, for Britomart suffers the same fate after a particularly hard blow:

> The wicked stroke vpon her helmet chaunst,
> And with the force, which in it selfe it bore,
> Her ventayle shard away, and thence forth glaunst
> A downe in vaine, ne harm'd her any more.
> With that her angels face, vnseen afore,
> Like to the ruddie morne appeard in sight,
> Deawed with siluer drops.
>
> [4.6.19]

Stripped of parts of their armor, the lovers are closer together not only because their fight is more physical but also because their uncovered bodies enable them to identify each other. The discord was conducted via the body; so the body becomes the source of concord.

Artegall of course knows nothing of Britomart, but the sight of her beauty removes all his will to fight. Instead he reads her body as a heavenly vision, and "At last fell humbly downe vpon his knee, / And of his wonder made religion" (4.6.22). This is not the only sense in which the vision of Britomart's body is a bringer of peace. For Scudamour, who has been fed with jealousy about Britomart's supposed relations with Amoret, the sight of her femininity resolves all fears and makes him worship her "as some celestiall vision." Much earlier, the same vision had stilled all of Amoret's fears.

44. See above, note 42.

Artegall's body is for Britomart an even more literal source of peace because she is at last able to give a concrete form to the image she saw in the mirror. This knowledge produces in Britomart, just as it did in her lover, a momentary fragmentation of bodily forces: "Her hand fell downe, and would no longer hold / The wrathfull weapon gainst his countnance bold: / . . . She arm'd her tongue, and thought at him to scold; / Nathlesse her tongue not her will obayd, / But brought forth speeches myld" (4.6.27). But, significantly, this fragmentation of love is only momentary. The identification of Artegall by name produces a blush on Britomart's face, but unlike the blushes of *Astrophil and Stella* and of Guyon in the House of Alma, this is described so as to suggest internal unity rather than disunity: "all her vitall powres with motion nimble, / . . . themselues gan there assemble, / That by the swift recourse of flushing blood / Right plaine appeard" (4.6.29). Britomart herself becomes a cosmic body consisting of forces flowing like the rivers, and any attempt to conceal her state from Artegall is fruitless, since her body has so effectively conspired against her delicacy. On this occasion alone is the image of "Continuall siege vnto her gentle hart" meant to suggest a good siege that will be triumphant.

As one might expect in a section of the poem devoted to union and reunion, the evils of Book IV are weaker than any other evils in the poem. Evil is depicted as the combination of an external monster and an internal state within a good or morally equivocal character, as elsewhere in *The Faerie Queene*. But in Book IV the external monster is much less significant than the internal state. For this reason the book contains no magnificent battle with a composite body of evil. Rather the evil characters seem in each case to be wedded to their particular victims. This union is the anti-image to the weddings of good characters.

The foursome of Ate, Duessa, Paridell, and Blandamour most fully realizes this interrelation between evil and its victim, though in a more spiritual than physical way. Ate and Duessa are themselves a wedded pair of evils, between them representing a composite machine designed to undo the unwary. Together they represent an evil version of opposites united in one. Ate is the principle of doubleness and disagreement, while Duessa is the bait which can assume opposite forms so as to breed war where there was peace. Ate enables Duessa to create opposing sides in battle, and Duessa "was as it were her baude, / To sell her borrowed beautie to abuse" (4.1.31). The doubleness of effect is not only the result of the separation between Ate and Duessa but is also inherent in each of them by herself. Duessa, as we saw in Book I, is an emblem of doubleness, an unresolved combination of opposites. Ate is double in every part of her body:

> Her lying tongue was in two parts diuided,
> And both parts did speake, and both contended;
> And as her tongue, so was her hart discided,
> That neuer thoght one thing, but doubly stil was guided.
> Als as she double spake, so heard she double, . . .
> And as her eares so eke her feet were odde,
> And much vnlike, th' one long, the other short,
> And both misplast; that when th' one forward yode,
> The other backe retired, and contrarie trode.
> Likewise vnequall were her handes twaine,
> That one did reach, the other pusht away,
> That one did make, the other mard againe,
> And sought to bring all things vnto decay.

[4.1.27–29]

The implications of this physical picture are complemented by her power to enter the bodies of others, for her greatest pleasure is to stir up strife between people "That she may sucke their life, and drink their blood, / With which she from childhood had bene fed" (4.1.26). The physical union involved in this eating and drinking typifies the internal power of evil in Book IV.

Paridell and Blandamour are perfectly symmetrical with Duessa and Ate because they are similar to the two women and complementary to each other. Blandamour has a "fickle mind full of inconstancie" (4.1. 32), and Paridell is as false as Duessa. While they are friends, they are as interchangeable as Cambell and Triamond. When Paridell is unwilling to fight with Britomart over Amoret, Blandamour gives up his lady, Duessa, and fights for Amoret himself. When Blandamour is too exhausted to approach Scudamour, Paridell takes his place and casts their friendship into physical terms which suddenly seem coarse and self-serving: "do not dismay / Your selfe for this, my selfe will for you fight, / As ye haue done for me: the left hand rubs the right" (4.1.40). The physical image seems to suggest bodily union, but in fact turns into just the sort of friction which rubbing can produce.

The complete symmetry of their interchangeability seems to be the cause of their strife. They spend too much time rubbing the left hand and the right and too little time achieving real union. This failure is suggested by other strands of imagery. The fight with Scudamour is described with the ubiquitous water imagery, but in this case the contrary billows strike each other without uniting: rather, "each abacke rebowndes / With roaring rage," and only Scudamour easily stands up again. There is a similar image of contact without union between Paridell and Scudamour when they have fallen out with each other:

> As when two warlike Brigandines at sea,
>   With murdrous weapons arm'd to cruell fight,
>   Doe meete together on the watry lea,
>   They stemme ech other with so fell despight,
>   That with the shocke of their owne heedlesse might,
>   Their wooden ribs are shaken nigh a sonder;
>   They which from shore behold the dreadfull sight
>   Of flashing fire, and heare the ordenance thonder,
> Do greatly stand amaz'd at such vnwonted wonder.
>
> [4.2.16]

The flashing fire again represents the sort of friction produced by rubbing of the hands.

The sequence of evil monsters in Book IV, Care, Lust, Sclaunder, and Corflambo, all appear in close proximity in Cantos Five through Eight. By Spenserian standards they are impotent and colorless, not because the poet's inspiration was failing but because he was more interested in the effect of these monsters upon their victims than in a display of iconographic brilliance. In keeping with the recurrent image in Book IV of bodily union between two characters, Spenser joins each of these monsters physically with its victim. Like the great good concords of Book IV, these physical unions result in a loss of the self and the birth of a third principle, i.e., the monster and victim united. The description of Care is brief and uninteresting, but the force of Care within Scudamour's mind is treated at length. The physical features of the blacksmith's shop are meaningful only in terms of Scudamour's mental state. The iron wedges which Care makes are "vnquiet thoughts, that carefull minds inuade" (4.5.35). The hammers and the bellows are means of disturbing the knight's sleep, and the tongs wake him up just when his dream is becoming intolerable. Once joined with Care, Scudamour is fragmented within himself. He ends up resembling one of Care's implements, "like heauie lumpe of lead," and not at all resembling himself: "in his face, as in a looking glasse, / The signes of anguish one mote plainely read, / And ghesse the man to be dismayd with gealous dread" (4.5.45).

Lust is joined even more closely in body with his victims. In allegorical terms Aemylia's meeting with Lust was a confrontation with herself because, eloping despite her family's objections, she finds Lust instead of her squire Amyas. But in very concrete terms, Lust is joined with his victims because he eats their bodies. His own body is that of a carnivore and cannibal: "his wide mouth did gape / With huge great teeth, like to a tusked Bore: / For he liu'd all on rauin and on rape / Of men and beasts" (4.7.5).[45] Aemylia has escaped this complete union via cannibalism because there is still in the den a hag more susceptible to his advances than she is, the hag having essentially been eaten away already.

Amoret, who has the strength to flee, is still less susceptible to union with Lust. But she does seem partially his victim in the fight with Timias:

> Thereto the villaine vsed craft in fight;
>> For euer when the squire his iauelin shooke,
>> He held the Lady forth before him right,
>> And with her body, as a buckler, broke
>> The puissance of his intended stroke.
>> And if it chaunst, (as needs it must in fight)
>> Whilest he on him was greedy to be wroke,
>> That any little blow on her did light,
> Then would he laugh aloud, and gather great delight.
>
> [4.7.26]

In this way Amoret's body is joined with Lust's, for her chastity becomes his armor. Only extremely careful fighting by Timias is able to disengage Lust from his armor. This wit on the squire's part becomes the allegorical equivalent of a nascent ability to distinguish lust and chastity, though the very dilemma is a sign that he has some difficulty in making this distinction.[46]

Sclaunder, like Care a specific image of dissension, though in this case among individuals rather than within, is described in terms of an overflowing body: "she was stuft with rancour and despight / Vp to the

---

45. Thomas P. Roche, Jr., in *The Kindly Flame*, p. 137, sees in these lines a "graphic description" of the male genitalia. Such a possibility would form an interesting part of the present argument, though I am not certain that the anatomical reference is so clear.

46. Of course, the physical inextricability of Amoret and Lust is allegorically significant for her own development as well.

throat, that oft with bitternesse / It forth would breake, and gush in great excesse" (4.8.24). The physical force she exerts upon the bodies of her victims is a kind of inundation that gradually travels over each part of the body:

> noysome breath, and poysnous spirit sent
> From inward parts, with cancred malice lind,
> And breathed forth with blast of bitter wind;
> Which passing through the eares, would pierce the hart,
> And wound the soule it selfe with griefe vnkind.
>
> [4.8.26]

Union with her is a result of contagion. This contagion is capable not only of spreading to other characters but even, as Spenser slyly suggests, to us, for he chastises us for having evil thoughts about Arthur entertaining Amoret and Aemylia in Sclaunder's house: "some rash witted wight, / Whose looser thought will lightly be misled, / These gentle Ladies will misdeeme too light, / For thus conversing with this noble knight" (4.8.29). In these days, with temperance so rare, Sclaunder's contagion has spread everywhere.

Corflambo, who conquered Amyas in just the way that Lust took Aemylia, unites with the bodies of his victims by the power of his wounding sight "Full of sad powre, that poysonous bale did breede / To all, that on him lookt without good heed" (4.8.39). As in the Petrarchan love ethic, which so often described the lady's eyes as basilisks, Corflambo is an expression of loose love and has the capacity, once having entered a woman, to have "captiued her thought." Thus when at their appointed assignation Aemylia met Lust and Amyas met Corflambo, they were in a sense meeting each other. The squire's heedless eagerness to join with a lady of higher class is the result of lust, and her power over him was gained by a basilisk-like Petrarchan flirtation. The potential union of each of their bodies with the monster represents a mock physical union with the beloved.

Book IV closes with two unions: the marriage of the Thames and the Medway, which forms a cosmic conclusion, and the joining of Marinell and Florimell, which forms a personal conclusion. Both express physical union and transcendence of the body's multiplicity in the One. Just as the House of Alma, in a book concerned with the single individual, takes that individual and refracts him so as to include all of history and geography, so the marriage of the Thames and the

Medway does the same for the pair of individuals. The essential image is of course the union of the Many and the One, but this image is shaped by the fact that it is a wedding of two in which each brings a world of multiples together. For this reason the references in the canto are extremely inclusive: countless nations are represented, history is seen in the Scamaunder, which still contains the blood of Greeks and Trojans, geography is represented with all the parts of England as well as such distant areas as South America, and also included are the wonders of civilization like London, Oxford, and Cambridge.

But more important than the range of references is the method by which they are joined. The flowing of water is throughout Book IV (and all of Spenser's work) an image of organic union. Here in a canto so concerned with grandsires, sires, and children, the force connecting these generations is the literal flowing together of their forms. Thus near the beginning of the procession is Ocean and his consort Tethys, "For all the rest of those two parents came, / Which afterward both sea and land possest" (4.11.18), and at the end of the procession come the fifty Nereids, who are all united in being the daughters of Nereus, eldest born of Ocean and Tethys. The image of the wedding is of rivers

> All which long sundred, doe at last accord
> To ioyne in one, ere to the sea they come,
> So flowing all from one, all one at last become.

[4.11.43]

This is in essence the form of Book IV, a contrast to the historical, dynastic method of earlier books which turned the individual into an infinite sequence by means of the act of redemption, the scope of the mind, or the fruit of the womb. The Thames and the Medway do not unite for the sake of "children" they may bear. Rather their union is the celebration of the cosmic chain which permanently unites all of nature's forms. All of life, and all of Spenser's poem, is the ceaseless movement from the One to the Many back to the One, and so on. The means by which this endless chain is made and affirmed is the union of one with one. The disjunction between two individuals who ought to be united is a kind of dissonance in the cosmic harmony, a break in the universal electric circuit. The Medway had for a long time denied the suits of the Thames. Now that they are united, all the waters can flow together.

The two Florimells, in contrast to many other figures in Book IV, are united in body but diametrically opposed in spirit. Through this paradox, the two can image forth the whole range from personal discord to cosmic concord. The reason for the prominence of the Cestus tournament in Book IV becomes apparent in the contradiction between the two Florimells, each of whom is in some way physically represented there. The opening cantos of the book strongly emphasize the negative aspect of discord, but it is important in the face of this denunciation that the virtue of knightly combat and striving is not similarly discredited. Hence we have this tournament which is a meeting of good and bad strife.

The Florimells, one represented in body and the other by that girdle which perfectly fits her body, present the whole range. False Florimell, allied with the most fickle knights, stirs up the strife, but the girdle, which represents the real Florimell's body in a way that False Florimell cannot copy, purges the tournament of discord. Even the first mention of the girdle by the Squire of Dames to Blandamour and Paridell turns their strife into union as they prepare together to win it for False Florimell. The girdle has a power of its own apart from that of anyone who might win it or hold it: "That girdle gaue the vertue of chast loue, / And wiuehood true, to all that did it beare; / But whosoeuer contrarie doth proue, / Might not the same about her middle weare" (4.5.3). The only person to whom it is subject is Florimell, for this power of discovering and binding virtue comes directly from her spirit and her body, though more remotely from a still chaste Venus who has not yet committed adultery with Mars. Thus if False Florimell is one equivalent of Florimell's body, Cestus is another. Cestus is truly united with Florimell's body because it alone is not deceived by the false union with Florimell's body that the old witch created. In the form of her girdle Florimell is herself present at the tournament judging the wanton ladies and the contentious knights, saying, as the Squire of Dames cynically interprets it, "*Vngirt vnblest.*"

In affirming Amoret's body and rejecting False Florimell's, Cestus succeeds in dividing the good knights in the tournament from the bad and in destroying much of the power and appeal which False Florimell had won. That the girdle chooses Amoret, Britomart's lady, is in perfect keeping with the fact that Britomart has won the tournament, while Blandamour, who is False Florimell's knight, has made an undistinguished showing. And once Cestus has made its choice, False

Florimell suddenly becomes a highly unsalable piece of merchandise. She is offered to all the truly successful knights of the tournament (i.e., the virtuous ones), but one after another they refuse her. She retains the power to stir up discord, but ultimately is forced to choose a knight—the nearest thing to an act of sincerity she is ever driven to— and chooses the falsest of all, Braggadocchio. In this way, the virtue of real Florimell's body has the power to bring union out of discord to both the good and evil camps.

The power of Cestus to unite those who ought to be united is just what the real Florimell lacks. She and Marinell are both essentially imprisoned, she in Proteus's cave and he in a false misogyny which is seen in physical terms as an expulsion of woman's love from his heart, a mistake that leads him to "loue him selfe alone." The imagery which describes this double imprisonment ties it in strongly with the concepts of physical union and corporeal transcendence. Florimell becomes Proteus's prisoner in Book III in an episode emphasizing the flaw of multiplicity in the sea god. Book IV, on the other hand, treats the sea as the primal image of union. Florimell is literally trapped between these two significations. Her dungeon is surrounded by a sea which is multiple and frightening: "wall'd it was with waues, which rag'd and ror'd / As they the cliffe in peeces would haue cleft; / Besides ten thousand monsters foule abhor'd / Did waite about it, gaping griesly all begor'd" (4.11.3). Water is also evoked in the images of the Thames and the Medway, the prototype of universal union and generation.

Between these two significations stands Marinell, also belonging to the sea as grandson of Nereus. The endless gems of his "rich strond" suggest the sea's fruitfulness, but at the same time they are multiple, cold, and infertile. Florimell's complaints have some of the uniting power of the sea to erode obstacles. At the same time her imprisonment represents an obstacle to the flow of the sea, for we are told that when she complained, "ruth it moued in the rocky stone" (4.12.5), and she herself says, "Yet loe the seas I see by often beating, / Doe pearce the rockes, and hardest marble weares; / But his hard rocky hart for no entreating / Will yeeld, but when my piteous plaints he heares, / Is hardned more with my aboundant teares" (4.12.7). At this point, then, Florimell's sea of tears cannot erode Marinell's obstacles and flow together with him.

Fittingly Marinell undergoes his change at the feast of the Thames and the Medway, for that is the great celebration of the union of all the waters. The trials of the love, once it is born in him, lead him almost to death and to much the same kind of torture that Florimell is undergoing. He tries to imitate the sea in constantly flowing around the rock upon which Florimell is imprisoned, but alone he cannot produce union. Neptune purges the sea of its protean element and eliminates the one obstacle to the perfect flowing together of the waters. This physical union restores life to both their bodies. Thus the seas are simultaneously the principle of the One, the two, and the Many. The One is their single, common source, the Ocean, or love, "that leads each liuing kind"; the two is the Thames and the Medway, Florimell and Marinell, all the pairs which are united by love's force; the Many is the endless progeny of the seas,

> So fertile be the flouds in generation,
> So huge their numbers, and so numberlesse their nation.
> Therefore the antique wisards well inuented,
>   That *Venus* of the foamy sea was bred;
>   For that the seas by her are most augmented.
>   Witnesse th' exceeding fry, which there are fed,
>   And wondrous sholes, which may of none be red.
>
> [4.12.1–2]

Thus we return to the figure of Venus, who in Book III represented half the origin of forms, early in Book IV the hermaphrodite, and now in addition all the progeny which result from the sexual union implied by the hermaphrodite.

In the transcendence or flowing together of individual bodies, which can represent the most mysterious and abstract religious truths, Spenser reminds us that he also finds the most concrete assertion in the universe: sexual reproduction. By returning to the Many in this final canto of physical oneness, the poet again emphasizes that this is the book of paradox, of the simultaneous presence of opposites. The human body is not only paradoxical in structure, being at once united and fragmented, but it is also a generator of paradoxes: it is at once the image of individual identities, like those of Red Cross or Britomart, and the means by which self and identity are transcended, whether in the Neoplatonic ladder from the profane to the sacred or in the sexual act itself. Since Book IV is a union of paradoxes, it becomes clear at the end that the transcendence of the body is only a means for the production of more bodies.

7

The transformation of Spenserian multiples into unities is not confined to the processes of the last three books. The breaking down of single individuals into multiple worlds and of single concepts into multiple groups of allegorical figures stands as a central principle for the method and meaning of the whole poem. In the case of the Graces, we saw Spenser explain a rich and ambiguous unity—Venus—by unfolding her into three clearer constituent parts, and then reuniting the trinity in a figure—Colin's shepherdess—rich and ambiguous, but more palpable because of the process by which she had been generated. The process of the whole poem can be compared to this unfolding and reinfolding, but in the poem's overall design Spenser deliberately leaves the reinfolded figure outside the text of the poem. All the multiplicities of the poem's fabric—and no English poem is richer in them—point outside the text toward a larger personage who never appears.

This external personage can be identified variously: the perfect gentleman, Gloriana, or Arthur, who appears in the text but clearly has some special composite function. Each of these figures is steeped in imagery suggesting the Many returning to the One. The figure of the perfect gentleman appears in Spenser's description of his purposes to Sir Walter Ralegh: "the generall end therefore of all the booke is to fashion a gentleman or noble person in vertuous and gentle disci- pline."[47] Spenser here implies that all twelve virtues are essential parts of the gentleman and that the heroes depicting them can form the composite parts of the gentleman's anatomy. He is speaking very much in the tradition of Castiglione, whose *Book of the Courtier* is structured upon the idea that hypothetical perfection is inherently multiple. Count Lodovico says at the outset:

> To recognize true perfection in anything is so difficult as to be scarcely possible; and this because of the way opinions vary. Thus there are many who like to hear someone talking a great deal and who will call him an agreeable companion. Some will prefer reticence; others an active and restless man; others one who always acts with calmness and deliberation; and so everyone praises or condemns according to his own opinion, always camouflaging a vice under the name of the corresponding virtue, or a virtue under the name of the corresponding vice. . . . Still I do think there is a perfection for everything, even though it may be concealed, and I also

47. Spenser, *Poetical Works*, 3: 486.

think that this perfection can be determined through informed and reasoned argument.[48]

From these presuppositions, Castiglione structures his work, allowing each conversant to have his say in defining composite perfection. For Spenser, the composite quality of corresponding virtues and vices is pregnant with meaning, itself suggesting a world of moral precariousness: Is Guyon in the Bower of Bliss temperate or prideful, and is Florimell, when pursued by Arthur, inconstant or chaste? The "vertuous and gentle discipline" is a difficult composite perfection.

According to the Letter to Ralegh, Prince Arthur in particular is the image of this composite perfection, and here Spenser's intention is clearly composite and reunifying:

> So in the person of Prince Arthure I sette forth magnificence in particular, which vertue for that (according to Aristotle and the rest) it is the perfection of all the rest, and conteineth in it them all, therefore in the whole course I mention the deedes of Arthure applyable to that vertue, which I write of in that booke.[49]

As has often been pointed out,[50] Spenser's portrayal of Arthur is far from a perfect fulfillment of these promises. Yet the description tells us a good deal about Spenser's poetics even if Arthur does not play this role in the poem as we have it. Though he traverses the poem, his beginning—the vision of Gloriana—and his end—the union with her—are outside its bounds, and it is through those acts that he can become the perfect composite form reunifying the poem's multiplicities of virtue. This technique typifies Spenser's medievalism, for, as Rosemund Tuve pointed out, "magnificence" is a composite virtue in the traditional medieval scheme.[51]

Gloriana, equated with Queen Elizabeth, is perhaps the clearest instance of Spenser's reaching beyond the poem for a personalized composite unity. Faery is Gloriana, and Gloriana is Queen Elizabeth. This is true not only in the vague and general sense suggested by "And thou, O fairest Princesse vnder sky, / In this faire mirrhour maist behold thy face" (2. Proem. 4), but also in such concrete terms as in her composite depiction in the characters of Gloriana and Belphoebe.

48. Baldesar Castiglione, *The Book of the Courtier*, trans. George Bull (London: Penguin, 1967), p. 53.
49. Spenser, *Poetical Works*, 3:486.
50. Lewis, *Spenser's Images*, pp. 137–40.
51. *Allegorical Imagery*, pp. 57–145.

Thus Spenser asks her, "In mirrours more then one her selfe to see, / But either *Gloriana* let her chuse, / Or in *Belphoebe* fashioned to bee: / In th' one her rule, in th' other her rare chastitee" (3. Proem. 5). But perhaps the broadest and fullest indication of this composite method is that which borrows directly on the image of the rivers:

> Then pardon me, most dreaded Soueraine,
>   That from your selfe I doe this vertue bring,
>   And to your selfe doe it returne againe:
>   So from the Ocean all riuers spring,
>   And tribute backe repay as to their King.
>
> [6. Proem. 7]

Spenser's poetic flights, his world of characters and images, are the rivers, which flow from a single source, either himself or his paragon, and ultimately relate to a single object, either as an offering to Queen Elizabeth or as a unified picture of the composite perfect man.

The present study has emphasized how the allegorization of the human body tends to break down a single individual into a world of multiple meanings and drives. But it should not be forgotten that this process has an almost inevitable complement: the reunion of many individuals in a single, larger, composite body. Thus Donne's fragmentation of body and self in the *Devotions* is not opposed to but rather inextricable from his belief that "no man is an island," that a baptized child is "thereby connected to that body which is my head too."[52] And in a less optimistic vein, the fragmentation of a Sejanus or a Coriolanus is balanced by the image of a composite human body of the state, in which the citizens, themselves with multiple bodies, are component organs. All the images of fragmentation in *The Faerie Queene*, whether of the individual, like Alma, or of the single concept divided into a multiplicity of individuals, like Malecasta's six courtly knights, have their own inherent reunification. One might argue endlessly whether Malecasta generates the Gardante group or they her. This is less important than the realization that for every multiple there is a unity, for every Priamond group an Agape, for every Lucifera a band of deadly sins.

This endless flux from the single figure to multiples and back, is the essence and the uniqueness of Spenserian allegory. The special triumph of the poem is not only the implementation of this idea but also the

---

52. *Devotions upon Emergent Occasions*, Meditation 17, p. 107.

success with which Spenser manipulates the narrative so that neither the single nor the multiple ever seems an arbitrary excuse for the other, a pure piece of ornamentation, or a flat-footed explication. The Spenserian hero moves through a world which is determined by this flux. Good characters with the internal fortitude to be immune to or triumphant over the single antagonist are brought low by the antagonist's personified multiple subdivisions, and good characters with the skill and diversity to fend off the multiples often lack the internal strength to combat the single. We must exist in a world which contains both essences and shadows: our contemplative power must grasp the hidden essences, and our active power must negotiate the terms of life with the shadows.

The human body is a crucial image because it is single and multiple at once, and because it is the midpoint in a great hourglass structure. When Spenser anatomizes (and the very word suggests the union between multiplicity and the body) Alma or describes emotional reactions within Britomart in cosmological terms, he is demonstrating that the body is a multiple world. But when he points outside the poem to abstract perfections or composite characters, he is using the same process of anatomizing to unite the multiple world into a human body. Spenser's poem is centrally concerned with the process of anatomizing and reuniting, and all the anatomy (in both senses of the word) in the fabric of the poem demands the reunifying effect of composite perfections which must, for their very ineffability, remain offstage. Yet these perfections are human, however we may choose to identify them, and the emblem of their humanity is their generation out of two mortal parents: the world and the human body. Thus Spenser for all his orthodox Neoplatonism, is seeking not only the One but also the Many, for perfection in his terms is human and multiple at the same time as it is single and immortal.

Afterword

It should come as no surprise that a work like *The Faerie Queene*, at once microcosmic in technique and grandly cosmological in scope, should point to an external goal too great to be contained within the poem. The microcosmic idea, for all its glorious history and intellectual grandeur, is inherently limiting. The human body is a very small thing, and despite the vividness of Renaissance poetic imagery, the infinity of the world and the heavens cannot literally be contained within it. All the imaginative thought and poetic creation wc have considered here, then, partakes of an esthetic by which great things can be captured in smaller proportional replicas. Such is perhaps the keystone of Renaissance poetics: the absolute equality of aspiration and limitation.

The image of a cosmic human body was dear to the men of the Renaissance because they felt imaginative synthesis to be identical to proportional reduction. The drive toward the creation of diversified but limited wholenesses is expressed by the creation of whole ranges of analogous *cosmoi*. The present study has tried to describe only a few of these. The equations of world, society, and man-made creations with the human body are only the beginning, for *cosmoi* like these and many others more spiritual, are capable of innumerable correlations which have not been discussed here. Yet equally as interesting as these objective terms which the human body has offered to metaphor and allegory is the insight which its use suggests into the Renaissance imagination.

Above all, the use of these analogies and the creation of these wholenesses suggest a belief that the universe, in something like its totality, can be captured in a poem. This belief underlies much Italian poetic theory of the sixteenth century. Guarini, in his *Compendium of Tragi-comic Poetry*, is one of many who creates an esthetic that is also a cosmology:

> There is nothing of any sort in this world subject to perception and alteration which does not participate in this rare gift of imitation. Beginning with the creation of the world, does it not appear that when the divine workman produced it he wished in some sense to imitate? and not merely because he produced it in conformity with the divine idea that had been in his breast from all eternity, but because in the celestial production he made it in the semblance of eternity, in that it could not be injured or altered. . . . Then in forming man as a little world, the divine voice of the same divine artist indicated that he was pleased with the work of imitation, saying: Let us make man in our own image, after our own likeness.[1]

The familiar parallel between the poet and God is more than a mere further step in the chain of analogies. The parallel demonstrates that poetic aspiration can be realized, and though this aspiration may seem as grand as God's creative design, it is also limited by the analogical system, i.e., by the process of imitation. A great overreacher like Tamburlaine finds his aspiration unrealizable, while his creator produces in him a successful mimesis of the cosmos, proving that poetic aspiration is realizable. In this system of analogies, the Renaissance poet develops the capacity to grasp infinity as none of his characters ever can, but in return he must be content to play by the rules of imitation.

Work as diverse as Sidney's lyrical sonnets and Spenser's chivalric epic unite in the creation of miniature wholenesses because those microcosms, whether conveyed completely or in *chiaroscuro*, are the only means for grasping the total universe. This esthetic is nowhere clearer than in Tasso's *Discourses on the Heroic Poem* (1594):

> But for all that, one is the world which includes so many and such diverse things in its bosom, one its form and essence, one the knot which joins and binds its parts in discordant harmony together; and lacking nothing in itself, it contains nothing that does not serve as either necessity or ornament. Likewise I judge that the excellent poet (he who is called divine for no other reason but that resembling in his works the supreme Artist he comes to participate in His divinity) can create a poem in which, as in a little world, can be seen here troops in the field, there land and sea battles, attacks on cities, skirmishes and duels, jousts, descriptions of hunger and thirst, tempests, fires, prodigies. . . . Nevertheless, the poem that contains such a variety of material is one, one is its form and soul. All these things should be com-

1. In Allan H. Gilbert, ed., *Literary Criticism: Plato to Dryden* (Detroit: Wayne State University Press, 1962), pp. 505–06.

posed in such a manner that each thing relates to the others, each corresponds to the others, each depends either necessarily or apparently upon the others; so that if one part is taken away or changed, the whole is destroyed. And if this be true, then the art of composing a poem is like the laws of nature in the universe, which is composed of contraries (as we see in the laws of music); for if there were no multiplicity, there would be no wholeness and no law, as Plotinus says.[2]

This belief in the *discordia concors* arises out of the Renaissance vision of a more complex world and a desire for more inclusive poetry. That search has as its immediate complement a sense of limitation as well as a need for the limitation offered by unity.

The human body becomes one of the prime images of this unity. As great as the world, as divine in its inception, as close to the image of God, it is still small, familiar, and in most respects comprehensible. To the Renaissance esthetic it offers the hope of combining aspiration and unity. Giraldi Cinthio, in *On Romances* (1549), defends the unity of a particularly diverse literary form by prescribing adherence to the image of the body:

When the writer has planned where he is to begin his work, he ought to exercise great diligence to see that the parts fit together as do the parts of the body. . . . In putting the framework together, he will seek to fill up the hollows and to equalize the size of the members. This can be done by putting the filling matters in proper and necessary places, such as loves, hates, plaints, laughter, jests, grave matter, discords, peace-makings, ugly and beautiful things, descriptions of places, times, persons, fables feigned by himself and drawn from olden times, voyages, wanderings, shows, unforeseen events, deaths, funeral rites, lamentations, recognitions, things terrible and pitiable, nuptials, births, victories, triumphs, single combats, jousts, tournaments, catalogs, marshaling of troops, and other similar things which perhaps are such that it would be no small task to detail all one by one. There is nothing above or under the heavens or in the depths of the abyss that is not at the command and under the judgment of the prudent poet who can with varied ornaments embellish the body of his work and bring it not merely to an excellent but to a lovely figure. With these he gives the parts a just measure and decorous ornament, in such proportion that the result is a disciplined and well constituted body.[3]

The sheer magnitude of Giraldi Cinthio's list should suggest what a miracle of construction the body was felt to be. Its principles offered the

2. Tasso, *Discorsi dell'Arte Poetica e del Poema Eroico*, ed. Luigi Poma (Bari: Laterza, 1964), p. 140.
3. *On Romances*, trans. Henry L. Snuggs (Lexington: University of Kentucky Press, 1968), p. 24.

poet the opportunity to include everything in the universe with no fear
of fragmentation or disorder, simply because God had included every-
thing in the universe within the body of man without causing the form
or content to be disordered. Thus the human body becomes itself one
of the objects for which the Renaissance poet strives. Its esthetic perfec-
tion is as much the object of the poet's quest as the body politic is for
Sejanus or the macrocosmic body for Tamburlane. But the Renaissance
poets are more optimistic about their own quest than about those of
their characters. This is largely because the human body is inherently
small, while its analogues are inherently great.

Questing after an inherently small proportional cosmos represents as
important a part of the Renaissance esthetic as do the more optimistic
overreachings of humanism. The image of the vast contained in the
little is a commonplace of English Renaissance poetry, not only for
George Herbert whose whole poetic is based upon the image, but also
for more soaring spirits like Donne, Marvell, and Milton. Yet this sense
of containment, which is the essence of the image of the human body,
is ultimately as limiting as the size of the body itself. For this problem
there are two kinds of solutions, conservative and radical. The first be-
longs to Spenser (and indeed to nearly all the other poets who have been
considered here): the poet escapes the limitations of the individual man
and of the image of his by body creating a greater, though hypotheti-
cal, cosmic or human body which is proportional and analogous, yet at
the same time inclusive of all the other orders. Such a creation we find
not only in Spenser's Gloriana or Arthur but also in all those evocations
in Donne, Shakespeare, Sidney etc., of the body of the world, the body
of the State, or the body of a building. All these proportional replicas
are greater than the individual, much more undefinable, and yet subject
to the human body's proportional laws. Like Gloriana, they free the
poet from the limits of the individual, but they are still limited by imita-
tion.

The radical solution is one that points toward the death of the micro-
cosmic idea. By the middle of the seventeenth century, we can observe
a severe rejection of proportion, of limitation, of the willingness to
allow diversity to exist within unity. Marvell, Milton, and Traherne
illustrate three strands of this rejection. Marvell doubts more seriously
than any of his "metaphysical" predecessors whether the poet is, in fact,
such a Prometheus as to capture the world in the terms which Tasso or

Giraldi Cinthio used. Though obsessed with microcosmic ideas and with the power of the poet's mind, his work suggests that the poet is as lost in the diversity and chaos of the world as are his characters. If he is one with his fictive world, if he is "ensnared with flowers," how can he capture the universe any better than they?

Milton's epic is perhaps the most decisive break in English literature with the medieval tradition largely because Milton is prepared, as no one was before, to treat the cosmos on its own terms. Despite the imposition, as many have felt it, of a doctrinaire Christian teleology, Milton's cosmology is uniquely literal and empirical. If the cosmos is taken so clearly as a thing in itself, then the system of analogous *cosmoi* becomes little more than a moribund figure of speech.

Traherne, as Majorie Nicolson has pointed out,[4] is a radical because he rejects proportion in favor of infinity. Though as conscious of limitation as earlier poets, he always affirms the complete abstract power of man and of the universe to break out of limitation. The synthetic imagination occupies itself not with the capturing of wholeness, but with the celebration of uncapturable infinity. Poetic structure is no longer an hourglass, but rather a pair of lines forming an angle extending infinitely. He does not reject analogy, as does Milton, or the Promethean power of the poet, as does Marvell, but he does reject proportion or finitude:

> A Strange Extended Orb of Joy,
>> Proceeding from within,
> Which did on evry side convey
> It self, and being nigh of Kin
>> To God did evry Way
> Dilate it self even in an Instant, and
> Like an Indivisible Centre Stand,
> At once Surrounding all Eternity.
>> Twas not a Sphere,
>> Yet did appear,
> One Infinit. Twas somwhat evry where.[5]

In the face of these rejections, the human body as image of the world loses its power, for such an image presupposes that the poet is a godlike maker of worlds, that the meaning of worlds is to be found in an endless

4. *The Breaking of the Circle*, pp. 196–204.
5. Thomas Traherne, "My Spirit," in *Centuries, Poems, and Thanksgivings*, ed. H. M. Margoliouth (Oxford: Clarendon Press, 1958), 2:51–56.

series of reflections and analogues, and that totality can be grasped by proportion. The concerns of more recent times, the self-doubting creator, nature and the world viewed for their own sakes, the belief in chaos and ineffability, are innately different from the feelings which produced the microcosmic image of the body. The loss of the certainties about poet, cosmos, and proportion has not been consistent or total since 1650, but the poetry of the Renaissance is the last which celebrated all these certainties. All the rest is modern literature.

Index

Abrams, M. H., 205–06
Acidale, 217–19
Adonis, 243, 245–46, 254
Affections, 170–71
Agape, 259–61
Alanus de Insulis, 119–21
Alberti Leone Battista, 125, 140, 140–41*n*, 147
Alchemy, 212
Allegory: and multiplicity and unity, 4–5, 117–18, 186, 220, 275; of the body, 5, 9, 52, 137, 152–55, 158–59, 199–200; of human body and esthetics, 117–18, 124–25, 172–73; and method of contemplation, 121, 130; in St. Hildegard, 124; of geometry and architecture, 128, 135, 138, 140, 144, 153, 155–56, 160–61, 190; in *The Faerie Queene*, 129–34, 162–73, 201–14, 217, 218–21, 267, 273, 275–76; and scripture, 152–53; and poetry, 158, 160, 162, 178, 189; of beasts, 161–62; and parts of body in Sidney, 180, 182, 192; and cosmic machine, 206, 207, 212, 214
Alma, 139–44, 162–74, 211, 212, 216, 217, 229, 253, 275, 276
Amoret, 238–39, 242, 254–55, 258, 263, 265, 267–68, 270
Anaxagoras, 17
Anglicus, Bartholomaeus, 203
Anthropometry, 117–18
Anthropomorphism: of cosmos, 8, 9, 11–12, 24, 37, 44–5, 69–80, 212; of state,

62, 65–66, 72, 75–78, 81, 107, 113; of architecture, 135, 141, 144–50, 161; in *The Faerie Queene*, 163, 211, 212, 220, 228–29, 243–44
Arcimboldi, Giuseppe, 49*n*, 204–05*n*
Archimago, 223, 225–27, 232, 234
Architecture, 116–74, 189
Ariosto, Lodovico: *Orlando Furioso*, 160–62, 171
Aristotle, 31, 33–34, 64, 70, 117; *De Anima*, 33; *The Politics*, 64–65; *Of the Parts of Animals*, 65
Arm(s), 24, 25, 35, 79, 98, 251; in *Sejanus*, 94; in *Coriolanus*, 99, 102, 105–06
Artegall, 207, 209–10, 251–54, 255, 257, 262–64
Arthur, 171–74, 233–35, 249–50, 262; in "House of Alma," 268, 273, 274, 280
Astrology, 21–25, 35–41
Astronomy, 9, 29, 124
Augustine, Saint., 10*n*, 50
Austin, William: *Haec Homo*, 127–28

Baldus de Ubaldis, 77
Barker, Ernest, 62
Beauty, 125, 186, 188, 189, 190, 221; in nature, 144; in *Astrophil and Stella*, 189, 191, 197, 198, 199; in *The Faerie Queene*, 246, 251, 256, 263
Belly, 68, 94, 111, 123; fable of, 96–100, 108, 159, 209
Belphoebe, 216, 222, 238, 239–42, 274
Bereshit Rabba, 25